More

"Nothing brings people [illegible] d stories. There's an abundance of [illegible] t memoir. As Weso attests, food can bring back happy, loving memories of times that were far from happy. Even a tray of funeral sandwiches brings a kind of comfort. This is a wonderful, honest portrait of northeastern Wisconsin, enlightening even to those of us who call this area home."

—**JARED SANTEK**, Founding & Artistic Director, Write On Door County

Also by Tom Weso:
Good Seeds: A Menominee Indian Food Memoir

"These stories and recipes make us appreciate the past, make us long for the woods and waters today, and make us just plain hungry."

—**HEID E. ERDRICH**, author of *Original Local: Indigenous Foods, Stories, and Recipes from the Upper Midwest*

"Weso says his grandmother used to start fire each morning. I want to say, it is Weso who starts fire, but the fire he builds is for the written word. It is language that sparks this work to life."

—**DIANE GLANCY**, poet, playwright, and author of *Pushing the Bear: After the Trail of Tears*

"Weso's stories are much more than culinary tales or instruction. Plain-spoken and occasionally hilarious, Weso sparks understanding and connection. As a contemporary of Weso who grew up less than an hour away from the Menominee reservation, I learned more about tribal food, culture and family life reading this single slender book than I did in more than two decades as his regional neighbor. *Good Seeds* is a poignant, important book."

—**TERESE ALLEN**, *Isthmus*

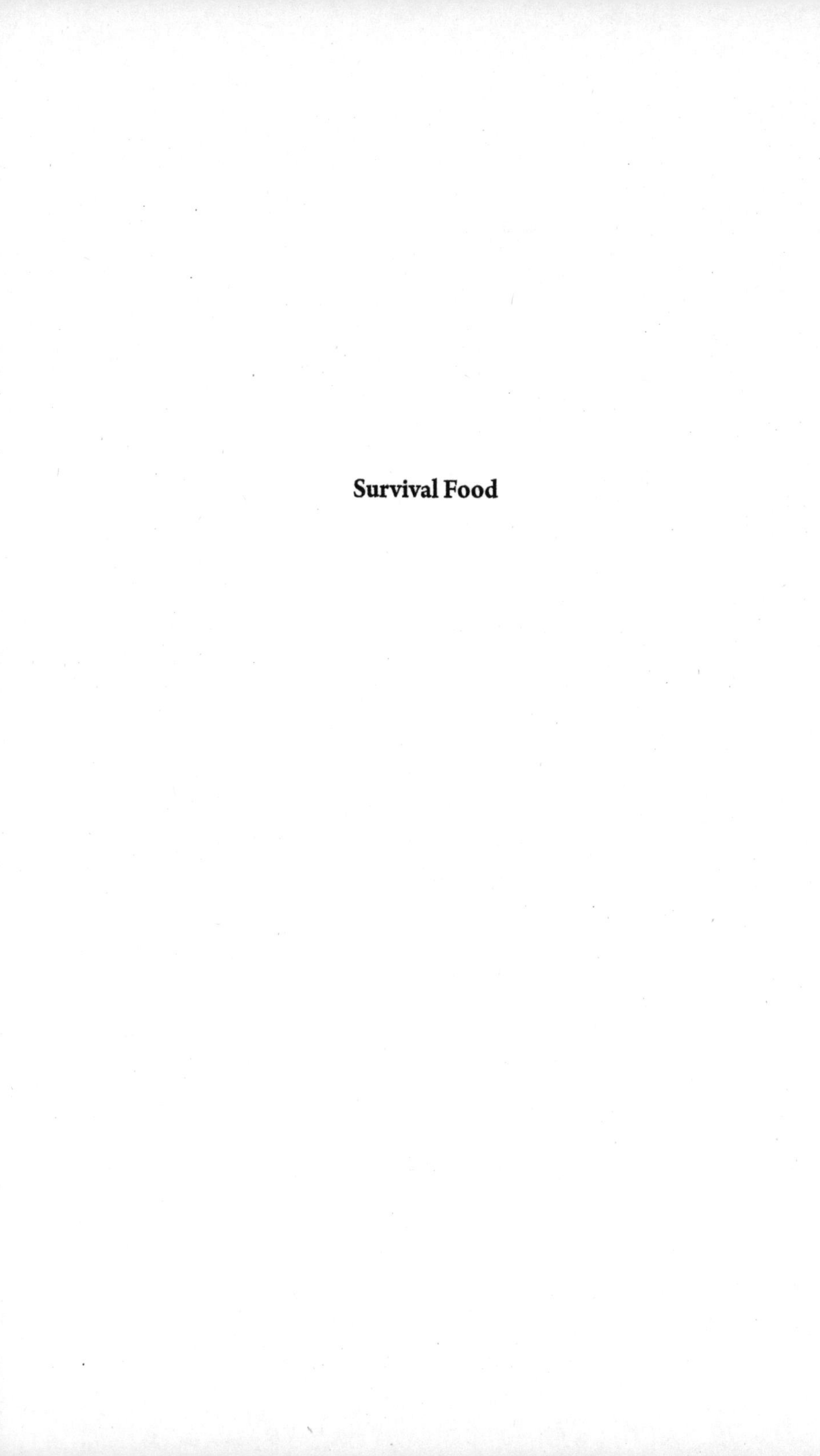

Survival Food

Survival Food

North Woods Stories by a Menominee Cook

Thomas Pecore Weso

WISCONSIN HISTORICAL SOCIETY PRESS

Published by the Wisconsin Historical Society Press
Publishers since 1855

The Wisconsin Historical Society helps people connect to the past by collecting, preserving, and sharing stories. Founded in 1846, the Society is one of the nation's finest historical institutions.

Join the Wisconsin Historical Society: wisconsinhistory.org/membership

Front and back cover image: Kari Lehr Art (www.karilehrart.com)

A modified version of "A Jailhouse Home and Frank's Magical Breakout" was previously published as "A Free Man: The Story of a Menominee Elder" in *Sapiens*.

Publication of this book was made possible in part by a grant from the Amy Louise Hunter fellowship fund and by support from the Wisconsin Historical Society Press Readers Circle. For more information, visit support.wisconsinhistory.org /readerscircle.

Printed in the United States of America
Designed by Percolator Graphic Design

27 26 25 24 23 1 2 3 4 5

Library of Congress Cataloging-in-Publication Data

Names: Weso, T. F. Pecore (Thomas F. Pecore), author.
Title: Survival food : north woods stories by a Menominee cook / Thomas Pecore Weso.
Description: Madision : Wisconsin Historical Society Press, [2023]. | Includes index.
Identifiers: LCCN 2023004205 (print) | LCCN 2023004204 (e-book) | ISBN 9781976600210 (paperback) | ISBN 9781976600227 (epub) | ISBN 9781976600227_q(epub) | ISBN 9781976600210_q(paperback)
Subjects: LCSH: Weso, T. F. Pecore (Thomas F. Pecore) | Menominee Indians—Food. | Menominee Indians—Biography. | Menominee Indians—Social life and customs. | Menominee Indian Reservation (Wis.)—Biography.
Classification: LCC E99.M44 W47 2023 (e-book) | LCC E99.M44 (print) | DDC 977.5004/97313092 [B 23'eng'20230] —dc03
LC record available at https://lccn.loc.gov/2023004205

♾ The paper used in this publication meets the minimum requirements of the American National Standard for Information Sciences—Permanence of Paper for Printed Library Materials, ANSI Z39.48-1992.

To all the children and grandchildren, nephews and nieces, and children to come, especially: PEmecewan, Josh, Curtis, and Frances; David, Allison, and Natalie; Daniel, MeiLing, and Aidan; and Diane Willie

Contents

Contents

Preface

Today's Sunday dinner consisted of turkey burgers, canned green beans, and gravy—a comfort meal that needed a packet of instant potatoes to make it complete. Our professional-level cook son, who is a winemaker by profession, will never be served such a meal. He does not have a history with food that includes daily Jell-O recipes (lime Jell-O made with cottage cheese and olives, for example, or orange with canned mandarin oranges) and Bisquick. Nor will he know the joys of squirrel stew, sturgeon roe fresh from the morning's catch, or steaming syrup in the springtime maple bush. He would relish the "slow foods" prepared during my subsistence upbringing, directed by my grandmother, mostly. My mother, a nontraditional college student during my teens, resorted to instant meals, and these have left their mark. I get nostalgic for Chef Boyardee pizza kits.

I grew up on the Menominee Indian Reservation in northern Wisconsin, where I am enrolled as a member. The reservation covers an entire county. It is located within a region of many settler descendants of German, Polish, and Swedish origins, and it is near another reservation, the Stockbridge-Munsee Community Band of Mohican Indians. All of these culinary traditions influence my interest in game, beer, cheese, and sausages, for a start. Commodity foods doled out by the government—blocks of processed cheese, canned milk, Spam—also shape my personal food profile.

According to scientists, the hippocampus part of the brain manages both formation of new memories and sense of smell. Food, a bouquet of aromas, provides a daily connection to the past. My life on the reservation intertwines with memories of subsistence hunting and fishing, gardens tended by my grandfather, and the bounty found in Wisconsin supper clubs. Cottage cheese, hull-corn soup, Pabst Blue Ribbon beer, mashed potatoes, chili poured over macaroni—all of these evoke the locations where and the people with whom I consumed them, as well as the delicious meals. I cannot separate foods from the moments in my life when I first tasted them. Each meal triggers memories. Some create new memories.

This collection of stories—beginning when I was five, continuing through my teen years, and ending in my adulthood—comes mostly from memories. But every story makes me think of the food connected to it. So this is a backward food memoir—the stories appear first, with the characters, and then the food memories and recipes. It is a personal food map of the Menominee Reservation and neighboring towns, with guest appearances by significant relatives and friends. Yes, some Indigenous mysticism occurs, as well as a ridiculous story about mescal worms. Canned tamales have as much power in my memory as my grandmother's wild rice with partridge stew.

When I was a growing child, everything that touched my tongue was new, interesting, and most often delicious. My previous book, *Good Seeds: A Menominee Indian Food Memoir,* told about subsistence meals from hunted, fished, and gathered sources. That book mostly covered my early childhood on the Menominee Reservation, up to about age ten. I did not stop eating, though, and not always were there storybook Woodland Indian meals available. This is the next installment of the Tom Weso food chronicle, set primarily in the more complicated time period of my tween and teen years.

An Adventure with Uncle Buddy

Because I was a difficult and unwanted child, I spent a considerable amount of time with my grandfather Kesōq, whose name means both "Sun" and "Moon" in English. His English name was Monroe, but he went by Moon. Grandma, a nurse at the Indian Agency hospital in Keshena, was unable to babysit during her day shift. All of her other children worked or were serving in the army. Thus, I was left with Grandfather Moon or my uncle Buddy. Both had decided tastes in cuisine, one bland and one spiced up.

Grandpa Moon also had a full-time job, but his days were spent in the woods traveling in his pickup truck. Grandpa represented the federal government for local administrative functions—he was town constable and justice of the peace and, during the tribal Termination era, state game warden. While watching me, Grandpa usually took me on patrol. This often entailed trips to diners outside the reservation, where I acquired a taste for meatloaf, sausage, sauerkraut, and other delicacies of our German and Polish neighbors. Some of our daily fare was from subsistence hunting, fishing, and gathering, as well as a large garden, but we also lived in the twentieth century amidst dairy and hog farms. Grandpa's work did mean long days, but they were not always filled with negative encounters. Sometimes, he officiated at marriage ceremonies in our living room while Grandma played

Mendelssohn's "Wedding March" on an Indian Agency record player. I was supposed to hold still.

To give Grandpa an occasional break, my maternal uncles took turns babysitting. Uncles Billy and Donny were in the army, stationed in Germany, so most of the relief babysitting fell to Uncle Buddy, the oldest and the least parental. Like his two younger brothers, Buddy was also in the army but on a different base and career track. In the mid-1950s, Buddy was still in the army as the world shifted from World War II to the Korean War. American battles across Europe and the Pacific and the humiliating retreat across Korea were fresh memories even while the fight against communism in Southeast Asia was just starting. Buddy had helped to liberate Auschwitz and then reenlisted for Korea. Despite this full schedule, Buddy spent considerable time at home in the late 1950s and early 1960s. People in the tribe said Buddy had ways and means of managing his military career.

Uncle Buddy also had experience with a range of international cuisines, and to him I owe my sense of adventure when it comes to food. In fact, *adventurous* would be a word to describe Buddy's entire approach to life.

From Grandpa and Uncle Buddy I inherit the Indigenous tradition of telling stories—from dawn to bedtime and beyond—that connect everything, so I cannot write about food without thinking of the people, the places, and the stories. Uncle Buddy did not just tell stories, though. His adventures became the stuff of stories.

In those days, Uncle Buddy owned a series of "hot rods," as Grandpa described them. Up until that moment when he permanently lost his driver's license—and perhaps just a little longer than that—Buddy always owned a heart-stopper car. Many were convertibles. He finagled car ownership as well as he finagled extra military leave.

One of his more memorable cars arrived years after his

babysitting days, in the 1960s. It was a two-seat English sports car, a forest green MGB. This particular model was made between the 1960s and 1980s. Grandma was still alive when he got it. I was walking home from Frank Skubitz's store in downtown Keshena when it zoomed past. Ahead of me, down the road, I saw Buddy pull into Grandma and Grandpa's driveway to drop off Cousin Mona, but mostly to show off the car.

That really was a car to die for. When the family gathered around it that morning, Buddy feigned a reluctance to brag about it, claiming instead, "It's a good hunting car." He said that rain or shine, that car would never wear its bonnet. "With the top down, I can shoot right from the driver's seat," he said. He pantomimed lifting a rifle to his shoulder and made an exaggeratedly slow pulling movement with his trigger finger: "Bang!" An imaginary deer fell dead.

Perhaps this car reminded him of an army jeep. It was almost the same shade of green. Built upon a light, narrow frame, it could skate over the muddy logging roads of the reservation. The narrow tires resisted hydroplaning by finding traction in mud puddles. The axles were narrow enough that the car fit easily between the deep ruts of most logging roads. The stiff racing suspension, however, made driving upon any dirt track a rough ride. This baby was made to cruise a European autobahn at high speeds, not crawl through the mud of an Indian reservation.

Ultimately, using that MGB for hunting proved to be the sporty car's downfall. On one particularly bad road, Buddy was surfing the deep, water-filled ruts looking for game when the small car suffered a bent axle. While most bent axles are not difficult to replace, vintage MGB axles have always been rare, especially in northern Wisconsin, and even more so on the Menominee Indian Reservation. That slight damage rendered the car inoperable. Since this happened decades before the Internet, it could not be posted for sale online to someone looking for a restoration project. Oh, sure, it still started and everything on it worked fine. Sometimes Buddy would sit in the driver's seat with a can of beer, letting the engine get warm to circulate the motor oil, and he would listen to distant American voices over the English-made radio. The car, however, could not move.

That MGB sat in my grandparents' yard for over thirty years. It may very well be still sitting there today as an expensive piece of lawn art—one of the finest pieces of British rolling stock ever made, just left to rust, the reddish brown metallic dust slowly mixing into the gravelly glacial till of a northern Wisconsin driveway. But this was not Buddy's first sporty car, nor would it be his last.

Here is where my adventure with Uncle Buddy begins, in the late 1950s when I was maybe five years old. I do not remember exactly what model of car Uncle Buddy brought home this spring day, so early that it was not even dawn. First we heard it, and then we could see its tires through our two steel-mesh-covered basement kitchen windows. Those windows sat only a foot above the ground, and they provided a limited field of view. We could hear the motor, though, through the brick walls. It rumbled with industrial authority. We all ran outside—my aunts and uncles and assorted cousins, along with Grandpa Moon and Grandma Jennie.

This car was shiny and dark, and the gathered family could see it was a two-door gangster car equipped with round fenders and a pointy, hungry-looking snout with chrome teeth. Maybe this was a Nash, as it had seat belts.

The automobile cruised along the front driveway, circling the house using the dirt drive like a hungry bass might eyeball and circle a bullfrog resting upon a lily pad. It came to a stop, and he killed the engine.

When the window rolled down, a cloud of cigarette smoke escaped. The first thing we saw inside was a shining built-in radio mounted above a chrome ashtray. The coiled metal tip of the cigarette lighter glowed bright red as Buddy pulled it out of its socket in the dash and used it to light a Winston held between his teeth. As a kid, electric fire impressed me a lot. I watched his every move.

When Buddy held the driver's-side door open with his left foot, he could even listen to the radio without a key in the ignition.

This car had whitewall tires. While most auto tires in the 1950s were whitewalls, these were not the mismatched set of baloney-skins ordinarily found on the reservation—four tires from four different tire brands and no spare. Here was a complete set of inky black tires, all the same model and brand, each one fully erect and topped with thick rubber tread. This was years before radial tires were invented, so these were stiff-wall, high-profile bias tires. Each one had a fat white stripe circling the chrome baby-moon hub caps. As a male-in-training, I knew these tires were exceptional. I had heard about them from the older boys at my school, St. Joe's. Plus, I'd seen exaggerated versions of these tires in cartoons and gangster movies.

This was a real-life film noir car, one like the gangster hero and occasional Menominee Reservation guest John Dillinger might have driven. He and his Menominee girlfriend, Billie Frechette, had frequented the area during the 1930s. This was no rez-runner wreck. This was a pricey American beauty, a White Man's motor-car built for cruising the White Man's smooth highways outside the reservation boundaries.

Right away, we could see that instead of a steel roof, it had fabric. That glistening dark fabric roof perfectly matched the shiny dark color of the car, while a set of chrome bumpers, fore and aft, bookended the curvy sleek beauty. I could see my face in the bumpers. The car looked much too nice for driving along dirt logging roads.

Uncle Buddy returned the key to the ignition, twisted it, and in response the car shivered alive, like Frankenstein's monster in the movies. The noise startled the wood ducks in the nearby creek channel, causing them to erupt into panicky, unsynchronized flight. Some combination of cylinders and carburetors made the car rumble until the ground underneath our feet shook in sympathy.

Buddy revved the engine a few more times, shaking the windows of the family home. The backyard filled with clingy white exhaust smoke, not unlike the white clouds of poisonous DDT that Indian Agency trucks sprayed on our town's gravel roads to kill mosquitoes. Sometimes children, like myself, would run through town behind those trucks, inhaling the poison. On those days, tiny mosquito warriors on their morning hunt fell from the sky while a few survivors fled to maintain their tribe. Now, the mosquitoes must have been confused by the smoky cloud coming from Buddy's car.

Buddy revved the engine a couple more times.

Suddenly, the roof of the car came loose from the windshield. We all jumped back. Buddy remained calm and reached to flick two handles mounted above the windshield. Then, using his left arm, Buddy pulled a lever mounted next to the parking brake under the left dash.

Gears embedded behind the back seat began slowly turning, sounding as though they were in agony as the roof began collapsing and retracting into an opening where a rear window should have been. The painful groaning became louder and more frantic as folds of stiff fabric and metal frames bunched up. Finally, the racket stopped. The roof was squashed into its own compartment. Engine off, Buddy jumped out of the car and ran around to each rear passenger side, snapping buttons down on the thick material, which finished hiding the roof.

"By God, by God," Grandma kept saying in English as she

watched this performance. Later, she whispered something quietly in Menominee to Grandpa, who answered back even more quietly in Potawatomi. Although I was almost fluent in Menominee, the only language spoken by many of my relatives, I was not able to understand it when uttered this low and fast. And I was not so good with Potawatomi, as I heard it only irregularly at ceremonies. Once, while Grandpa was talking to Grandma, they noticed me listening to their conversation. They asked in Potawatomi if I could understand what they were saying. Responding in English, I said, "No." This was how Potawatomi became the language for when Grandma and Grandpa did not want me listening.

From my limited stock of Potawatomi words, I knew they were amazed by the convertible car. Heck, me too. This was a first. How could the top of any car appear and disappear upon command? There was not a word in either of our languages for an automobile with a ragtop.

Some practical questions arose. What about rain and snow? It does both in Wisconsin, quite often, and sometimes on the very same day. It had just snowed two days earlier. Still, on this particular early spring morning, the brightening sky was already melting the scattered leftover pockets of snow and burning the morning dew from freshly exposed blades of grass. My questions were reserved for later.

Uncle Buddy had timed his arrival to coincide with our morning meal: buckwheat pancakes with Land O'Lakes butter and topped with either our own dark and earthy grade A maple syrup, my favorite, or the clear and viscous Karo Syrup, the favorite of my older brother. The other breakfast foods that day, like most, included homemade chunky-style applesauce, oatmeal served with slices of fried salt pork on the side and hot rendered salt pork grease drizzled over the top like icing on a cake, bacon and basted eggs, and any leftovers from the previous day's meals not already earmarked for Rocky the watchdog.

Rocky belonged to Uncle Buddy and lived with us. Grandma often threatened when I dawdled at meals, "Finish this up. Whatever you don't eat goes out to the dog." Rocky got fed twice a day, after breakfast and after dinner. Sometimes, before my grandparents found out, my younger cousin Jammer would eat his meals outside with the dog from the same bowl. I never did this.

Breakfast was our main meal of the day, and it was substantial. It was not unusual for the morning meal to further include a saucepan of reheated corn soup or slices of cold meat pie. Those were the days before microwave ovens. Our leftovers might include fried fish; hominy; boiled, fried, or mashed potatoes; and some kind of boiled, dried, fried, or roast meat like stewed squirrel. They also might include apple pie. Grandma made fruit pie for Grandpa almost every day. Usually, it was apple, but blackberry and raspberry pies were common, too. These fruits were all canned at home and gathered by our own hands. Occasionally, Grandma made her own favorite kind of pie, a lemon meringue.

Grandma's meals always followed the basic Menominee food pyramid. This was a four-sided pyramid built around four basic elements—sweet, salt, meat, and water. The actual presentation of those elements, what appeared on the table, was subject to Grandma's interpretation. Take corn as an example. We ate a lot of corn, and however it appeared—be it dried like a nut for a sweet snack, fresh on the cob, handmade into hull corn, store-bought hominy, sweet kernels out of a tin can, or dried multicolored kernels popped in sizzling hot fat—corn counted as the sweet component of our meal. Fish—boiled, dried, smoked, or fried—counted as meat, as did venison, squirrel, and anything else we could catch. So a soup made of dried corn simmered in spring water with pieces of venison and a pinch of salt combined all four of these elemental ingredients.

Grandma often made a meat pie for family holidays that was derived from a French Canadian recipe. It also combined all four of these dietary components into one, more complicated dish. Its meat and salt came from the savory filling and its sweet and water from the crust ingredients.

Near the end of any meal—whether it was morning, noon, or evening—adults would linger at the table with coffee and cigarettes. This was an important step, not to be missed. Coffee, or more correctly the water used to make it, marked the meal's ceremonial end. This completed the Menominee food pyramid. With that final cup, all four food elements were represented in the meal.

I had my own place at the aluminum kitchen table, always on one of the long sides, where I shared my space with other relatives. The ends were where Grandpa and Buddy sat as they drank strong coffee. My *kah-pe,* prepared by Grandma who sat right across from me, was one part coffee, three parts sweetened condensed milk, and a couple spoonfuls of sugar. That morning, between sips of coffee, and through the gossamer clouds of cigarette smoke from unfiltered Pall Malls (tobacco smoke carried prayers to the Great Mystery), the adults discussed Uncle Buddy's car from roof to tires and everything in between the bumpers. That conversation was conducted in three different languages: Menominee, Potawatomi, and English. English words were used because sometimes there are no simple Menom or Pot words capable of describing more advanced technology.

Following the conversation as best I could, I realized that the plan for the day was for my older brother and me to go off with Uncle Buddy for a ride in his new car. Buddy wanted to drive up past Cedar Dam and look to see if any trout were biting, maybe bait a hook. Everybody knew that it was too early in the season to even think about catching trout, because the mayflies had not yet hatched. But the sun was shining brightly. Early spring plants were greening under frost. We had Buddy's new car, and everything just felt right. Maybe we would find a few early trout.

By 8 a.m., the three of us packed into the front bench seat with me, the smallest, in the middle. We headed north on Wisconsin Highway 47, searching for one particular logging road that lay just past Neopit but before Camp Four Hill. It led to a secret fishing spot, a partially disassembled dam once used by the tribe for logging. It was a few miles past Camp 26 Road on the Little West Branch of the Wolf River.

All of my Indian relatives who owned cars, along with all of the non-Indian residents on the rez, kept fishing gear and an army surplus rifle in their trunks, in case fish were biting or a deer happened to appear. Another reason was that unpredictable animals could attack. Big-bore handguns, like a Colt .45 or a Ruger .44 Magnum, were commonly worn on the hip in case of a bear, badger, or hodag attack. Ask anyone from Wisconsin about hodags. Porcupines could also be a nuisance and made for tasty eating.

Once, while walking by myself down a dirt road in the woods, I happened upon a porcupine with its head caught in an empty pork-and-beans can. The label was still visible. Campbell's Pork and Beans was a go-to camping food, and the cans were often disposed of improperly. Many different kinds of animals would attempt to eat the half dozen beans and pork gravy stuck along a can's bottom crease. These, like most food cans, were too narrow for a bear's or wolf's head, but they have long tongues.

A porcupine has a thin head—the ideal shape to get into the bottom of a small can for that last morsel. The stiff quills on its head, however, make backing out of the can difficult. In this case, the porky I encountered was going around and around, trying to push the can off its head with its front paws while dragging itself backward using its rear paws.

At first, it seemed funny, and yes, I laughed, until I realized that the poor animal was terrified. Being five years old and naïve, I decided to help. I grabbed both sides of the can and slowly tried to pry the can off its head. Then I tried toggling it, levering it off, and bending it from one side to the other. Nothing worked. Trying to unscrew the can off that prickly head was the next step, but that did not work either. And by now, this porky was really irritated.

Treating it like my grandma treated a Band-Aid seemed to be my best last choice. So grabbing both sides of the can again, arms poised for a quick snap, I yanked that can back toward me hard and fast. The porky cooperated, albeit unwillingly, by doing everything in its power to back away, using all fifty pounds of its muscle. It must have outweighed me by ten. Only my two hands around the can kept it from getting away. When the can finally popped loose from its head, I fell backward on my butt. The porcupine fell backward on its butt, too. Both of us looked at each other in surprise.

The porky was the first to recover and obviously blamed me for recent events. It charged forward, quills erect, hissing angrily through bared teeth. I jumped up and began running back up the road. Surprised at being attacked by a slow-witted porcupine, I left my fishing pole. After a block, I looked over my shoulder and saw that the porcupine was gaining on me. Fright gave me the extra strength I needed to keep running and finally escape. After I told Grandma about what happened that night, I got my first .22-caliber rifle the next day, for defense.

I knew Uncle Buddy had basic survival gear—a hunting rifle and fishing pole—in whatever car he drove, and this was a comfort to me when we were in the more remote parts of the rez. On this particular morning, Uncle Buddy's car proved itself to be a great highway cruiser. He launched it into its overdrive gear near Volland's Farm (now Middle Village of the Menominee Reservation). I did not know what overdrive *was*, but I knew we were doing it. This was high adventure. The convertible roared up the highway.

Buddy leaned over and turned on the radio. From a speaker on top of the dashboard came the sound of White people's voices from outside the reservation. They followed us at high speeds as we left the highway for more narrow, twisting roads.

Radio was our contact with the outside world. We heard cheery beer-drinking polka music, much of it in German, from the Shawano radio station, and we heard sad beer-drinking, country-and-western music, always in English, from the rural town of Antigo. Those stations were our only two options in cars, but at home when it was dark, we could hear French voices from our northern neighbors in Canada. The big radio at home, the one kept in the separate two-car garage that we used for extra bedrooms, used to be a pay radio from an old hotel. My White stepfather had painted it gray after removing the coin mechanism. On it, I listened to music from Chicago, Detroit, Montreal, Pittsburgh, and other distant places, like Quebec, all around the Great Lakes.

In Uncle Buddy's car, we tried to tune into big-city radio stations but had no luck. We were trapped in the thick forest between two border towns. We got just the radio crumbs dropped from those radio towers. When we dipped between hills, the music dissolved into the thick white, almost paranormal noise of static.

Uncle Buddy gave the giant car a little gas, and it fishtailed around the curves, faster and faster. As we roared atop an abandoned railroad bed, Buddy accelerated through the mud puddles and splashed the trees on both sides. My brother and I laughed.

As much fun as this proved to be, it was also the source of our undoing. Not the splashing, but rather our treatment of the mud puddles in general as we violated the unspoken laws of the forest. Those spirits in charge of natural laws often forgive a little teasing, and they enjoy a good joke, too. But you should never try to provoke the spirits of the forest. Racing through the woods laughing with the radio blasting, we were forgetting to be respectful to the forest.

As a child, I had an imperfect understanding of the forest roadways, but I learned. Logging roads are normally used just during the frozen months, when heavy equipment will not sink into the hardened earth. During the first months above freezing, like that spring day with Uncle Buddy, they are impassable by civilian vehicles. The old railroad bed provided a solid but narrow roadway into the woods, up to a point. Then we had to take logging roads or follow old trails to get near the river to fish.

Logging roads have deep ruts that might appear to be shallow mud puddles, but they can be quagmires. Even during dry seasons, most of these roads are not friendly toward any kind of vehicle. Their condition results from their primary users, loggers employed by the tribal sawmill. It was not that tribal loggers were destructive. Quite the contrary; those Menominee loggers preserved the reservation for the current generation. Rather, it was the specialized multiton trucks and trailers used by the industry that tore up roads. Take the articulated log skidders used to carry logs out of the forest and stack them. These four- and sometimes six-wheel-drive vehicles are monstrously loud, smelly things made of solid iron. They shake the earth and mar the dirt trails carved between the trees. They leave potholes and deep, long parallel ruts. Then they expand and deepen those ruts as they move back and forth, working as long as there is daylight. The resulting gashes in the earth quickly fill with water from ground seepage because the reservation has such a high water table.

Grandpa once explained the forest to me: "Tommy, the reservation is more water than land if you see it from the air." In his official ranger duties, he had seen it from a plane. Mud was a constant element in my young life.

As long as a car's tires can reach the hard bottom of a water-filled pothole on a logging road and the carburetor can remain dry, then there is no impediment to forward movement. Sometimes, however, the pothole has such deep ruts that a car will bottom out. Sometimes these roads get so muddy that even logging operations are suspended until the ground dries out. Late autumn, winter, and early spring are the seasons preferred by loggers because there is less risk of equipment sinking on hard frozen ground. Ever since commercial logging was first established in 1850s Wisconsin, people have known not to drive into the woods after the winter thaw before the ground dries.

But even the worst logging road can be navigated with attitude, skill, and a superior machine. Uncle Buddy had enough attitude and skill, and we were testing out the machine. As we continued our joyride through the forest, he explained his strategy to his captive audience of two little boys. Driving through deep mud puddles, he said, requires a technique that is part scientific and part spiritual, but mostly a mindset. "We drivers judge where the deepest, treacherous ruts lie under the wide opaque pools on the road," he told us. "Even in dry weather, a car may get hung up. Dragging a car out of a dried logging road is just as discouraging as pushing a car out of a muddy one."

I listened as Buddy continued his lesson: "The best technique for pothole and rut driving is a uniform speed. Go too slow and you sink. Go too fast and you slip—and then you sink." He paused as he wheeled around another curve. "The science of mud-puddle driving also involves choosing the right path. Resist the urge to accelerate out of the hole. Steady, slow torque is best." I did not follow all the details, but what I learned was that you had to believe that you could make it, no matter what.

I believed in Uncle Buddy. Settling back in the warm bench seat, listening to the distant sounds of honky-tonk on the radio and feeling wind rush over my head, I was invincible, as long as Uncle Buddy was nearby.

We were fine right up to the precise moment when we were not. Perhaps one of the big whitewalls slipped into a rut or into a deep pool from a renegade spring. It did not matter.

The car jerked to a stop.

Our cinematic adventure ended. All of a sudden, where there had been a joyful polka, now there was eerie silence. No more sounds of splashing water and splatter, no more wind, no more radio, and finally, no more engine noise—just some metallic clicks and clacks as it cooled. Buddy had turned off the ignition to conserve gas and the battery.

I knew we were in trouble when Buddy jumped over the side—he did not use the car door—to assess the situation. After circling the vehicle, he tracked clots of mud onto the carpet as he returned to the driver's seat, this time using the door. I could see sticky, malevolent mud beneath the car's door. When Buddy closed the door, I watched a line of mud squish inside along the bottom of the door. The car was too buried for us to dig out and on too remote a road for us to expect any traffic.

Uncle Buddy's narration of pothole-driving technique had ended. With a couple of random curses, he attempted to free the car. First, he tried to drive forward, but the wheels spun uselessly. Then he put the gear in reverse and tried to back up. Again, the wheels spun uselessly. Buddy was silent for a moment. Then he said, "Nice day for a walk, nephews." I steeled myself for a long trek home through miles of mud.

Before starting out, Buddy rummaged in the car's trunk and dug out an army pack. He put a few things into it, including beer and some oddly shaped jars. He threw it on his back and scooped me up into his arms in one movement. He carried me much of the way, and my older brother walked. I do not know how long or how far we walked. Like all adults, Buddy seemed to know the way.

Eventually, after hours, we reached a fork in the road. Here, Buddy put me down, took off his coat, and spread it out on the side of the road where my brother and I could sit. The only sounds were the constant drip-plop-drip of melting snow falling from the thick forest of spruce, balsam fir, and cedar. It was too wet to build any kind of fire. Judging by the muted light of the sky, it was midafternoon.

Buddy sat down next to us. I was hungry. While a person can survive in the springtime woods on wild edibles, it is challenging to look for something to eat when you are already cold, wet, and miserable. Anyway, it was way too late to whine about things. I kept quiet.

Buddy opened his pack and pulled out a can of Hamm's beer. The Hamm's mascot was a genial black bear that would regularly get into troublesome, but not serious, jams. An Ojibwa man was the logo designer, and the familiar black bear was popular on the Menominee Rez. The happy bear cheered me up.

These early beer cans had solid flat tops. Sold as a "handy pack" cluster, they needed to be opened with a "church key," familiarly known as a can opener. A church key had a pointy end and left two triangular holes in the top of the beer can—one to allow airflow and one from which to drink. Buddy reached into his trousers and pulled out a large jackknife. Setting the can between his legs, he punched two thin holes in the top. Twisting the knife slightly, he widened one of the holes. The delicious man-made beer aroma woke me up. Buddy tilted the can to his mouth, took a long swallow, belched loudly, and sighed. I watched him as he finished the Hamm's with a second, shorter swallow, this time rewarded with a smaller belch.

"Time to eat, Tom-Tom," Buddy said as he dug in the backpack and found a murky jar of yellow, orange, and red swirls—something I had never seen before. "These are called tamales," he said.

I was certain that Grandma would not have approved of these tamales, but she was far away, and I was hungry. Tamales were always sold in tall glass jars, I would learn. In my youth, they were staples in neighborhood grocery stores. In the jar, they were crammed together standing on end, looking like wrapped bundles of dynamite. A thin wash of red-brown sauce was visible through the glass, and gravy pooled at the bottom of the jar.

Buddy pulled a whole tamale out of the jar and peeled paper from its outside. A pungent whiff of chili filled the air. These tamales smelled familiar, almost like the chili Grandma would make in the electric roasting pan at home, but with a smoky tinge. Buddy used his knife to scrape a clumpy layer of orange and red grease off the tamale, discarded the biodegradable paper into the forest, then handed it to me. He handed another one to my brother.

Gingerly taking the tamale, I gave it the smell test. Grandpa said that poisonous foods smelled deadly bad. This had a strong, but not unfamiliar odor. It looked like a thick yellowish-white cornmeal log, with the cavity stuffed with ground beef in a chili sauce. It tasted great. After that first tamale, I developed a routine for the second one. I stuffed the paper wrapping in my mouth and chewed all of the residual grease from it. I did not want to waste even one drop.

Recently, I bought canned tamales for research. Again, I chewed the wrapping papers to relish the greasy chili flavors. I also discovered that heating the tamales makes them taste better. These are not the worst food found in an American grocery store, but they are not terribly healthy, either. One can of tamales, a normal serving, contains at least one whole day's worth of sodium. These days, they are not that common either. Neither of the two major grocery stores in my hometown carry canned tamales—though they do have plenty of fresh and frozen ones. Perhaps the local Latino population does not approve of canned tamales. They are very mild in taste—not spicy, but more like a suggestion of Mexican tamales. It was, nonetheless, a perfect meal for a young, bedraggled explorer in the rainy northern woods.

After we ate, Buddy used his finger to wipe the knife blade clean and then licked his fingers. All of the day's events now seemed to be part of an exotic adventure, and I suddenly felt sure that we would make it home safely, just like in the movies I'd watched at St. Joe's. A full belly helped me be optimistic.

The three of us dozed there on the side of the road until almost dark, when I woke up to hear a loud motor idling next to us. Even with my eyes closed, I could tell from the sound of the muffler, or lack of muffler, that these were Indians. After indistinct voices exchanged some information, my brother and I were lifted into the warm cab of a pickup truck. I was squeezed in next to my brother, on Uncle Buddy's lap. Whoever found and rescued us from the deep woods on that cold wet night drove us all the way home to Keshena, almost from one end of the reservation to the other, over eighteen miles of hard roads.

I woke again when we got home. It was late at night—clear and whisper-quiet. Not even the dogs were barking, but every single light bulb at my grandparents' house, outside and inside, was burning. Warm yellow light poured from every window in the house like diffused search lights in all four directions.

Grandma was not pleased with Buddy, but before talking to him, she grabbed me as soon as I walked into the house. Carrying me into the boiler room, she made me stand in front of the furnace and strip off all my muddy clothes. Then she rushed me into the downstairs laundry room that also served as a spare shower room and scrubbed me down with industrial soap, Fels Naphtha. Whenever we were sick or got punished, we got scrubbed down with Fels Naphtha soap. Next, she fed me a bowl of cornmeal with a pat of butter, milk, and sugar. Since it was already so late, Grandma carried me to my bed, a rollaway kept in the foyer on the upstairs landing. She eased me between a set of clean fresh sheets, kissed my cheek, and wished me a good night. She sang a short prayer in Potawatomi over me. This landing was my special place, halfway between the comforting sounds of the living room and my grandpa in one direction and the comforting smells from the downstairs kitchen and my grandmother in the other.

I drifted off to sleep to the sounds of my grandma yelling Menominee and Potawatomi at Uncle Buddy late into the night.

Dried Corn

Spread fresh corn kernels evenly on a cookie sheet. Cook in the oven on low heat for 2 hours or until dried.

Venison Corn Soup

This is a relatively simple dish to make, after preparing the corn and finding a deer, dispatching it, and dressing it. Dried corn and venison can also be bought at a market. This soup, made of four ingredients, satisfies those requirements set forth by the Menominee food pyramid—sweet, salt, meat, and water. My grandma made it often when her sons brought home deer or similar game meat. Porcupine meat, when rinsed in brine to remove the gamey taste, may be substituted. In addition to meat, the old Indians in the North Woods also used bones from the deer's neck, ribs, and shoulder.

Serves 4 to 6 people

1½ quarts venison, cut in pieces—enough to fill the bottom third of a five-quart kettle
2 cups dried corn
1 tablespoon salt
1 gallon water

Place venison in the bottom of the kettle. Add dried corn and salt. Fill the kettle with enough water to cover all of the ingredients. Bring to a boil, reduce heat, and simmer for about 2½ hours. If you wish to make the soup easier to serve and more attractive, bone the venison, discard the bones, and add meat back to the soup. Serve when meat is tender.

Winter Tamale Pie

Most northern people do not make authentic tamales like the canned ones Uncle Buddy fed us on our forest adventure. Many people make a casserole version that includes the same chili spices, shaken from a can, and other ingredients easy to obtain even in winter. Fresh ingredients may be substituted, but canned corn, beans, tomatoes, and green chilis are late-winter staples. These also work during pandemic quarantines when trips to the grocery store are limited.

1 pound ground beef
½ of a medium onion, diced
2 teaspoons salt
1 tablespoon chili powder
1 (12-ounce) can pinto beans, drained
1 (15-ounce) can corn, drained
1 (6-ounce) can green chilis, drained
1 box corn bread mix, mixed according to directions and set aside

Preheat the oven to 350 degrees. Place ground beef in a skillet over medium heat. Break into small pieces with a spatula. Add onion, salt, and chili powder. Stir and brown the beef. Add pinto beans, corn, and chilis to the skillet. Pour mixture into a lightly greased 8 × 8-inch pan. Cover with the corn bread mixture. Cook 40 minutes, until the center springs back.

The Cabin by Cheese Box Curve

Wisconsin natives of any heritage are known as Cheeseheads—a term epitomized by Green Bay Packers fans who wear foam cheese wedges as headgear. Sometime before 1958, my Menominee mom, older brother, German American stepfather, Rod, and I lived together in an old dairy farm along Wisconsin Highway 47. This log cabin was located between Volland's Farm and the forest ranger station. We did not farm or keep cows, but rather we hunted and fished for protein. Rod had recently returned from a stint in Korea. He was jumpy, but perhaps his nervousness was also due to his involvement in the underworld. Years later, Grandma let slip that she suspected he was hiding on the reservation from both the police and the mob. That is what John Dillinger did, too, back in the 1930s.

Rod was an accomplished old-school printer capable of replicating government documents. I believe he was the subject of several official investigations, based on the number of times the police came to our farm looking for evidence of counterfeiting paper money. The police always searched for an electric-powered printing press. We didn't have electricity on our farm, and they never found Rod's small hand-operated printing press in one of the outbuildings. He could fit it into the trunk of his car when we moved to new towns. No, clever Rod was never convicted of anything.

Our farm was about half a mile south of the infamous Cheese Box Curve. The name became fixed when a semitruck hauling dairy products attempted the curve too fast and went off the road, landing on its side. Nobody was hurt, but dozens of boxes full of cheese spilled out of the truck and littered the highway like so many accident victims. The stench from unrecoverable cheese lasted for weeks. This was a major historic event on the reservation. In the other direction, our farm was maybe half a mile from the Crow Settlement Road and two miles north of the reservation town of Keshena.

Our farm was ancient, even back then. Its structures were built from logs harvested on the property—the house, the barn, and all the other outbuildings, except for the outdoor toilet, which was built from new lumber. All the buildings, except the toilet, had mice. But the toilet had its own issues. In the summer there were flies, and in the winter there were icicles. Sometimes a porcupine would take up residence in the rafters because it was attracted to the salt in urine. You had to look up before you walked in. Porcupines are formidable.

Every couple of months, our dog, Rocky, would tangle with a porcupine. He was never the winner. Rocky would come home with a snout full of quills and cry outside the door. Porcupine quills have tiny barbs along the shafts, and pulling one out is incredibly difficult, hence painful. In the olden days, the standard procedure was to pull the quills out from the other direction as they worked through the snout. This took a pair of pliers and a cooperative dog.

Poor old Rocky never learned about skunks, either. A few times a year, he would come home smelling of skunk. The first time this happened, Rod and Uncle Buddy gave Rocky a tomato juice bath, which wasn't as easy as it sounds. Rocky didn't like baths. He was a big dog, and he fought them both. The bath did not work very well anyway. Afterward, Rocky still stank and was banished to the barn. Eventually, he rolled around on the ground enough to be allowed near the house. The tomato bath was never attempted again—it was just too much work for so little benefit. The next several times the dog was squirted by a skunk, he was simply sent to the barn to deal with the smell himself.

In those days, electric power lines did not stretch to our part of the reservation. My mom had two glass kerosene lamps for light. The light was an almost but not quite sufficiently bright yellow orange. It gave off a warm friendly glow, albeit a smelly one.

The farm did have a water well in the backyard, positioned as far from the privy as possible. It was not one of those picturesque wells with a red metal hand pump, like they had in the national parks. Our well was a hand-dug, rock-lined shaft that extended to wet darkness below the water table, and it rose three feet above the ground. Water was drawn by lowering a bucket with an attached rope and then winching it back up with a wooden hand crank. The rope coiled around a wooden beam as it was turned by the crank. This beam provided extra leverage, and the heavy bucket would eventually come to the surface with little effort. It was a lengthy process, though.

Rod discovered that he could muscle the bucket to the surface more quickly by bracing himself against the rock-lined shaft and pulling the rope, hand over hand, not using the crank at all. He then insisted that my brother and I start pulling the bucket up to the surface without the crank. We couldn't, since a bucket of water weighed more than we did at the time, but that was his rule. One of my brother's chores was to fill a bucket with water in the morning and bring it back to the house. I was not assigned this chore because, as a little guy, I got in the way more than I could help.

We used that bucket of water for dishes, personal washing, household cleaning, and other chores. We consumed that water for drinking and cooking, too, until one morning a bucket of water was brought up with a healthy pine snake swimming in circles inside. After that, every few days, Stepfather brought home a milk can filled with water from a nearby spring for our family to use for drinking and cooking. The water always had the hint of a sour milk taste.

Rod would borrow a car from Bobby Perez, who later became my uncle, for doing chores, buying groceries, and going to town to pay bills. Then he added hauling water to the list. Looking back, I wonder if my brother did not put that snake in the bucket to get out of hauling water every morning.

For me, these days on the farm were wonderful, brief moments in time. The cabin was the perfect size for the four of us. In those days, my stepfather wasn't always physically abusive, and besides, he was gone a lot. My daily routine was idyllic—wake up, eat, and explore. Breakfast was usually cornmeal, toast, and coffee. The cornmeal took the form of a cereal gruel. I watched my mother boil water, add a handful of cornmeal, and give it a few minutes to cook, with some stirring. I liked mine with a pat of butter, homemade maple syrup, and fresh milk.

We used a lot of milk in our house. My coffee was half milk and several spoonfuls of white sugar. Stepfather bought raw, whole milk from a local farmer every week, and sometimes cheese. Perhaps he used some of his home-printed bills. Perhaps not.

We stored the milk, and anything else perishable, in the log milk house behind the cabin. It was built partly submerged in the earth and had a stout wooden door. To enter, we walked down a short flight of stairs, and in the northern climate, it was always chilly.

Without electricity, our only source of entertainment—beyond the sights and sounds related to our environment—came from a battery-powered transistor radio. Being so far from any city, the area's only two reliable radio stations were local. Starting in the early morning, before I woke, the station streamed polka music for the large German population. Then it gave local sports scores and announced tidbits of local news until midmorning, when it switched to easy listening music. The exception to this format was in the instance of a juicy scandal involving a local Indian—Menominee, Potawatomi, Ho-Chunk, Ojibwa, or a stray Sioux. Then the news was rehashed seemingly every few minutes. Uncle Buddy used to say that Shawano residents weren't prejudiced at all; they hated all Indians equally. The other items of repeated news were winter road conditions and weather reports. These were universally appreciated.

On Sundays, the radio played polka as usual—with lyrics like "In heaven there is no beer, that's why we drink it here"—until midmorning, when Catholic church services were broadcast, then Lutheran services, followed by Methodist services, and finally Episcopalian services until the end of the noon hour. Then, they switched to Lawrence Welk. Our radio consumption was dependent on how many batteries we could afford. We generally had radio for a week out of every month.

The farm stood two hundred yards from the gravel highway and was set back about a hundred feet from an old dirt road leading to a high plateau where Menominee clan leaders once met for council. My mom told me about this. The open meadow, once dotted with wigwams and tepees, had long since been turned over to cattle. The gravel highway, now Wisconsin 47, might have been more accurately described as a glorified foot trail. At its widest points, one and a half cars could fit. This was still better than some of the modern tribal roads that are simply dirt ruts for a single car. In the late 1950s, it would be a couple more years before this state highway was paved with asphalt.

But the road was big enough to be a source of amusement for our whole family. Traffic was so infrequent that we would gather to watch whatever was passing by. Any motor vehicle could be heard from a distance. This gave us time to run to the road to watch. We could tell a White car from an Indian car by the sound alone. Indian-owned cars, which were used in the woods, had dinged-up, noisy mufflers. White-owned cars, on the other hand, stayed on the highway and had intact mufflers that muted the engine noise.

Back then, the only trucks on this route were local delivery vehicles, often little more than enclosed pickup trucks. Certain neighbors' cars we recognized by sight, and we would give a friendly wave at the owners as they drove by. White cars and their drivers were commented on and sometimes ogled.

It was not until several years later, when I was maybe nine years old, that my grandpa started taking me to Antigo for lunch. We didn't go so often that it became routine, and the diner always remained special. Grandpa liked to study both sides of the menu, too. That was part of the experience.

We always ordered the open-faced hot roast beef sandwich—two slices of white bread cut into four triangles, topped with slices of beef and a scoop of mashed potatoes, each drenched with steaming hot, thick and shiny, brown, salty gravy. My grandma never cut my bread into triangles. And my mom did just once, when I asked her to after pulling the bread out of the toaster. It didn't feel the same, and I never asked again. The diner entrée was accompanied by a small dish of canned corn. Grandpa really enjoyed the perfectly smooth scoop of instant potatoes whose only flaw was the offset dimple used as a gravy reservoir. It was the purity of form he loved, rather than the flavor, like how hot fudge on soft-serve vanilla ice cream always looks better than it tastes.

All these years later, I have conflicted feelings about Antigo. Some of my favorite relatives lived there. It was close enough to Keshena that my grandparents and I, in the late 1960s, would regularly eat Sunday dinner with Aunt Lorraine and Uncle Jim. Aunt Lorraine made twice-baked cheesy potatoes, which, after my mom's dehydrated potatoes straight out of a box, tasted like something delicious from outer space. Their middle-class one-car-garage home with a small porch had an arch dividing the living room from the dining room. As I was used to the bleak ninety-degree walls of our German Gothic home, my school at St. Joe's, and my church in Keshena—with thanks to the Jesuits for their preference for judgmental architecture—the curves and individuality of Aunt Lorraine and Uncle Jim's house were something strange indeed.

On the other hand, my teenage years in Antigo include some uncomfortable memories, like being dragged into a bank on Main Street to withdraw money from my trust fund so that my out-of-work stepfather could float another one of his get-rich-quick schemes. My early years in the simple cabin by Cheese Box Curve were all too brief.

Aunt Lorraine's Twice-Baked Cheesy Potatoes

This simple dish takes a bit more time than a typical potato dish, like boiled potatoes, but it is worth the effort. When I was growing up, potatoes appeared at every meal. Cheese also was ubiquitous in this land of dairy farms and occasional cheese truck wrecks.

Serves 6 people

6 russet or other baking potatoes
¼ cup lard, shortening, or vegetable oil
½ cup (1 stick) butter, softened
½ cup cream or sour cream
½ cup milk
Salt and pepper, to taste
½ cup grated cheddar cheese
Green onions, diced (optional)

Rub potatoes with lard and prick each with a fork. Bake potatoes for 1 hour in a 400-degree oven, until still firm but cooked through. Remove from oven and slice lengthwise. Arrange on a baking sheet to cool. Scoop out insides of potatoes while still warm, leaving the skins intact for later use.

Put potato insides into a bowl with softened butter, cream, and milk. Season with salt and pepper. Stir and mash until mixture is the consistency of mashed potatoes. Fill the potato skins with mixture. Top with cheddar cheese and bake 15–20 minutes at 400 degrees, until cheese melts. Add diced green onions for more color, if desired.

A Turtle Story, Jammer, and the Beach

When developers presented blueprints of the School View Addition to the Menominee Tribe in the late 1960s, few people knew this area was already known as Banana Island by the locals. The tribal administrators had an ulterior motive for the project. The tribe built the Addition—its first suburb—to entice big-city Indians to move from fast-paced metropolitan areas to the rural reservation. My family was among the first to inhabit one of the houses.

That first tribal meeting to raise the prospect of building the suburb addressed an old problem on the reservation: housing. With a more suburban neighborhood, though, no one knew what a change in food culture would come to this remote Indian reservation. Nothing, however, could change the area's proximity to the Wolf River. It continued to be a source of protein-rich fish and other animals, including turtles, for families living at the subsistence level, no matter what people called the area.

The architectural firm proposed rectangular housing clusters built on what they thought was an empty landscape. Blueprints for single-story ranch homes were readily available, which was another selling point. Ranch-style houses, even those with basements, were easy to erect from standard materials, and this type of construction did not require any specialized technical skills.

However, the reservation was not a blank canvas. A pine grove stood on the site. There were already memories deeply embedded within this landscape, such as foot paths dating back to before the arrival of European settlers.

Also, there were a few glitches in the blueprints. Some basic amenities were overlooked, like playgrounds, sidewalks, and green spaces. And it had limited road access. Still, the plan had unexpected success, as many families moved into the houses. The Banana Island neighborhood was officially renamed the School View Addition, which was most often used because, after all, Banana Island seemed so un-Menominee.

This brand-new and isolated neighborhood had a preexisting foot trail network through the forest. This connected Banana Island to the rest of the reservation and to an older Indigenous trade route around the Great Lakes northern woods. Once inside this development with a car, however, there was no easy escape—only two exits. As a consequence, children and adults regularly used the informal trails to travel from here to there and back again.

Without green spaces, the quarter square mile of undeveloped land between the river and the main highway (north of Banana Island and south of the one-time Indian Agency hospital) became a playground for all ages, particularly two scenic points: the Beach and the Roots. The Beach was more popular with young children. They could wade into the water there and play in the sand. By comparison, to get into the water at the Roots required a dive from a fair height into deep, fast water. The Roots was popular with teenage boys. There were just two ways of reaching either of these spots, by river or by foot trail. The lack of roads kept the local cops out. Besides, they did not ever get out of their cars.

The Beach was located on a sharp, sandy curve along the east shore of the Wolf River. Altogether, this sandy bank was maybe twelve feet at its widest and about twenty-five feet long. Unless you knew of this place, you might walk right by and never know it was there. A thick stand of spindly pussy willows and red twig dogwood kept it hidden from the river travelers on both sides.

Strawberries, black-eyed Susans, and oyster root grew on the high, sunny bank. Oyster root, or salsify, is a commonly foraged food, plus it has a pleasant grassy appearance.

This beach was the result of an eroding natural river levee and the constant deposition of river sand from upstream rapids. The curve was not shallow or slow, by any means. Bathers could safely wade out about five feet from the shore. Just a few feet farther out, the river quickly reached a depth over an adult's head. Maybe twenty-five feet beyond the shore, past the middle of the river, a sand bar with swift currents on either side provided a strong teenaged swimmer's goal. The water around the sand bar was only a few feet deep. After any hard rain, swimming out to the sand bar and back was a struggle. Nobody, to my knowledge, ever drowned at the Beach, but I came close when I decided to go swimming alone once after a fierce rainstorm. Getting to that sand bar was not so hard, but getting back against the current proved otherwise.

There were bigger dangers than drowning to worry about at the Beach. One of the horror stories passed around among the kids involved a young girl and a snapping turtle. One sunny afternoon, the girl was out playing with a group of friends in the water where the willows begin their growth, and she stepped on the back of a snapping turtle. Adult snapping turtles average around a foot long and can weigh up to thirty pounds. They are fearsome beasts. While generally shy and docile around humans, they will bite when surprised. They have bony jaws that can open surprisingly wide, as well as fast-moving heads and necks. Plus, snapping turtles are determined. This one clamped down hard on the girl's toe and would not let go.

Screaming in terror, she and her friends dragged the creature those few feet to the shore and then up the bank. Little did they know that grabbing a turtle's tail and yanking just makes it bite down even harder. One of the girls had relatives living in Banana

Island, so she ran to get help. Some older boys quickly returned with a .22-caliber rifle. They shot the turtle a couple of times until it finally died, but it still would not release its grip on the girl's toe. One boy had a knife. They removed the turtle's head by severing the thick neck muscles and then sawing through the neck bones. Next, the jaws had to be pried open. I heard that she lost her toe. Maybe it fell off then, or maybe it developed gangrene and had to be removed later. At this point, I suppose it does not matter. I was not a witness, but I did hear this story a couple of times from different people. It scared the hell out of me, and I always kept alert for giant turtles.

From the Beach it is possible to see Banana Island within the river, upstream about four hundred feet. Yes, it really is shaped like a banana. It is not some friendly piece of yellow fruit, though. The gravelly mud shoals surrounding the island looked like prime snapping turtle country, so I never swam in that direction.

One early spring day, in the warmest part of the afternoon, but well before any snapping turtles woke up hungry from their winter hibernation, my cousin Jammer and I, filled with young male exuberance, were taking our time following a forgotten trail along the river. We were looking at the sights and enjoying the day. We were so tired of the long, unforgiving Wisconsin winter that it hurt. That day, finally, a beautiful blue sky above glistened with bright yellow sunshine. The temperature approached the midfifties. In Wisconsin, anything over forty-five degrees is officially T-shirt weather.

Jammer and I were sitting on a slight hill above the river, downstream from the beach. Our seats were comfortable piles made of last year's leaves among the scrub oak and white pine forest. Bright red wintergreen berries peeked out beneath their low-growing, evergreen leaves. We often chewed the leaves for their minty taste, and sometimes our parents brewed tea from them. In the dappled sunlight away from the mild wind, it really was quite beautiful. The river, an inviting blue background, became our goal. All of this anticipation, all of this temptation, was too much for us. We decided to go swimming.

Thin sheets of ice still floated past, propelled by upstream forces. Trapped on the surface, they performed slow-motion somersaults among the brush along the edge of the shore. We watched these natural gymnastics. When the river is this cold, it is absolutely clear. Motionless piles of aged, hardened snow on the north side of the trees made us even more determined to take the first swim of the season.

Still, we dallied and observed the river life. River redhorse, the name of red sucker fish that grow to be about two feet long, cruised the shallow gravel beds on this early spring day, fat with eggs. Like all suckers, this fish can be identified by its fat lips. Additionally, they are the only red fish in these waters. In the spring, they lazily paddle within reach of human hands, two feet out and two feet down. Like the brown bullheads that are revered among the Ojibwa, these fish make bowl-like nests in the river bottom where they deposit their eggs. Both suckers and bullheads use their tails to wave away the fine silt and sand. Bullheads are mainly found on silty bottoms, while redhorse are found on gravelly sand bottoms, but they often overlap. The redhorse eggs are deposited and fertilized in a process that takes one female and two males working together—the female sandwiched between the two males as they vibrate in unison. The resulting eggs and milt fall into the nest and are reburied by the fish that originally made the nest.

My friend Bud liked to eat suckers. Most people do not, since suckers have a bad reputation as bottom-feeding trash fish that taste like mud. I do know that given the right preparation, redhorse can be tasty. They live in the same fast, clean waters where trout live, which is a plus. But they also have lots of tough-to-remove scales and many small bones. They are just too much trouble to mess with for most people. Bud, however, had a way to clean them with a minimum of work.

He fileted the fish, which eliminated the need to scale, gut, and remove the heads. He then removed the flesh between the skin and the entrails—a process requiring knife skills that are uncommon among trout eaters, who simply gut their catch. The resulting redhorse filets were filled with tiny sharp bones and were still inedible. But Bud had a solution for that, too. He put those filets into a meat grinder. By turning the hand crank, he processed the flesh and bones into a lite-gray, gloppy paste of uniform consistency. If he had eggs and some bread or cracker crumbs, he would add them to the mix. If not? Hey, no problem. Bud would simply skip that step and jump forward to the next, which was forming gooey patties. He placed these on a flour-covered plate, dusted both sides, and dropped them into a black iron skillet filled with an inch of sizzling lard. Bud fried the patties until they were a golden brown. After salt and pepper, he served those steaming fish piles between slices of store-bought white bread with a spread made of mayonnaise and hot-dog relish. They were delicious. Still, it took an awful lot of work to get them ready to eat, and the processing part of it seemed so wrong. It was much easier to catch, cook, and eat a trout.

Fish are a major part of the Menominee diet because of the Wolf River and its tributaries. There are sandy ripples on the river bottom at Banana Island, caused by the shifting currents. Seen from above, these peaks and valleys become a three-dimensional diorama filled with tiny white clams, tiny white snails, and reddish brown crayfish, all going about their business. Occasionally, a school of minnow-like river chubs will dart by at seemingly near supersonic speed in fish formation, inches below the surface. If you throw a rock into the water at the school, they will scatter in all directions, only to reform just as quickly. They are members of the carp family with a diet that includes live and dead creatures.

They eat mostly water bugs living in the river around them, but any kind of insect will do. Low-flying deer flies are a delicacy to them. In the springtime, young males also make nests in the shallow gravel beds away from the main current. They do not use their tails. Chubs use their mouths to form depressions by picking up small pebbles and digging a hole. They deposit those same pebbles around the edge of the hole, creating a nest.

Once, on a bet, I swallowed a dozen chubs, one after another, alive and headfirst. They swam around in my belly for several days. I could feel them. For a week after that, every time I belched I could taste fish. It was not a good taste, either. I do not care what Bear Grylls of *Man vs. Wild* might say. I will never do that again.

In those olden days, wading along the slower, shallower, sandy bottom of the river near the downtown Veterans of Foreign Wars Park, I could find huge but empty off-white and sometimes yellowish clam shells that were bigger than my grandma's biggest dinner plates. The meat inside must have been larger than my young, clenched fist. I always wondered who or what ate those clams. I never dared.

So on that beautiful spring day, after retelling our previous exploits and several rounds of dares and double-dares, Jammer and I worked ourselves up to a swim in the icy river. First, we needed to undress on the beach. I watched Jammer as he took off his shoes and socks, stuffing his socks into his shoes and placing them together on the sand. I did the same, item by item, self-consciously leaving my clothes next to his. Next, he removed his shirt, folded it, and placed it on top of his shoes. Again, I matched him move for move. Next was his pants, which he folded and placed atop the shoes and shirt. I did the same, tossing my underwear on top.

The river was cold, frigid in fact, as we should have expected. Still, we managed to man up and wade to a depth above our knees but still well below our private parts without too much trouble.

This gave us another opportunity for dares and double-dares. One might think that standing naked in midriver arguing with your first cousin about who was going under first would make you self-conscious and attentive to your surroundings. It did neither.

We were not alone in the woods. Jammer and I were so involved in this game of testosterone chess that we did not realize that some girls were standing next to our piles of clothes. They had been watching us from the riverbank, the same riverbank that we were facing. If only we had looked up. The sneaky girls were all younger than us. I think they were related to this guy Chester who lived down the street from me—maybe they were his sisters. Jammer and I saw them at the same moment, and simultaneously fell to our knees in the cold water, covering our man parts. The girls pointed their index fingers directly at us, laughing, while prodding our clothes with sneakered toes. They taunted us, "Eww, Jammer, does your mother know that you are back here in the river all naked and being nasty in public?" The water was really cold, and I felt very small. Suddenly, two girls each grabbed a pile of our clothing. At first, they slowly backed up the path, making whooping noises. We swore at them. They whooped louder. We swore louder.

This situation, any situation involving girls, was confusing for me as a young man. Only now, looking back from a distance of over fifty-five years, can I admit it was a little funny.

Jammer looked at me and said, "To heck with those girls, I'm not going to let them steal my clothes." Since I would have gotten into all kinds of hell if I showed up naked at home at any time of the day, I quickly agreed. It was Jammer who was the first to charge the beach and rush over the grassy embankment in an attempt to retrieve our clothes.

We chased the girls along the path—them laughing and us swearing. We had already used up our stock of swear words while standing in the river and were now repeating them, creatively combining them for the eighth or ninth time. Since we were barefoot, we could not catch up to them. Just before the path reached the street, twenty feet from my home and public view, they dropped our clothes on the trail and ran down the street screaming with laughter.

We quickly and quietly put on our clothes and appreciated how the girls were not being completely hateful. They could have taken our clothing home with them. They were only teasing us. We never plotted revenge on those girls, and to my knowledge, they never told anybody about us. That afternoon on the Beach stays with us.

Turtle Soup

Little distinction is made among species of turtles for this recipe. All turtles in the Great Lakes region are edible. The meat is rich, red flesh. Turtles are difficult to catch because they are difficult to approach. They usually submerge and swim away long before you get close enough to dispatch one. Here are instructions for cleaning and dressing a turtle, and then the recipe.

The larger turtles seen around Banana Island were usually snapping turtles. A large snapper has up to seven kinds of meat, and depending on where the sample is cut from, they may taste somewhat like pork, beef, veal, chicken, shrimp, fish, or goat.

Serves 4 to 6 people

Meat from one medium-sized turtle, cut into small pieces
1 gallon water
1 small white onion, quartered
Salt and pepper, to taste
½ cup (1 stick) butter
2 tablespoons flour
1 (3-ounce) can tomato paste

To Clean the Turtle

Using a sharp knife, blunt stick, bone saw, or hammer, cut the head and feet off the turtle. If this is a snapping turtle, be extra careful, as the jaws may snap shut if you touch them. Place the carcass on its back on a board, and then nail or tie the tail to one end. Cut away the skin on the lower edge of the back shell. Cut the belly plate loose. Remove the skin from the neck, tail, and quarters—these are the edible parts. Discard the organs. Remove the tenderloins from the top and bottom shells and rinse all edible pieces with water. Alternately, wrap the entire turtle, without cutting it up, in cheesecloth and simmer until cooked through.

To Make the Soup

In a large pot, boil cleaned turtle meat in water. Skim as it cooks. Add onion, salt, and pepper. Simmer for 2 hours or until meat is tender. Remove meat with tongs and let cool. (If you do not let it cool, the meat will be too tough to cut.) Chop into bite-sized pieces. Reserve the broth.

In a saucepan, melt butter. Stir in flour to thicken. Take about 2 cups broth from the pot and add to the saucepan, mixing until it is a creamy consistency. Add tomato paste. Season with more salt and pepper to taste. Add turtle meat to the saucepan. Simmer on low for 10 minutes or until heated through. Stir and serve.

Steamed Oyster Root (Purple Salsify)

Oyster root, otherwise known as purple salsify or Tragopogon porrifolius, *is a root vegetable member of the dandelion family. Its early blooms are a sign of spring. The plant grows well in gravelly, disturbed soil, like that on the beaches of Banana Island and other shorelines along the Wolf River. It can also be found along highways and trails where seeds take root in open ground. This is one of the plants of a subsistence diet in northern Wisconsin.*

The root is long, thin, and white. It has been described as tasting like an oyster. Maybe—if oysters taste like parsnips. It is easily identified by the purplish dandelion-looking flower growing from its center. As the flower dies, the head becomes a puffball of seeds resembling a giant dried dandelion flower. The prepared plants can be steamed or boiled. They could probably be grilled, too, if large enough roots could be found. The plant is commercially available and can be purchased online. Some chefs use it in beef and veal recipes. On the rez, salsify most often lands in the stew pot. Use them in soups, stews, and roasts as you would parsnips, potatoes, or rutabagas.

Oyster roots
Water
1 tablespoon lemon juice
Salt, pepper, and butter, to taste

After digging the roots from the ground, peel them and place them in a pan of water and lemon juice. This will stop them from browning. Cook as you would carrots—either steam or boil in water—until tender. Serve with salt, pepper, and butter if being used as a side vegetable.

Wintergreen Tea

Wintergreen, or teaberry, has a strong, minty flavor and makes a delicious tea. Like willow bark, it also contains an aspirin-like chemical that relieves pain. The berries and leaves can be chewed, or the leaves can be made into tea.

Collect and clean 10–15 leaves for each cup of tea. Boil water and remove from heat. Add leaves to the teapot and let steep for 10 minutes. When cooled, pour out and drink.

Commodity Foods and Mom's Cooking

The completion of the first phase of tribal housing stirred local resentments over a new demographic. Menominee residents from the cities filled the new School View Addition neighborhood. Some reservation residents were uneasy with the cultural values held by those returning from an urban diaspora. Some were members of an organization called Determination of Rights and Unity for Menominee Shareholders (DRUMS), formed in 1970 to regain federal recognition. They were not as militant as the American Indian Movement members, but they weren't pacifists, either.

Some detractors of DRUMS began referring to the Banana Island neighborhood as Commot Lane. This pejorative nickname referred to the large number of inhabitants, perhaps all of them, receiving government-surplus commodity foods. In local dialect, the word *commodity* was shortened to "commot."

Qualifications to live in these low-income tribal housing units were based on a complicated mathematical formula using federal income guides and the total number of residents per house. Approval to move into one of these new homes also could prequalify that family to receive commots. The tribe had streamlined the two application processes, so bundled paperwork for one program followed the applicant from one program office to another. The intent was to provide as high a standard of living as possible for these Menominees as inducement for them to return to their northern homeland. My mother and stepfather took the steps to house us and to acquire commots.

Things were hectic for my family in 1969. For three days a week—Monday, Wednesday, and Friday—I was alone. On those days, my mom commuted fifty miles each way from our home in Banana Island to Green Bay in order to work on a teaching degree at the University of Wisconsin. What was even more difficult for her, and the family, was that she did not drive. For eight semesters, three summer practicums, and a couple of internships, she bummed rides from a revolving list of students and factory workers who also drove those hundred miles daily. She managed to make all of her required collegiate special events and teaching internships, too. Just getting back and forth from home to school was a monumental hurdle for her to overcome, never mind all of the required classwork and studying. At the time, for that summer anyway, my White stepfather was gainfully employed as a tribal cop and took his meals elsewhere. My four siblings, two brothers and two sisters, also made their own accommodations to our rapidly dissolving family life.

So we entered an era of grocery-store quick, if not fast, foods. Despite the circumstances, my mom made sure that we ate a wide variety of foods, albeit the most convenient ones. She favored the ones being mass advertised on television, which she considered the most sophisticated.

Let me give you an example. She normally kept four different kinds of store-bought bread available in our household larder: white, rye, potato, and raisin bread with icing. We did not eat Indian frybread, at least not at home. Mom did not make frybread at all, except twice when my two sisters were there to help. Although this pan-Indian recipe is found across the country—from Navajo land in Arizona to the Prairie Band Potawatomi in Kansas to our tribe, the Menominee in the northlands—my mother opted out. One reason? Making frybread is a daunting chore. It requires preparing, tending to, and cleaning up after a large pot of boiling grease. It was something that my mom did not feel like tackling. I do not ever remember my grandma making frybread, either. My sister still makes an excellent Menominee-style frybread, though, using a sweet dough made with bleached wheat flour and yeast. Navajos use Blue Bird flour. Each tribe puts their own unique twist on the recipe.

At our house, if there was any frybread, it was made elsewhere, and besides, it seldom lasted long enough to appear at any meal. The primary bread eaten at our home was a national brand of supermarket white puff bread, the kind made in thousand-loaf batches, and it was almost always Wonder Bread. Loaves of this brand had, in my opinion, an underrated value. I thought the bread was perfectly pliable, having the right amount of give and yet stiff enough to construct a thick sandwich.

Even my full-blood grandparents ate only supermarket white bread. We often visited the local bakeries, but we never bought artisan white bread there. Wonder Bread was baked elsewhere and shipped everywhere. It could have been a coincidence, a monopoly, favoritism, or simply consumer preference, but very often, at least around the Shawano-area supermarkets, Wonder was the only sliced white bread for sale in the supermarket. It lay on bread aisle shelves—row upon row, stacked heels front to back. Its white plastic wrapping was imprinted with red, yellow, and blue dots that I always saw as balloons. It was the wrapper's tagline, "Building strong bodies 8 ways," that hooked my mother, who considered it the healthy alternative. For her, buying Wonder Bread at the supermarket was visual proof to the outside, White world that she loved her family, despite her absences.

This particular brand of white bread, in my opinion, made the best grilled cheese sandwiches. Not only did Wonder Bread grill up nicely and brown toastily, but it was also the perfect-sized canvas. A whole slice of cheese cut from an eight-pound rectangular block of commodity cheese completely covered the slice of bread, from corner to corner. When the cheese and the bread were the same size, there was no danger of gaps—no need to add little orphan scraps of cheese to fill up that empty corner of the grilled cheese sandwich. In a perfect grilled cheese sandwich, like Mom's, the melted cheese would bulge between toasted bread slices in a fragrant, yellow-orange ooze.

With our coffee in the mornings, we ate toasted rye bread with butter made in a local Shawano dairy and fruit jelly or jam slathered on each slice. My mom made and "put up" many kinds of jellies, jams, and fruit preserves with fruit that had been gathered by the family during those infrequent times that my stepfather could hold his temper. Despite him, we managed to can all of our own jams, jellies, and fruit preserves. We ate a lot of chokecherry jelly because the fruit was so easy to gather. This shrub produces a very tart, small cherry that is easily found and gathered. They really are so tart that they cause you to choke, like a persimmon before the first hard frost. They require cooking and lots of sugar. Mom and we kids made a delicious jelly with this often overlooked fruit.

Chokecherries are a stone fruit, much smaller than red or black supermarket cherries. And they are particularly sour. They do not grow very tall, but this shrub produces massive amounts of cherries, growing on the sides of thin branches connected by thin stalks. Chokecherries left to their natural state on the shrub tend to be either red, very hard, and unripe or purple, soft, and ripe.

Chokecherries do not seem to get attacked by many insects, but I have seen dogs eat them. Yes, I really have. I once saw a clever German shepherd mix jump a couple feet upward alongside a shrub and grab a fruit-laden branch with his mouth. Then, he let the branch drag across his teeth as it snapped back into place, leaving a handful of cherries in his mouth. These he chewed and swallowed.

The only difficult thing about making chokecherry jelly is separating the inedible seeds from the edible juice and pulp. I guess that is what children are for. We kids fought each other for the privilege of helping. Mom had an aluminum cone with many small holes. After rinsing the cherries with water, we dumped them inside this perforated metal mortar and "worked" them with a wooden pestle. As the cherries were crushed against the sides of the cone, juice and tiny bits of purple-black fruit drained through the perforated sides, down the bottom of the cone, and into a waiting container. Afterward, the leftover almond-smelling seeds and the dripping pulp were dumped outside in the backyard along the edges of the woods in hopes of growing new chokecherry shrubs. The remaining thick, purple slurry, like a thick grape juice, was then processed with sugar on the stove and canned for later use. A year's worth of homemade jelly for a family of seven could be "done up" in one day with enough cooperation. Chokecherries really are that easy. Chokecherry jelly plopped on top of a slice of warm toasted rye bread with melted butter is a treat.

I also liked a scoop of refrigerator-cold, homemade applesauce spooned directly out of a quart-size mason jar as a topping on toast and on oatmeal, too. We put up all of our own applesauce. I was so spoiled with homemade sauce that even today I do not buy store-bought applesauce.

We got our apples two different ways. Some years, our entire extended family would move to the Door County peninsula and work as migrant workers at one of the orchards. We began our harvest season picking tart cherries. They are red and beautiful, and they make wonderful cherry pies. The cherry-picking season wrapped up about the same time that apples began ripening. Some orchards had both cherry and apple trees. In those days, there were many apple orchards looking for pickers. Jamaicans, Whites, American Indians, or Mexicans—it did not matter. The fruit needed picking. Usually, we stayed in camp housing, but one season we had a big house on a farm to ourselves. With the beginning of fall and school, I attended the local elementary school in Sister Bay.

Windfall apples were usually free to workers. That was the first way we obtained apples. The men in the family collected the extra bags of apples from the orchards, but it was the women, with Grandma in charge, who made applesauce and canned dozens of jars after the family had moved back home.

The second way that we got apples was picking them in the woods. Wild apples have more unique tastes and textures than orchard apples. We ate many of them raw, but being wild, they often suffered insect damage. So, to avoid eating bugs, we would trim our apples. Sometimes, a few slices of apple were all that remained after the trimming. All of our wild applesauce was chunky, made of different-sized pieces. Wild apples required a lot more time and effort to gather and prepare than orchard apples. Our return on all that work was not so much the jars of applesauce—it was the family time spent working for them.

We picked our apples from a couple of wild groves. Our favorite picking spots were easy to get to, close to roads. These wild orchards in the West Branch area of the Menominee Reservation were associated with early failed attempts at farming by Catholic Indians. Abandoned, they are mostly frequented by black bears, some of whom are ill-tempered and hardly welcoming. In general, black bears have little regard for social decorum. It is best to leave all bears with plenty of apples to eat, or even better yet, leave the orchards alone. Our favorite groves had few bears.

The rye bread of our youth was not the inoffensive and anonymous modern light rye bread for sale in local big-box stores today. The rye bread of my youth was available only in small-town bakeries, where I could see the men who had just baked it covered in flour dust. You made eye contact with those bakers when you picked out your loaf and paid for it. You had to—the bakers also worked the till. The change from your purchase would be covered in flour dust. It was a dead giveaway of your visit to a sweet shop.

We ate dark, thick slices of sweet rye bread, fresh baked by the children and grandchildren of European immigrants, especially on meatless Fridays. Although nobody in my immediate family was a practicing Catholic—indeed, I was the only one to attend mass at St. Joe's and always against my will—Mom still followed Catholic practices whenever it was convenient. This meant, unlike my grandparents (Grandpa insisted on meat at every meal), we did not eat meat on Fridays.

On Fridays, like thousands of other Wisconsin residents, we ate lots of rye bread with oven-baked fish sticks, along with a macaroni-and-cheese salad garnished with frozen peas for lunch or dinner, and sometimes for both meals. Both the mac salad in the fridge and the fish sticks in the freezer stored pretty well, while no bread ever lasted long at our house. Food did not go to waste, and we ate a lot of bread.

Both the mac salad and the fish sticks had simple preparations—so easy that Mom did not have to be home to provide a healthy home-cooked meal. On her school days, she did not get home until late, sometimes not until ten o'clock. A cold mac salad could even be bought the day before at the supermarket deli. I liked the kind with the tiny squares of cheddar cheese.

Fish sticks, sold in the freezer aisle, could go right from the home freezer into a preheated 425-degree oven. A fish stick—and who does not like fish sticks?—tastes fairly good right out of the hot oven or sitting on a serving platter at room temperature or even cold out of the fridge as a leftover. I liked them placed on slices of rye bread smeared with Kraft Sandwich Spread, which we used just like straight-out-of-the-bottle tartar sauce. It is reminiscent of a thick Thousand Island dressing. Uncle Donny liked this kind of spread on a couple of cold Oscar Mayer hot dogs split lengthwise and served on rye bread.

Back in the day, every box of fish sticks came with a small package of green roughage inside a cellophane bag, made from chopped-up pickles and spices. There was always plenty of room for this condiment package in the box of fish sticks, since they made the cardboard box three times the size actually needed to hold the fish. According to the special condiment instructions, you emptied this package into a mixing bowl and whisked in a scoop of mayonnaise to make tartar sauce. The few times that we made tartar sauce from this pickle packet, Mom used Kraft Miracle Whip instead. Much later, I learned from Uncle Buddy that if you really want tartar sauce, but do not have any, you can just chop a sweet pickle into any brand of mayonnaise.

My mom also liked potato bread. This kind of bread could be found in many local supermarkets, sliced and packaged in plastic wrap, but Mom preferred to buy her loaves still warm and just sliced from one of the bakeries in Shawano. I still think potato bread with the iconic white potato powder dusted on the top of the loaf was the best choice for her Tuesday lunch of ground bologna spread.

Of all the different things that she made for us to eat, this is what I most fondly remember. Some people on the reservation call these ground bologna sandwiches "funeral sandwiches" because of how regularly they are served at wakes. Since Mom bundled all of her classes on Monday, Wednesday, and Friday, she was able to be home on the other days and do home stuff with us. Tuesday morning was ground bologna day. It all began right after breakfast when the dishes and kitchen table were clean. This was the first step: make room to work. Next, Mom found a heavy, silver-gray chunk of steel in a bottom cabinet. This old-school food grinder was powered by a hand crank.

In one episode of *Popeye Meets Sinbad*, a vintage cartoon from the 1930s, Popeye's friend Wimpy follows a duck through the sixteen-minute film trying to entice the bird into a grinder in order to make burgers. In a 1950s *Three Stooges* short, when Curly drops bullets into an old-time food grinder and turns the hand crank, it becomes a machine gun. He uses the food grinder against the villains and saves the day. As a kid, I understood that this was a mythic piece of kitchen equipage.

That food grinder once belonged to my grandmother. I watched her use it on Sunday mornings to make hash for our breakfast from the Saturday leftover beef roast, leftover potatoes, and a whole white onion. I am not exactly sure how my mom came to have it after Grandma retired, but eventually she gave it to Uncle Buddy. Upon his death, I received it as a keepsake from his estate. For a couple of years, this food grinder sat unused in my Kansas pantry while we relied upon our Cuisinart. But it was a working man's tool, an heirloom, and it was meant to be used. We gave it to my daughter. I hope that she will give it to one of her children, keeping this food grinder in the family.

Mom's grinder needed to be attached to a stout table using the vise-like clamp. The next step in making ground bologna sandwiches was to find a ring of bologna. In Wisconsin, this is a common food item. Mom always used an Oscar Mayer all-beef ring bologna for her mince, but other fine varieties of ring bologna exist. Garlic-infused ring bologna is common, as are turkey varieties. Mom did not use those other varieties, as she was traditional, but she knew they were out there.

She cut the bologna ring into large pieces and dropped them, one at a time, into the rotating grinder. All of us kids competed to turn the hand crank, like in one of those World War II movies where the desperate Filipino troops turn the crank of a hand-powered radio deep in the jungle. The grinder crank turned an internal auger, which forced the solid food into a rotating disk containing small holes that turned anything it came into contact with into a mince. Shredded meat dropped out of the end of the grinder into a large mixing bowl. Mom and one of us kids kept this rhythm going until we ran out of ring bologna. Finally, Mom dropped spoonfuls of Kraft Miracle Whip into the grinder, followed by a well-drained dill pickle—never a garlic dill and never a sweet pickle. Adding the wet ingredients at the end helped rinse all the meat from the auger.

Then Mom turned to the huge mound of ingredients in the mixing bowl. She used a wooden spoon to fold the ground ingredients into each other until she was satisfied with the smooth consistency. This meat spread was put into an empty plastic margarine tub and covered with plastic wrap to stay fresh until the moment when the sandwiches were actually put together.

Another of our family traditions was eating raisin-bread-with-icing toast on weekend mornings. Getting the bread to toast properly in our toaster without the drizzles of icing melting and falling off was a matter of compromise and timing. The compromise was that the degree of doneness was dependent on the amount of icing desired. Mom always kept a small bowl of white sugar and cinnamon mixture at the breakfast table to top the toast, to make the raisin-and-icing toast even sweeter.

Through the natural process of bread attrition at our house, there were times when raisin bread with icing was the only bread left from which to make sandwiches. Raisin bread made a good platform for our homemade spread of peanut butter and maple syrup. Hydrogenated peanut butter, rather than one with a layer of oil, is imperative to keep this mix from being too runny. Just mix a couple of tablespoons of peanut butter in a small bowl and add maple syrup for sweetness and consistency.

Raisin bread with icing is less successful as a platform when used for a sandwich made from Kraft Sandwich Spread and sliced hot dogs—or Miracle Whip, sheets of head lettuce, and Oscar Mayer bologna. These sandwiches did not taste bad, just weird.

Once a week on Friday nights, after getting home from Green

Bay, Mom did the bulk of the family grocery shopping at the Super Value Store. This was when the Super Value was located downtown, behind the Main Street bakeries, ice cream shops, and shoe stores and across the street from the county library, in the building now occupied by the Shawano Police Department.

I used my mom's weekly shopping trip as an opportunity to visit Main Street and the three places in town that sold records. From my meager allowance, I saved enough money to buy something new, either a 33⅓ rpm LP or three new 45s. The record shop near Main and East Division had the best selection of albums and 45s in town, but they had no listening stations, unlike the Woolworth's at the corner of Green Bay and Main and the Schultz Brothers'. In my youth, that building, made bright on the inside with fluorescent lighting, used to smell like it was filled with cotton candy.

My aunt Nita bought an album from that record store on East Division, the one without listening stations. She thought it was a country-and-western album. The name of it was *Electric Music for the Mind and Body* by Country Joe and the Fish. She listened only partway into the first song, then gave the record to me. To me, at fourteen years old, that album was an epiphany. Years and years later, I met the daughter of the guitar player for the Fish at an education conference. She listened to my proposed master's thesis about entheogenic substances and gave me some valuable advice. In return, I got some firsthand knowledge of a band I followed most of my life.

At the Woolworth's listening station, I could listen to a 45 before purchase. Going to Woolworth's was a social occasion. I could hang around and listen to what other kids, White kids, were listening to and maybe even talk to a girl, or at least look at some. This store had an ancient and stained wooden floor that creaked, and inside, depending on where you stood, it always smelled like popcorn or fried hamburgers with onions. A cigar-store Indian stood watch in the middle. There was a long counter with stools attached to the floor where I could spin, keep time, and almost dance without getting up. They served Coca-Cola from an old-time soda tap. For an extra dime, I could get a scoop of ice cream and have a float.

On Friday nights, after paying the bills and grocery shopping, Mom made her last in-town stop at a bakery to buy three loaves of bread: a loaf of rye, a loaf of potato, and a loaf of raisin bread. She always had the bakery slice the bread. Sometimes she would buy hard rolls for the next day's breakfast. I could see the bakery from across the street at Woolworth's. As soon as I saw my mother inside, I hurried over to catch her before she paid for the bread. If I was fast enough, she would buy me a cream puff or a warm apple turnover slathered with vanilla icing.

In the 1960s, Shawano was still a major resort area, and Friday nights were always hectic. Working people cashed paychecks, bought groceries, and paid light and phone bills while carloads of young people cruised up and down Main Street in borrowed cars. Local farmers came to town, stopping at the banks, the hardware stores, and the farm supply places.

On downtown Shawano sidewalks, Polish and German farmers mixed with sophisticated tourists from the cities. People came to Shawano from all over Wisconsin and Illinois, with car radios blasting. They honked at window-shopping local girls. They admired each other's muscle cars, like Plymouth Road Runners, Chevy Camaros and Chevelles, Dodge Chargers, and Ford Mustangs. They circled like great white sharks, traveling to and from the Shawano County Park Pavilion seven miles away. The twisting road followed the lakeshore, and long convoys of out-of-town tourists formed. In the summer, the county park had live music on Wednesday and Saturday nights. The park also had a tavern that served 3.2-percent-alcohol beer, or what was called *near beer*, to eighteen-year-olds who were nearly adults. Even better, the county park had a beach that still remains popular as a sunbathing spot—it was a great place to meet girls from all over.

Shawano taverns, by contrast, served real, full-strength beer to customers twenty-one years old or older. These Main Street joints left their front doors propped open to beckon unwary passersby with the tinny sounds of honky-tonk, the clinking of ice striking metal in cheap cocktail shakers, the titter of flirty voices, and the musky adult smells enhanced by aromatic spirits. Sometimes at dusk, when walking past those dark spaces toward the island of light at the Five and Dime, I strained to hear feminine laughter. Sometimes I would slow down and try to poke my head inside, attempting to see one of the women hidden in the shadows.

Maybe once a month, my mother and sister would bake bread for the household larder. At times, it could even be once every four or five months. Mom's cinnamon and raisin rolls were really good. We made entire meals from them. Mom rolled out a sheet of dough and buttered it liberally. (We did not use oleo margarine, as it was still illegal in Wisconsin.) Then we heavily dusted the dough with a mixture of cinnamon and white sugar. Just before rolling the dough into a cylinder, Mom sprinkled on a handful of raisins. Once the dough cylinder was formed, she sliced it into sections about an inch and a half thick. These were placed on a greased pan and baked until crisp.

When Mom did bake, she always baked several loaves of white bread in addition to a couple of baking pans of white dinner rolls. All of this was made from the same batch of yeast-risen dough. She used commodity flour, commodity lard, and commodity raisins, when needed, to bake our bread. Other families used the same ingredients to make frybread. While the baked goods were still hot from the oven and slathered with butter, the six or seven of us could easily eat an entire loaf of bread or pan of rolls. Mom called them dinner rolls, but they tasted best cold in the mornings. On Sunday mornings, we ate those rolls with a pat of butter and a spoon of chokecherry jelly accompanied by a cup of coffee with evaporated milk poured from the can and a couple spoonfuls of sugar.

I believe my mom thought her homemade bread was not as good as the store-bought Wonder Bread because it did not build healthy bodies eight different ways. She was wrong, though. Hers was so much better.

Our neighborhood was known as Commot Lane because of the residents' dependence on the government-rationed commodity foods. What went unsaid was that, except for the tribal elite, almost everybody else on the rez during those years also depended on the same government-funded cuisine. When people ask about Indigenous foods, they do not realize the profound influence of twentieth-century realities like these.

This government program had two goals: provide low-income families with nutrition assistance and, more importantly, provide financial support to farmers by creating a market. When the price of certain goods fell below a predetermined level, the federal government stepped in and bought any unsold goods. These goods were then donated to people who could not afford them at that price. Items distributed as commodity foods varied by region. Commodity foods could include items as diverse as fresh dragon fruit, fresh kiwis, ground bison, and fancy bakery cakes.

A list of those foods distributed to needy families on a monthly basis often included items like lard, white flour, yellow cornmeal, white rice, pasta, dried beans, dried split peas, boxes of cornflakes, dehydrated potatoes, dehydrated milk, dehydrated eggs, raisins, corn syrup, American processed cheese, canned peanut butter, canned beans, canned pork, canned beef, and canned chicken, as well as the usual flavors of canned vegetables—tomatoes, corn, green beans, peas—and canned fruits such as peaches, pears, and fruit cocktail. Cans of thin applesauce gruel were also available. The unsweetened pineapple juice came in gallon cans that required church keys to open. The juice tasted of metal quickly after being opened. The canned apple juice was much better.

My family used the lard in our daily cooking. Adding lard to dough makes for wonderful pie shells, and we had some kind of fruit pie every day when I stayed with my grandmother. All of those pies were made from our own put-up fruits. We had many quarts of canned blackberries, raspberries, cherries, and apples from which to choose. We had venison meat pies on most Sundays. Deer meat was provided by male relatives.

While many pastry chefs still prefer using lard to butter, most home cooks have reduced its overall use. I did not know this from my family's cooking. One of the traditional North Woods recipes for chili includes a half cup of lard as an ingredient. It certainly does give this Wisconsin Indian dish a rich finish. Now when I make chili, I remove as much fat as possible and use lean meats.

We used commodity cornmeal to make a hot breakfast cereal. I liked it best when served with butter placed on top of the cornmeal and with whole milk poured over the whole thing. Served with toast, it is a satisfying meal. Uncle Buddy made a delicious corn bread using government lard, government cornmeal, and a can of government corn. He was quite proud of this dish.

One of my mom's recipes, and another one of my favorites, was her white rice and hot dogs. It is pretty simple. She just cooked the rice according to package instructions. The trick was that a few minutes before the rice was finished, she added a half dozen all-beef wieners, cut into one-inch pieces. Then she seasoned the dish with salt. Our family was brand loyal and used only Oscar Mayer all-beef hot dogs. Later, I learned that this dish tastes even better if you substitute Nueske's wieners from Wittenberg.

The commodity dehydrated milk was problematic. Mixed according to the directions—add a certain amount of dried milk to a certain amount of clean water, shake well, and chill—it tasted funny, perhaps because of its nonfat status. Nobody liked it. Some people discovered that if you mixed a certain amount of dried milk and water with a certain amount of real, fresh whole milk and then chilled it, the result was a barely tolerable milklike beverage that still tasted bad. Nobody liked it served this way either. Some people added dried milk to their dogs' and cats' food. Those pets did not voice any complaints.

Because these boxes of dried milk were distributed monthly but so seldom used, my family built up a stockpile of unopened milk boxes. The solution to this was staring me in the face. Yogurt was just becoming a commercial success in middle America, and I was buying several containers a week. Eating yogurt marked you as a liberal. While visiting a guy in Green Bay, I noticed his yogurt maker. As soon as I got back to Shawano, I found one at the health-food store on Green Bay Avenue and bought it. This machine made one quart of yogurt, in four eight-ounce jars, over eight hours. We would mix up some dried milk and water in the evening, strain it through a metal wire sieve, add a little starter to the batch, cook it, then add it to the machine. In the morning, we had delicious fresh yogurt. It was indistinguishable in taste and texture from the Dannon yogurt that we used for the original starter. From then on, we had fresh yogurt every day, and after several months, we ran out of the dehydrated milk and had to ask relatives for donations, which they readily gave. I used maple syrup to sweeten the yogurt.

As a teenager, I experimented with commots other ways, too. I am not a great fan of pancakes, and I thought that I could whip up something better. In a large bowl, I mixed together about a third of a package of dehydrated eggs, a handful of dehydrated potatoes, a handful of white flour, and a handful of yellow cornmeal. I added water to this, forming a slurry—not thin and not thick. I dropped spoonfuls of this into a very hot, well-greased, cast-iron frying pan. As soon as bubbles formed on the top of the pancakes, it was time to turn them over. When the edges crisped, they were done. Served hot with butter and with the bottle of corn syrup, this was a much-improved pancake breakfast.

The commodity peanut butter was packaged in large cans, and nobody liked it. It was too thick, like a crumbly, spent mortar. Peanut butter cookies were pretty common on the reservation, as a last resort.

Some people brewed homemade hooch from the government-supplied raisins, assorted fruit juices, and bottles of corn syrup. People are always inventive, but I never had the initiative.

Commodity dehydrated potatoes were good. We were already buying Betty Crocker instant mashed potatoes at the supermarket. There was no taste difference between that type of supermarket instant potatoes and the government dehydrated potatoes. Regular potatoes that you had to peel and cook were obviously better tasting, but the government potatoes were done as soon as you got the water hot. Besides, Grandpa Moon honestly liked the instant potatoes better.

The canned chicken was tasty but looked bad. The boned meat came enveloped in a yellowish embryo of chicken fat. This was not something that you wanted to eat right out of the can. First, it had to be heated up to degrease it. Once heated, juices drained away from the meat. Then, the chicken was ready to eat. We ate many wonderful meals of canned chicken meat, dehydrated potatoes, gravy made with the chicken juice, and canned corn.

Out of the three, twenty-nine-ounce cans of meat—chicken, pork, and beef—I thought the pork was the best tasting and the least gross-looking one. The pork had the least amount of congealed fat or packing juice. When the can was opened by removing both lids, the pork slid effortlessly out of the can as a cylinder of meat. It held its shape and was easy to cut into thick slices for subsequent grilling or frying. Crumbled up, the commodity pork was delicious for impromptu meals with reconstituted potatoes, canned peas, and gravy.

I did not care for the canned beef. To me, this one of the three commot canned meats was the grossest looking. When a can is first opened, even at room temperature, unappetizing ribbons of thick yellow congealed fat are clearly visible. Also, the odor is nasty. I could not get past the appearance and smell to enjoy eating canned beef.

A collection of commodity foods were visible in most homes in our neighborhood—I was in most of these homes at some time or another—and a similar collection could be found in other reservation neighborhoods. Even though frybread, one of the common denominators in Native cuisine across the country, was not part of our family's tradition, our neighbors and relatives filled in for this lapse.

Healthy Frybread

This recipe uses vegetable oil instead of lard and is slightly healthier than older, more traditional frybread recipes. Enjoy these in moderation.

Serves about 16 people

4 cups white flour, or experiment with replacing ½ or 1 cup of the white flour with whole wheat flour
4 tablespoons baking soda
½ teaspoon salt
3¼ cups vegetable oil—¼ cup to make the dough and another 3 cups to fry the dough
1 cup warm water, give or take

Mix dry ingredients in a large bowl. Slowly add ¼ cup vegetable oil to dry mixture to achieve an oatmeal-like consistency. Slowly add warm water, a little at a time, until the dough sticks together. Roll dough into about 16 fist-sized balls. Put the dough balls in a large mixing bowl. Cover the bowl with a towel and let stand for 10 minutes. Using your hands, form balls of dough into large, thick pancakes. Without crowding the pan, fry each piece in hot oil (at about 375 degrees) until it is golden brown on both sides. Flip as needed. Cool slightly on paper towels and serve.

Acorns, Ticks, Bud, and the Black Bear

The School View housing development became a Menominee version of the great American melting pot. Its new residents, from cities as well as the reservation, latched onto the older, more descriptive name of Banana Island for their community instead of the new official one. But no bananas grew on Banana Island.

South of Banana Island, the area bordered by the river, the state highway, and the county line was a forgotten mixed forest of second-growth white pine and scrub oak. Scrub oak is a generic term that refers to several kinds of tall woody brush—short trees, to some—that bear acorns. Bear oak is the predominate variety to grow in this part of the reservation. Several natural clearings in this forest were filled with blackberry thickets and tall islands of staghorn sumac—habitats favored by wild turkey. Scrub oak, similar to blackberries and sumac, grows best on disturbed soils, like those after a big fire.

As children, we played with toy pipes like the ones Popeye the Sailor smoked, made from acorn husks with the meat removed and hollowed lengths of river cane stuck through the side. Acorns were an important part of an old Indian's life. To begin any recipe with acorns, the outer shell must be removed. Once shelled, acorns are a major plant source of proteins and fat. A type of bread can be made from baked, finely crushed acorn meat. Blanched acorns can be added to soups. Cooked like this, acorns have a mouthfeel resembling chickpeas. Fresh acorns can be picked and eaten raw from the tree as a handy snack. Fresh raw acorns taste like Brazil nuts. Certain varieties are sweet, while others can get very bitter from natural tannin. When salted to taste, the flavor of roasted acorns is more complex than salted peanuts—less meaty, lighter, and sweeter, with an outside crunch and a tender inside. Once baked, the texture and taste are reminiscent of macadamia nuts.

Many creatures depend on acorns. Unsurprisingly, black bears eat lots of bear oak acorns. White-tailed deer eat the fallen acorns and, by standing on their rear legs, the tender tips of the tree branches as well. Acorns are the preferred food of wild turkeys. Many types of insects eat acorns. Almost all of these animals eat their acorns after they have ripened and then fallen to the ground. Most, except a few hearty insects, avoid eating the green acorns still on the tree. Those can be intensely bitter and mouth-puckering, like an underripe persimmon.

My cousin Jammer and I christened the forested area near Banana Island "Wood Tick Alley" because of the sheer number of ticks. Wood ticks prey on warm-blooded animals like bears, deer, turkeys, and little boys. Riding our bikes through these low brush-filled trails left our lower torsos covered with wood ticks. Even our bikes were covered with ticks. As soon as we were in the clear, we began to pull them off, shake them off, scrape them off, anything. You had to get them off. You didn't want one to bite. Wood ticks bury their heads and jaws into your flesh and drink your blood. The longer they are attached to your skin, the bigger and more purple they become. Humans usually find and remove them pretty quickly. Sometimes you might find one engorged upon some poor forgotten dog. Purple, as big as a small mouse, and shaped like a pear, they hang by their buried jaws like some obscene fruit from hell. And when they are filled with blood, they drop to the ground like an overripe fruit. If stepped on, they leave a huge blood spot on the ground.

By my teen years, I already had personal experiences with wood ticks. This happened while living at my grandparents' house when I was a little guy. My playground included the grassy slopes of Chapel Hill and the brush-filled swamp that lay between their house and Rabbit Ridge. I didn't know it then, but this also was first-class wood tick habitat. I thought that wood ticks lived in the woods—so, by staying out of the woods, I'd keep clear of wood ticks. I mean, they are brown and invisible against a piece of wood. Why would a brown tick live on green grass and low brush, anyway?

When a tick bites a person, it generally does so in certain areas, like along the waistband or where socks cling tight around the ankles—places on the body where they aren't easily noticeable. During tick season, the first thing Grandma said whenever I came in from the outside was to check for ticks. After walking into the furnace room, standing in front of the giant boiler, and checking my pants legs and ankles, I would put any discovered ticks inside the burn box. If a tick is placed onto a piece of burning wood, it will rapidly swell up before exploding in a satisfying pop.

Sometimes a tick would visit in the middle of the night. My bed was on the second-floor landing directly across from the bathroom. The upstairs bathroom door wasn't a solid one-piece door. Instead, it was a set of double doors, like those old-time saloon doors in western movies. I liked going through those doors. This bathroom had a large window and was well lit, unlike the bathroom in the basement. One particular morning, at five years old, I woke up and went into the bathroom to urinate. I pulled my pants and underwear down around my ankles and stood in front of the stool. Taking a firm grasp of the situation, I happened to look down. A tick had embedded its head into my head. Doing what anybody else would do in that same situation, I screamed and ran out of the bathroom, down the stairs, and into the kitchen, crying and screaming hysterically. My pants were still down around my ankles. By the time I reached the kitchen where Grandma was standing, her back to the stove and terror in her eyes, every other member of the family had also been alerted and was either in the room or just getting there.

It was left to Uncle Buddy to deal with me. He carried me back upstairs into the bathroom, stood me up, and then lit a Winston cigarette with a book of matches. He waved the glowing end near the tick's backside. I could feel the heat. It started to wiggle. Next, putting the cigarette between his lips, he reached down, grabbed the tick between two fingers, and pulled it out. The tick had a bit of my flesh in its jaws. I started to cry again. Buddy put the wiggling tick on the edge of the bathroom sink, lit a match, and then used it to burn the tick until it popped. After this execution, he opened the door of the medicine cabinet and found a bottle of Mercurochrome. Opening the bottle, he painted the tip of my penis orange-red with the dropper inside the bottle's cap. Tick and match both went into the toilet and were flushed away. All that made me feel better but, to this day, more than sixty years later, I still carry scars from that encounter.

So, I was pretty sensitive to wood tick habitat as a young teenager in Banana Island's wooded areas, as long as they lasted. To make room for this new human habitat near Banana Island, the tribe had to destroy the earlier, natural one. After new construction, most of the trees, brush, and blackberries had been cut down and removed to several huge burn piles. Living bundles of tangled roots, bigger than an adult man, were yanked out of the earth with a D6 Caterpillar and a stout iron chain. These roots were added to burn piles. After being covered and insulated with sand, they took a long time to ignite and burn. The landscape was marked with gaping holes where piles of unwanted organic materials burned for weeks. The smoke and caustic ash from those burn piles lingered longer. At night, dull orange pockets of dying light glowed in the darkness. It looked like a battlefield.

Most wild animals, including the resident bears, were driven out of this part of town by those impromptu smudges, although some stubborn individuals had to be physically removed by hand. Those few black bears still coming around a year later weren't actually living or feeding here anymore, but it didn't stop them from being nosy, cantankerous, or simply oblivious tourists and walking through the neighborhood like they owned it. Black bears blunder through one mess and move onward to the next. They have untidy habits and make awful neighbors. They are very curious wandering loners.

That curiosity makes them dangerous. It leads them into unpredictable situations that are out of their control. They can and do lash out when surprised. Even an accidental swipe by a frightened black bear can be a mortal wound. Full-grown adults have no natural enemies, not even humans. Like most animals, they will avoid human contact if at all possible, but, make no mistake, they aren't teddy bears. While just a few of them are left in this part of the reservation, even one transient bear is too many for any neighborhood.

Bears eat a lot of everything and seldom discriminate. Maybe that's not completely true. My aunt Nita says, "Reservation bears will not eat oranges or lemons." She should know. Her family members are bear hunters. Acorns, blackberries, and insects, like bees and grasshoppers, are important parts of black bears' diet. Get rid of the food and you get rid of the bear. Ever since most berry bushes, grasses, and low brush have been removed from Banana Island, the general insect population has declined.

In response to this habitat removal, area wood ticks have learned to live on the weeds inhabiting the unkempt edges of lawns, where they wait to feast on passing, ownerless rez dogs and wandering children.

One day, when I was thirteen or so, a bear wandered into the Banana Island neighborhood. It was one of those particularly gorgeous Wisconsin days, the kind of ordinary day that was common before global warming, with big white puffy clouds set against a bright blue northern sky. For whatever reason, I chose that exact moment to leave my bedroom where I had been suffering a yearlong case of teenage angst. Upon moving in, I had painted my bedroom ceiling red, two of the walls white, and the other two walls blue. I seldom left my room as it was equipped with a stereo. I would lie on my bed and listen to Black Sabbath while wishing that I had painted my room differently. This was before the band kicked Ozzy out for using too many drugs and destroying their image.

On this day, walking out of the kitchen door on the north side of the house and into the driveway, I saw a small crowd gathered on the southeastern corner of our block. From this distance and angle, it looked like they were gesturing and pointing in my direction. They weren't, but I had to go over and look to make sure. This was relatively soon after the first phase of the housing development was completed—so soon that people said the paint was still wet. This Banana Island neighborhood was where the forest met the town, the old foot trails intersected recently paved city streets, and natural plants grew alongside suburban geraniums.

The crowd had gathered around one of the few white pines left standing within this southeast corner. That tree is still there—a reminder of these events, though like me, it must be nearing the end of its life cycle. My family's home stood on the opposite, northwest corner of the block. I carried my Sting-Ray bike out of the mud room, down the steps, and onto the gravel driveway. Then, I pedaled over to see what was happening.

In the few moments it took me to get there, the crowd got noticeably bigger. Pulling in at the rear of the crowd, I leaned my bike against a tree. It once had a kickstand, but kickstands were for sissies and a few days after getting the bike, I took the kickstand off and threw it away.

Walking over to join the crowd, I met up with a neighborhood chum and asked him, "What's happening?"

He pointed at a tree with his lips. "There's a bear cub near the top of that white pine, maybe three-quarters of the way up."

Weaving my way through the crowd, keeping my eyes pointed upward, I could definitely see a bear cub hiding from the crowd behind a bough-laden limb, quite a long way up that tree. It might have been looking for a bee's nest. Honey-coated bees are a treat to black bears.

The crowd was arguing over what to do about the bear cub. One sizable group didn't want to do anything. The cub would either climb down on its own or the mother would appear to get him once everybody went home and "left the damn thing alone."

Someone said, "The mother bear is probably watching us right now, getting mad. Everybody should just go home!"

Another group, smaller than the first but louder, thought that we should do something, anything, to keep the bear cub safe from all this human contact. Someone from this group said, "That bear cub needs our protection to keep it safe. Somebody should notify the forest service and call the police."

The last sizable group of people also wanted to do something, anything, to keep that bear from causing any harm to *humans*. To them, bears, like burglars, were immediate threats that needed to be handled by the local officials. "What about the children?" someone asked. They also wanted the forest service and the police called to humanely and quickly shoot the bear.

A few people standing on the crowd's fringe just wanted to shoot the bear "for its own good." There were several volunteers to do the shooting. I saw a few rifles present and edged away from them. I knew some of those people were serious, and at least one of them had already taken a shot at the bear cub before the crowd had gotten large.

The arguments over this cub's destiny—indeed, his life—

were now a verbal calliope, going around and around, increasing in volume every circuit, for maybe another fifteen minutes, until the Keshena Volunteer Fire Department appeared, siren wailing and ancient red bubble light rotating dimly. The village's old dull-red vintage pumper truck had served on some unnamed air force base during the Korean War. This was genuine army surplus, and for this emergency, it was manned by only one person, the driver.

The firetruck pulled up and the driver dismounted from his seat in the open-air cab. Standing beside the truck, he reached behind the seat and pulled out a bright red fire helmet from a wire mesh basket. He put it on his head and adjusted the straps. It said CAPT in big black letters. I wondered if the helmet came with the truck and if this guy was really the captain.

When he walked in front of the crowd, he took command of the situation. He got the facts and assessed the tone of the crowd. He then devised a plan—get the bear out of the tree. He told the crowd that he would hook the pumper truck to a nearby fire hydrant and use that high-pressure line to hose the bear cub off of his perch and out of the tree.

Several people immediately objected to this idea: "What about the bear?" After being ejected from that height, his fall would be fatal. "We could use a net to catch the bear," the captain responded. But nobody wanted to be anywhere near a falling bear cub and risk having it land on their head like an angry cat.

It was a good thing for all concerned that after checking the truck, the captain realized he didn't have a net or anything that could serve as a net, anyway. Since most everyone on the reservation lives on the ground floor, there was little need for a rescue net to catch jumpers or even a tall ladder for climbing anywhere.

Most of the crowd finally agreed that this bear's continued good health was the most important consideration at the moment. It couldn't stay in the tree, but the plan to hose it out of the tree was put on hold.

Other impracticable ideas were considered, such as tranquilizing the bear (but where would we get a tranquilizer gun?) or shooting the limb off, out from underneath the bear (but we'd need an elephant gun to break that branch).

"Okay then," the fire captain said, "somebody has to climb up that tree and bring that bear cub down, by hand." He looked around at the crowd. "Who wants to volunteer?"

I knew right away that the basic problem with this plan was that while a bear cub looks cute, chubby, and cuddly, like a happy human baby, in reality, they are sixty-pound pit bulls with forty-two teeth, four of which are large incisors, and twenty sharp claws attached to four strong legs. And even if the bear cub was small enough to be handled relatively safely, by grabbing him by the scruff of the neck for instance, the mother bear was almost certainly lurking in the background nearby. Mother bears average four hundred pounds and are never safe to handle. They are built like that monstrous hound of the Baskervilles and can go quickly, and sometimes for no reason, into a full-on demonic attack. It doesn't matter how many teeth the mother has. Her mouth is big enough to bite your head in half. A charging black bear of any size or gender is no joke, but mother bears especially don't like humans touching their offspring, period. Nobody wanted a mother bear to see them holding her cub. Plus black bears can follow scents like a bloodhound and have good memories. They have been known to hold a grudge.

Members of the crowd looked at one another, and several people, including me, standing all the way in the back, verbally declined when they met the fire captain's eyes. The guys with guns didn't volunteer, either.

Finally, from deep within that awkward silence, this tall-for-his-age, scrawny guy who lived a few houses down from me said that he would give it a try. While Bud and I were already friendly acquaintances—I had known him for about five years—this was still way before we started hanging out together. It was before our gang found out that Bud could regularly get us beer. Later, we would often visit him, first for the booze and then to hit on any of his several good-looking sisters. Those girls were all tough, certainly tougher than I was, and I never got anywhere with them. Bud was a couple of years older than me. He was the younger brother of Lee Boy, my older brother's friend. Bud's real name was Earl and his middle name was Lee, and so of course, he was always "Early," or sometimes we called him "Early Squirrelly."

Already active in the Golden Gloves amateur boxing league on the rez, Bud was tough enough to take a joke. He had one pair of glasses—government-issued thick, black plastic-framed glasses. They looked like a pair of those x-ray glasses listed for sale in the tiny lurid advertisements on the back pages of certain magazines. These were regular tribal-issued glasses, however. Based on what I knew about how my older brother and Bud's older brother treated him, Bud was probably defending his manhood and goaded into accepting this challenge.

"The first part of getting that bear cub down, and the hardest part," said the captain, still wearing the fire helmet that identified his rank, "is that first ten feet up." He pulled on one of the two short ladders attached to the truck, where the roof should have been, lifted it up over his head, walked to the pine tree, and leaned it against the tree trunk. The ladder reached only ten feet up the trunk. "If I used a longer ladder, one with an extension, no way could I lean it against the tree—there are too many branches in the way," he explained. "We can't start cutting any of those branches because it would drive the bear farther up the tree, and that would mean a longer climb up and a possible longer fall down."

Bud walked over to the ladder. He was offered some rope to tie the cub with and some leather gloves. Bud took the rope, stuffed it under his belt, refused the gloves, and began to climb the aluminum fire ladder.

Reaching the last rung easily enough, he grabbed a nearby branch with his right hand to begin the long climb upward—but first, he took that first crucial step from the metal ladder to the tree, from human culture to natural biology. After a few jeers from one section of the crowd—"Jump, jump, jump!"—he finally pulled himself up onto another thick branch, keeping as close to the trunk as possible. Now officially on the tree, he stopped, looked around at the crowd, and made a face like a crazy person. From a different group in the crowd he got a few cheers—"Oi, oi, oi!"—as he began climbing upward, handhold to foothold, foothold to handhold, upward, from branch to branch, one hand and one foot never leaving contact with the tree. Climbing a white pine is simple enough, in theory. The branches grow alternately out from the straight trunk in regular steps. Actually, climbing a white pine is deceivingly easy. You can get pretty high up the tree with little effort, and white pines can grow tall.

Bud made his way up the tree slowly at first and then faster after a few moments, without any incidents. A few people, mostly his friends, still called out for him to jump. Someone else in the crowd insultingly called him "monkey boy," which got some laughs. Somebody else answered, "Na-boo, Sabu," which got even more laughs. This came from an old movie about a jungle boy living in the wilds of India that played on the local television channel. In the movie, a character was named "Sabu" and the phrase "No Sabu" was uttered. *Na-boo* was a nonsense, or teasing way to say no, from the root word *nah*, then made to rhyme with Sabu. Those words became bastardized on the playground as "Na-boo, Sabu," and it became a put-down.

Generally Bud's ascent was so smooth and so uneventful that the crowd began losing interest in him. Background noise increased. As Bud neared the bear cub, however, the conversations withered. Upon reaching the branch where the bear was sitting, Bud had the crowd's undivided attention again. The bear cub reacted to Bud's presence by crawling still farther out on the limb, the limb bending under its weight.

Black bears spend a considerable amount of time climbing and sitting in trees. They can and do fall, but they don't usually fall all the way to the ground. Even if the tree limb did break, the cub would probably just fall to the next one underneath and grab hold. Bears are like cats in that way, surprisingly nimble and fast.

Bud, on the other hand, was no Tarzan, and he would probably bounce from branch to branch all the way down to the ground. Mind you, all of this was happening two-thirds of the way up this tree, so maybe fifty or sixty feet in the air.

Bud moved to the same branch as the bear and, wrapping his legs around the trunk behind him, bent over the limb, with his upper torso adding to its total load. The limb bent even more downward. Those branches were still green and pliable, not old and brittle—a good thing for Bud. Reaching out, he grabbed the cub from behind, by the scruff of its neck.

The cub started to cry. Several people looked around, but there was no sign of the mother bear on the ground. This would have been the moment that the bear would have charged if she were going to charge.

Bud pulled his body inward, straightening up while still hanging on to the tree trunk with his legs, and balanced the struggling cub on the tree limb at arm's length. The crowd, still growing, cheered. The bear struggled. Bud, showing off, freed one arm to wave. But now came the hard part. He had to climb down the tree, holding a struggling bear cub with one hand and branches with the other.

Bud began his descent using the same technique he used to get up the tree—handhold to foothold, foothold to handhold—except now in reverse and using only one arm and one hand. The other arm and hand were occupied by a struggling sixty-pound bear cub. At first, he got lots of encouragement and advice from the crowd. His journey downward was agonizing to watch, as his rhythm was screwed up. Shouted words of advice finally stopped. Slowly and, from the look on his face, in apparent agony, Bud worked his way down the towering white pine. Now, the words of encouragement, though much fewer, became noticeably more heartfelt.

Twenty-five feet from the ground, almost all the way down, with the front of his shirt and jeans covered in sticky pine sap, perspiration, and bits of bark, Bud finally lost his grasp on the cub. The cub landed on its feet like a cat and ran between startled members of the crowd into the nearby forest. Mama bear must have been just out of sight.

I looked at Bud and our eyes met. He also saw the bear cub escape into the woods having suffered no harm from this human contact.

The last fifteen feet to the ladder took him longer than the previous sixty feet had. His arms and his hands were numb. He moved as though he were still carrying that bear cub, with stiff, exaggerated formality. Nobody said anything. He would either make it or he would fall the last twenty-five feet.

All I could hear was the crowd breathing. When Bud took a step down, the crowd collectively sucked in its breath. He finally reached the ladder and found the rung with his foot. He looked too stiff and too sore to even bend over to see where he was going. The climb down the ladder was awkward—he used only one hand to clutch at the aluminum ladder, while the other one, numb and clumsy, he used like a trapeze artist would use a balancing pole.

When Bud finally reached the ground, my brother walked over and punched him in the arm, the numb one. Lee Boy punched him in the other. I watched the three of them begin the short walk home.

The crowd thinned slowly, most people seeming unable or unwilling to let go of this momentary distraction. Mission accomplished, the captain loaded his ladder on top of the truck's metal braces and strapped it down. He looked around, took off his helmet, and placed it gently in the wire mesh basket behind the seat. He then jumped up onto his perch.

The dim bubble light had revolved during this entire encounter. The truck started right up, no hesitation at all. Looking around once more and paying me no attention, the captain turned on his siren, put the truck into gear, and drove back to the station. The rising and falling siren marked his diminishing trail with light and sound.

Sumac Juice Drink

Sumac is a valuable plant. According to the old ones, various parts of this plant possess several health benefits. For example, the sap can be rubbed on the skin as an insect repellent. Personally, I think it's too sticky for that purpose, although I've added green branches to a campfire to drive mosquitoes away. Sumac branches have a milky sap, and the plants grow as hilly red colonies in open fields and meadows. Poison sumac, in contrast, is a solitary plant with white or green berries that grows in swamps. Avoid any contact with poison sumac. At best, you will start to itch. At worst? Possible death. Never eat anything that you can't positively identify without consulting an expert.

Fresh sumac berries make a delicious fruit drink that is naturally high in vitamin C and sugars. Both staghorn and smooth sumac have hairy red berries. Berry clusters from the smooth variety may be darker red than the staghorn variety. Those berry clusters can be dried and used later to make a fruity-tasting tea. Sumac berry tea can be substituted for pink lemonade.

All of the measurements in this recipe are approximate. You can add more or less of any ingredient. Yes, there will be sections of sumac branch that get caught in the liquid. Don't worry—they add complexity to the drink. High-end wine makers add grape stems to their must, or freshly squeezed grape juice, for the same reason.

1 gallon sumac berry clusters—it is okay to leave a couple inches of stalk that may remain after breaking a cluster off the bush
4 gallons water
Sugar (optional)

Gather fresh sumac berry clusters. Fill a large kettle with the berry clusters. Visually inspect and remove anything unappetizing, like caterpillars and any excess woody parts. Fill the kettle with water, rinse and swish berries using your hands, drain, wait a few minutes, then repeat. This removes stubborn ants and other hangers-on.

Once berries are clean, add enough cold water to cover the berry clusters. For 5 minutes, crush berry clusters using a stout sumac branch or baseball bat, as if making thick, unreasonable butter. Strain the liquid using a sieve and/or a clean kitchen towel—the finest filter available. (Sumac has tiny hairs like the prickly pear that may be unpleasant to some.) Taste and dilute, if needed, with water. Add sugar if desired. Note that most people find this drink pretty sweet already. Serve chilled, and enjoy the day.

Roast Acorns

Most acorns are too bitter to eat raw. Prepare the acorns by shelling them and boiling them to remove the bitter taste. Boil, drain, rinse, and repeat until the taste is mild. Alternately, you can soak the shelled acorn meat in water for several days, changing the water until it becomes clear. Taste for bitterness. Acorns are nourishing, but they are labor intensive.

1 quart shelled acorn meat
2 teaspoons salt

On a salted cookie sheet, roast the acorn meat at low temperature (200 degrees) for 1 hour or until crunchy.

The Roots and a Royal Lesson in Gratitude

My cousin Jammer first showed me the trail leading to the Roots, near Banana Island. From there, through the woods, it is a few hundred yards farther north to the old Indian Agency hospital. It is possible to see the Roots from the upstairs windows of the old hospital.

The southern end of the banana-shaped island, across the river from the hospital, is fifty feet wide. Thick brush covers it, so it is indistinguishable from the brush-covered shoreline. If the water level were one foot lower—if Balsam Row Dam had not dammed the river so many years ago—there would be no Banana Island today. This brush is a place for foraging greens, edible shoots, and teas. Most of all, I remember it as my playground until I began to get older.

The Roots is a special place where an eroding paleolithic levee borders a sheer riverbank, about ten feet above the river's surface. Erosion at the outside center of the curve has worn a V-shaped crack. Through the years, this crack has grown to expose a tangle of white pine roots from a small grove.

Those white pines grow in a semicircle around this spot. With an average life span of two hundred years, these trees are older than the reservation. Indeed, since their maximum life span is about four hundred fifty years, these trees may have been growing here before the time of Jacques Marquette's 1673 arrival. All of these trees lean inward, toward the east and away from the river. A few of them are tilted at an absurd angle of 45 degrees, challenging gravity. Many daring Menominee youths have climbed to the very tops of these trees, around sixty-five feet from their bases. I was not one of them.

As erosion occurs, the exposed roots of the pines bend outward, away from the trees and over the river. With so many different trees and root systems combined, these root clusters have formed a wooden spiderweb suspended above the water, hovering from about four feet above the river to a few strands that reach into the air around twelve feet above.

Some of these roots are long, gray, and bony-looking—in my youth, they reminded me of giant spider legs clawing at invisible things. They waved in the wind. At night, between dark and dawn, when they put on their hidden faces, they seemed especially creepy.

In the warm and friendly sunlight, these extended roots became diving boards. Swimmers carefully balanced on those trembling roots and then leapt into the deep channel. The gnarly roots were perfect natural launching points, strong enough to carry the weight of a teenager but with lots of stiff bounce. Still, this was not a spot to play casually. The water was too deep and fast for young swimmers. This was where the bigger kids hung out. The only way to reach the water was by diving between the tree roots. Even getting back out of the water was difficult, as it involved a hard swim upstream, after the current had taken you downstream, and then after reaching the bank, there was a scramble up a steep slope.

One morning while biking past, I saw that at least one unknown daredevil had carefully balanced a ramp among the exposed roots. That must have been a hair-raising stunt on its own. About five feet down the dirt path, the daredevil had laid a long sheet of plywood to form the ramp, tilted upward. Eventually, many young men rode their bikes down the short steep hill and propelled themselves at full speed onto the ramp, then flew upward over an audience sitting among the roots. Man and machine flew through space until splash-down.

I never heard of any girls trying that ramp. This was an adolescent male thing, and lots of girls watched. Once airborne, a rider was better off separating himself from his bike while flying through the air. Hitting the river from a height of fifteen feet or more while straddling a bike could result in painful groin injuries. The aftermath—diving and retrieving the bike—did not seem to be as much fun as the actual stunt. Jammer and I were way too cool for such hijinks. Anyway, our bikes were too nice to abuse in that fashion. But we watched the foolhardy showboats with some envy.

Everybody in our Banana Island gang had access to a Schwinn Sting-Ray bicycle. These models were made only between the years 1963 and 1981. The bike was factory-equipped with ape-hanger handlebars and a banana seat.

The Sting-Ray was the sports car of bikes. The comfortable banana seat was too small for two but perfect for one. The bikes were small but versatile, and they gave us mobility compared to other neighborhood gangs. We used them like dirt bikes, racing along logging roads and ancient Indian trails. A Sting-Ray is light enough to easily portage over any impassable terrain. In fact, they are sure-footed enough to maneuver down the middle of most small streams. They were nimble enough for us to navigate through the forest, dodging trees. We rode over small logs with no problem. And the bikes easily lent themselves to flying off of hills and ramps, unlike other bikes, which were longer and heavier on the front forks and prone to tumbling end-over-end and crashing. A Sting-Ray, being short and low, resisted tumbling.

Jammer and I used our Sting-Rays to explore the area south of Banana Island. On one of our expeditions, we found evidence that people once lived back along the river north of the Shawano

County line. Pedaling through the woods, we rediscovered forgotten beaches and several dilapidated lumber buildings that had become piles of rotting wood. Most of those buildings were so far gone that even the ghosts had gotten lonely and moved on. We had no fear.

Thick brambles, tall purple thistles, and short hairy ferns grew out of one decaying pile of lumber, square-headed nails, and shredded black tar paper. Poking a foot into it, we saw hundreds of roly polies and other bugs run back into the shadows. Nearby, we found an outdoor privy. There were holes at ground level where the walls had been eaten through by porcupines, who consume the salt contained in human waste. The remaining thin wooden slats were bleached and beaten by the weather. The privy shook in the wind but remained standing. That proved the owner put a lot of effort into its construction. The door was closed. We worried that some ghost might be seated inside, taking their time, perhaps looking at the newest styles pictured in the Montgomery Ward catalog. We did not look inside. Anyway, we knew the sides of the dirt hole inside may have washed away over time, as is common with any old hole. This made it dangerous to approach, as we might have fallen in. I can think of few things worse.

Farther on, we found another opening in the woods and another collapsed building, this one sitting only ten feet from the river's edge. The remains of an ancient dock were visible. We could see a couple of posts still rising above the surface.

The shallow river bottom was sandy and the current mild. The yard was an acre or two of tall-grass prairie, brightened with pale green milkweed pods and piercing red staghorn sumac leaves. A privy was once located here, too, away from the house near the edge of the woods. Only the prolific stinging nettles on all four sides of the filled-in hole clued us in to its presence. Thick brown clouds of waist-high amaranth and green blackberry canes helped identify the garden area. Several apple and cherry trees were growing along the edges of the forest clearing. We did not see any hand-dug well, but Jammer said there was probably a spring nearby, or maybe the former residents had taken their water directly from the river. Back in those days, any time before the twentieth century, it was still possible to drink the river water.

Ferns grew in the shade on both sides of this old path among blackberries, poison ivy, and plantain. The old Indians said plantain, which they called "White Man's Foot," only grew where the White Man had stepped. This plant is a low-growing green herb with a rosette of broad, spinach-looking leaves. There are two varieties: the broadleaf and the narrow-leaf. They are similar looking. The broadleaf variety has edible leaves that look and can be cooked like spinach. Served with butter and salt, they do not taste bad, but neither do they taste good. The leaves belonging to the narrow-leaf variety look more like dandelion leaves and are bitter. Both kinds of plantain can be used as medicine, as the leaves make an effective poultice. This plant grows in disturbed soil. It has a single seed-bearing spike, maybe a foot tall, growing from the center. Its seeds have several short hairs and will stick to fabric, only to fall off later. Jammer and I called this plant wild corn and christened our rediscovered trail Wood Tick Lane after the number of ticks we removed from each other.

Everything changed when the housing development was completed in the midsixties. Jammer's parents moved away from Banana Island, and so my cousin missed becoming a member of our neighborhood gang. I made new friends.

Sometimes our gang hung out in Herman's mom's basement, listening to him play the blues on his guitar. We were all way too cool to listen to the top forty, or to the ubiquitous country and western heard on the radio and through the doorway of every local tavern. All of us owned kazoos, inspired by Country Joe and the Fish. A head shop on South Broadway in Green Bay had a box full of them for sale on the countertop, and we had all purchased our own instruments. Breaking them out at a moment's notice, we filled the air with our melodious countercultural statements. Herman's mom let us hang out in her basement any time. My stepfather would not let any of us hang out at my home, so this was a real oasis. We carved out a space in her basement, cordoned it off with psychedelic tapestries, and filled it with cast-off furnishings. We had a small record player and Herman's fire-engine dog for company. Herman's mom owned an adult male Dalmatian. This dog was no man's best friend, however. This was one miserable, very mean, son-of-a-bitch dog. It did not like any of us. Oh, he loved Herman's mom—always licking her hand—and she loved him. "Oh my, you're my big Butchy dog," she would say. "Yes, Mama loves you." But around the rest of us, that dog was constantly trying to bite us. Not nip, but seriously bite.

Butch the dog made it clear that he was the man of the house, and he did not want any of us around. We all got bit, even Herman. If you did not keep an eye on him—and face him directly—he bit you. He had no problem with other people, only us. This was personal.

Collectively, we tried to train Butch using food scraps and dog treats. Butch knew what we were trying to communicate to him and how we were trying to do it. He would take a treat from Herman's hand, but he would not chew it. He would drop it to the floor instead. When any of the rest of us tried, Butch just growled viciously and refused to take our offerings. "Screw you guys," he seemed to be saying. Butch was funny that way. He never barked at us. He seldom even growled. But he was sneaky, trying to get us to lower our guard around him so he could bite us.

We tried locking him out of the basement one night. When we were leaving to go home, we came up the stairs and opened the door, and the dog attacked us. He lunged down the steps. Herman grabbed his collar when he landed at the bottom and held him long enough for the rest of us to get away.

The only times that we were safe from Butch were when he got stoned. Then he was a gentle, good-natured, friendly dog that sat around with us, listening to music, grooving—doing guy stuff with us. Was this animal abuse? Yeah, maybe whoever first taught that dog to get high was guilty, but it kept him from biting.

One time, my buddy Mooch directly asked Herman who taught the dog to get high. "I think it was one of my mom's first boyfriends after she got divorced from my dad," he said. It was left to the rest of us, though, to suffer through that damn dog's addiction. I remember my first time meeting him—I extended my hand to let him sniff me, and he bit me instead. But after a joint? Then we were best friends, at least for an hour or so.

Butch recognized marijuana protocol. We would be in the basement, sitting in a circle, about to pass around a marijuana cigarette, and that dog would come running over, tail wagging and ears bouncing. He would join the circle. It's like Butch had ESP and knew when we were about to smoke. The only other times the dog came running over to us were times when he was trying to bite us.

When it was his turn, Butch would lift one of his floppy ears. This was the signal for whoever took the last hit to blow the smoke into Butch's ear. He had us trained. After a couple of hits, Butch would try to stand but instead kind of stagger and collapse on the floor with a silly grin. Then he really was one of the guys, letting us pet him, shaking hands—normal dog things. Once, he put his head on my lap and looked up at me adoringly. After dozing pleasantly, Butch would wake up, start jonesing for a buzz, and then be just as miserable as he was before.

We managed to survive Butch and his teeth, individually and as a group. One of our more creative accomplishments was to gather old construction materials from Keshena and build a small cabin in the woods. It was along the river between the Beach and the Roots. It was not much, but to us, it was a mansion on a small hill. It became our hangout—a place to dream and a place to talk.

At least five generations of people have gathered at the Roots. This popularity is partly due to its natural beauty and partly to its relative closeness to the tribal courthouse, which used to be the early Indian Agency hospital. It was a very scenic place and well known. Almost everybody in the tribe eventually visited the hospital and, when that closed, they would have business at the courthouse. This place made a convenient spot to hold a conversation, wait for an appointment, or find a ride. There were trees to sit on and people to talk with. You could listen to the river.

Getting to the Roots from the hospital and courthouse building on the old foot trail seemed easy enough. First, a waist-high guardrail needed to be negotiated. It separated the paved lot from nature. The old and the infirm could just walk around it. Then, one needed to go another seventy feet past a few crab apple trees, over some downed limbs, through a small grove of white pine, and up the sandy lip to the top of the levee. There was a well-established trail the entire way, except for the guardrail area. To get there, I thought, I just needed enough balletic grace to overcome a few obstacles. In this unlikely place, I made a close friend.

On one special morning, not quite noon, I was just leaving the dentist's office. The traveling dentist made his office in the courthouse. He was there only a couple of days a week. This was the only dentist for several thousand people, and it was difficult to get an appointment. On this occasion, I had not needed any painful drilling or Novocain shots, so I was leaving the building with a smile, feeling good. Going down that last, long flight of concrete steps, I ran into a guy I knew named Royal. He was just about to start his climb up those unforgiving stairs to enter the building.

I had seen Royal around town. He was a social person, and Keshena is not a very large community. Even if you do not know a specific person, you know *of* them. Royal used to hang out at the downtown VFW park along the river, where the older kids staked out their territory. And even though I did not go to many of the tribal events aimed at Indian youth, he was always at those few events that I did attend. So I saw him around town enough to nod and say hello in passing.

Royal lived across the river from my grandparents in downtown Keshena in the same foster home as my cousin Steve. As a small child, Royal had contracted polio, and now he was confined by an upper-body brace. He used crutches to walk. On this day, he was balancing on two crutches held under one arm and using the other arm to clasp the metal handrail and hop up the stairs, one step at a time.

I do not know why this encounter was any different from the other times I'd seen Royal, but on this day, I stopped to really talk with him. After pleasantries, he asked what I was up to. I told him, "Going to the Roots to smoke a joint." Not knowing if he smoked or not, I impulsively asked him to join me.

He smiled a sad smile and said that he could not. He replied sarcastically, "I have too many legs."

In my benevolent mood, I said, "I'll carry you piggy-back." Before Royal could raise any objections—I do not think anybody had ever made such an offer to him—I circled around to be one step below him, backed up, grabbed him, and lifted him onto my back, in one fluid movement. As a young man, I could be quite graceful.

To my surprise, Royal was not heavy at all. I carried him through the muddy, obstacle-strewn path that rendered crutches useless. While worldly—he knew the cities and the rez, and he did almost everything a person without an upper-body brace could do—Royal told me that this was the first time he had ever been in the woods. Getting to the Roots was a big deal to him. I hadn't realized this until he spent the next several minutes telling me. We sat together and watched the eddies swirl, the minnows flicker, and crows fly by. With him there, everything seemed new.

This spontaneous encounter began a lifelong friendship. I learned many important things from Royal—about patience and gratitude, among other things—lessons that I still struggle with. Over the years, we had several adventures together in Green Bay and in Milwaukee, as we drove around in my Volkswagen. Later, Royal got a good job with the tribe, married, and raised a family. They had a nice home, and he built a good life.

We stopped hanging out, not for any particularly good reason. We were still friends, but I just no longer regularly ran into him. My path led elsewhere.

Steamed Shoots of Broadleaf Plantains (White Man's Foot)

This is a recipe for the herbaceous plant, genus Plantago, *not the banana-like plantain of tropical climates. This plant can grow in your front yard as well as along rivers, roads, and new gardens—any place where the soil has been disturbed. It has a pleasant flavor similar to asparagus.*

Collect about a pint of the central spikes that grow from the center of the plant, selecting those that have closed buds, like broccoli, rather than openly blooming ones.

Serves 4 people

1 pint plantain shoots
2 tablespoons olive oil (or butter or lard)
3 cloves garlic, minced
1 teaspoon (each) salt and pepper, more to taste if needed

Wash shoots carefully and pat dry. Heat oil in a large skillet on medium high and add garlic, salt, and pepper. Cook for 2 minutes. Add plantain shoots, stirring to coat evenly. Cook another 4–5 minutes until shoots are heated through and softened but still firm. Serve warm with potatoes.

White Pine Needle Tea

The reservation is filled with pine trees, so finding a vitamin C–rich tea is easy. Avoid the poisonous evergreen pines—yews, Ponderosas, and Norfolk. Pick fresh needles for best results, although dried pine needles can be used.

½ cup pine needles
1 pint water
Honey (optional)
Lemon (optional)

Clean needles by washing them and wiping away all dirt. Boil water in a saucepan. Add pine needles and simmer for 20 minutes (cooking too long destroys vitamin C). Remove from heat and let steep for another 20 minutes or let sit overnight. Add honey and lemon to taste, if desired.

Bud's Commot Breakfast Scramble and Weaponized Eggs

After the first stage of the Banana Island housing development was completed, for a brief moment in the statewide news cycle, our new neighborhood became a tourist destination. We residents became celebrities. Local and state representatives, as well as federal bureaucratic types from Madison and Washington, DC, came to look around. They wanted to kick the tires of this new-concept suburb with matching floorplans and commots in the pantries. This political theater would soon become a media circus, and our family home almost became center ring.

On this particular day, I was in the living room with my stepfather—an unusual situation. Perhaps our proximity had something to do with the well-publicized notice of the governor's arrival. We were seldom in the house at the same time, due to mutual dislike.

As we sat in the living room, we looked out the front windows. The television—mounted inside a large wooden cabinet that also held a stereo—was tuned to WBAY, broadcasting out of Green Bay. Governor Pat Lucey was on a fact-finding mission to Banana Island, and talking heads were giving live updates on the progress of his bus caravan. We knew this could be just a photo opportunity with local Natives. Indians are always newsworthy—except when they are not.

We heard that the governor was due to arrive any minute. Then, right on cue, we saw through the windows a fancy Greyhound bus pulling into the neighborhood. It parked almost directly across the street from our house.

Stepfather got up from the sofa, pulled the shades down in the living room, and closed all the blinds. Peeking through the slats of the blinds like criminals, we watched the governor exit the bus and walk across the weed-choked road. He could have visited plenty of houses closer to his bus, but he decided to start with us. He came directly to our front door, escorted by a phalanx of highway patrol officers. Television camera operators and several reporters surrounded the governor on our cement steps, taking notes and snapping pictures.

We watched through the slats as Governor Lucey vaulted up our three cement steps, with no apparent hesitation, and pounded at the front door with an urgent knock that sounded like the police. Stepfather became more and more panicky as they approached. I looked across the living room at my stepfather, who possibly had criminal associations, to see what he would do.

Lucey pounded again. Stepfather did not say anything and pretended that nobody was home. The third time was a simple tap-tap-tap, a courtesy knock. And then we lost our potential moment of fame. Pat Lucey went down the street to the next house.

Later, Stepfather complained, "I'm too busy to talk with some politician."

These were the first new homes built on the reservation in many years, and this was the first new housing development on a Wisconsin Indian reservation ever. The paint in our homes was still slightly tacky, the insides still smelled of fresh-cut pine, and piles of construction debris sat ready for pickup on our struggling lawns. Banana Island was becoming a bubbling cauldron, the place where Menominee identity was recast and reforged.

We were no longer fur trappers and mighty warriors. We lived in a new century.

In time, I made a good friend: Earl Lee, also known as Bud. I learned many valuable things from my best friend and Banana Island neighbor. Indeed, without his friendship and guidance, I doubt that I would have survived my adolescence. He was also an inventive chef who specialized in the commot ingredients in our cupboards.

Bud and his older brother Lee Boy were both Golden Gloves boxers and had traveled extensively around the state for amateur matches. They were in their fighting prime—both in their early twenties. These bouts occurred in faraway places like Green Bay, Milwaukee, Kenosha, and Racine. I had been to Green Bay a couple of times, but all those other places were only names on a map.

Bud and Lee won many of their boxing matches, but not all of them. Nobody who entered a boxing ring ever really won, I thought, since every boxer took some kind of beating. I took enough regular beatings at home at the hands of my stepfather. I had no interest in boxing. I could see, however, that all of their experiences on the road had earned Bud and Lee Boy a worldliness lacking in most other kids. Bud took me under his wing. He taught me to think about a situation instead of just reacting, when to be tough—to stand firm and fight—and when to run away. These were lessons in manhood that I would not learn at home.

My initial introduction to Bud took place a couple of years before either of us moved into the new homes at Banana Island, when I was fourteen or so. It was on a Saturday morning, in the late spring or early summer. I was living with my mother, stepfather, brothers, and sisters outside of Shawano in a house next to the highway. On this day, my older brother and I had been dumped off at our grandparents' house by my stepfather. My older brother decided to visit his friend Lee Boy at his family's apartment in the upstairs part of the old Catholic government boarding school. That school had closed in 1952. Part of the school had been converted into a tavern, in addition to apartments. I tagged along.

Altogether, about a dozen buildings, garages, storage buildings, and livery stables associated with this industrial school were still in use. The Gothic federalist-style brick buildings were impressive, and this building was no exception.

The entire place, although substantial, seemed abandoned. Even the water tower sat unmoving. While all of the buildings were still being used for other purposes, they seemed desolate without hundreds of children occupying them.

This particular brick building sat on the deserted southeastern edge of town. To its north was a hidden spring that fed Keshena Creek. Before the dam on Balsam Road was constructed in 1926, that swamp had been a meadow with a spring-fed brook running through it. That brook ran right past my grandparents' home. Rising out of the man-made swamp were two hills, Bean Hill and the long slope marking the site where Keshena's band of Menominee once lived. The state highway ran north and south a quarter mile to the west of the tavern. To the east, behind this fortress, was a forest of white pine. Then it was pine forest and swamp all the way to the next county. At night, this area was dark and isolated, with only a few outside lights, and the only visitors came in loud, rumbling cars. As a teenager, I never wandered around the deserted buildings at night. Family stories did not inspire confidence.

Once after our evening meal, Grandma referred to this building complex and said in Menominee, "Nothing good ever happened there." Deaths had occurred in these buildings, in the old Catholic days. Some of these deaths were accidental. Others, who knows?

Every older Catholic edifice hides more than a few building flaws. Aside from my grandparents' home, I knew if any place in town were really haunted, this would be it. The buildings seemed sad to me, although others might disagree. Some still remember the thrill of receiving a formal education as they sat in rows, dressed alike. They looked forward to learning more modern ways of doing things. My mother, for one, enjoyed the lifetime of camaraderie she gained through the miseries of boarding school life in Keshena and later on in Lawrence, Kansas.

But besides a few pleasant memories, the former boarding school students must have amnesia, as government and church schools for Indians were places of abuse and ethnocide. This unnatural place destroyed the forest. Then the harsh glare of sunlight killed the ginseng. The shaded canopy was replaced by fenced meadows for grazing cattle. Even at fourteen, I found this collection of out-of-place and mostly abandoned structures depressing. I did not hang around this part of town, even though the fields seemed inviting enough in the daylight.

Well, once I did hang out there, much to my regret. One late night, I sneaked out of my grandparents' home. I met up with Jimmy B. from across the street, and we walked around town in the shadows of early morning. Eventually, we ended our tour of Keshena at the water tower behind the old government school. Climbing the tower at three in the morning was no problem whatsoever. Walking around the steel scaffolding that circled its belly in the predawn darkness was not a problem for us, either. Climbing down was the problem, and eventually the police got involved. Even worse, they called my grandmother. Needless to say, this was not one of the best memories of my youth.

So I was prudent when visiting the home Bud's mother had made in one of these old boarding school edifices. Half of the building's downstairs was taken up by the bar, a forbidding place. The other half of the downstairs area was living space that was only sporadically occupied. On one visit to Bud's home in the government school, we toured the tavern with the owners. Bud's family was related to them, which was how they got the place.

In the daylight, this building seemed empty of ghosts. For a few hours, the aura of horror and dread was replaced with dusty cobwebs and trails of mouse droppings. Where darkness surely held unimaginable terrors, the daylight burned them away as sunlight burns away the dew.

The downstairs tavern had a long, backward J-shaped bar top running the length of the building. The owners had purchased this distinctive counter in Green Bay and brought it back to Keshena in sections on a pickup truck. The short end of the reversed J faced the front door, a set of double doors on the west side. Facing east toward the building, the tavern took up most of the building's first floor and all of the left, or north, side. The other parts of the first floor, on the right side of the building, were vacant living spaces. Bud's family occupied the only living space on the second floor.

The entrance to the upstairs was a door on the left, near the front. That door was protected by a small, shingled roof, maybe four feet square, which provided a little shelter. The door was water-damaged and had been hastily patched with whatever thickness and color of plywood was available—parts were painted white and other parts were not painted at all. Also, because the door did not close properly, there was a constant draft, which sometimes produced a howl. Beyond providing a barrier to windblown precipitation, that door offered little protection from the elements. In the winter, a snow drift accumulated just inside the door. At the landing at the bottom of the stairs, a small pool of melted snow would freeze, slick as a skating rink. The steps got drier and the footing got better higher up. In the summer, the situation was almost the same, except the ice was replaced with a layer of mud. The steps became less dirty as they rose.

At the top of the stairs, a cold, black pay telephone was mounted chest-high on the wall. This phone's users were probably the reason for the shabby condition of the downstairs area. People from the tavern came upstairs to use this phone. The cord connecting the handset to the coin box was wrapped in a steel cable. This rotating dial pay phone was an antique, even then. Walking past it, I always checked the coin return bin for spare change. On the wall next to the phone were numerous handwritten phone numbers and small doodles—some written in pencil, some in ink. Bud once showed me a number written in lipstick. A pencil dangled from the phone, tied to a length of string. Many of the numbers on the wall were preceded by a phrase like, "For a good time call. . . ." Most of those doodles were X-rated. At the time, I did not fully understand them, but they seemed interesting.

There was no door at the top of the stairs leading to the apartment. A door had once been there, as doorjambs and hinges remained where it was once attached. At the top of the stairs, one simply walked into Bud's family kitchen. Their apartment was stitched together out of a group of second-floor offices, like an apartment/train hybrid. Some rooms branched off from a hallway, and some rooms opened into other rooms. The rest of the upstairs offices were dusty and unused, and any previous occupants were long since dead.

Sometimes the constant draft from the front door was welcome. In the winter, it was not. But it was not a big problem because, except for the open kitchen, all the other rooms had solid doors and were heated with radiators. They seemed warm enough. This narrow and cramped apartment had remarkably high ceilings, dirty plaster walls, thin white wainscoting, and a rolling wooden floor covered with dirty clothes.

The first office space, perhaps originally a teacher's lounge, had been converted into the kitchen. An aluminum table shoved against the wall served as the kitchen table, with mismatched kitchen chairs on three sides. Only one chair was empty and available for sitting, as the others were stacked high with household junk. The table was piled with dirty dishes, many of which were serving double duty as ashtrays. Many of the cigarette butts had lipstick stains, Bud's mother's.

On the east wall was a small hand sink for washing dishes. It was mounted on the wall next to a small handmade counter where clean dishes could be stacked. For cooking, there was an old gas stove connected to a tank of liquid propane stored in a narrow closet a couple feet away. Some frying pans and other kitchenware hung from nails pounded into the plaster wall. The refrigerator was a small ivory-colored box with a tall, round condenser, the cooling element of the refrigerator, mounted on its top. It was the old-time kind where the top was bigger than the bottom.

The bathroom was a typical office bathroom. The walls were painted a dirty industrial green, the same color as the walls at Grandma and Grandpa's home. The paint for both must have come from the same batch of government surplus. Their bathroom had four stalls, four sinks, and a tile floor. Near the door, a shower head had been installed over a drain in the bare cement floor. The drain was thick with hair and bits of soap. I felt really bad that these guys lived this way.

A few years later, when Bud's family moved to the 'burbs about the same time as mine, their new home in Banana Island rapidly acquired a similar patina of neglect. It was as if the family was stalked by some ghostly slob. In only a matter of weeks, their home took on a weathered and lived-in look. It even seemed abandoned. Still, it was a step up from the tavern building.

While his mom owned just one car, the family's Banana Island driveway could not hold all of the cars pulling in and out. Bud had lots of relatives, and their cars were always spilling out of the gravel driveway. The barely established lawn suffered immediately. Alarmed, Bud's mom sent him and Lee Boy outside to reseed along the driveway. But no matter how much grass seed they planted, the lawn simply never had a chance. It could not grow beyond a few sprouts, and things only got worse with time.

To warn drivers to avoid those newly reseeded parts of the lawn, Bud and his brother drove crude fence post branches into the ground with twine stretched between them that announced their purpose—stay off the grass. So visitors parked even farther away from the driveway, which made the dead patches of grass even larger. In three months, the lawn surrendered. A once-thickening emerald green lawn soon became a gravelly patch of dried mud, with tire ruts radiating outward in all directions.

Bud's family's homes—both the government building and the new suburban rancher—were always messy on the inside, too. In Banana Island, this was a flaw in the house's design. There was not any kind of mud room—no place to contain the outside messes of the six people coming in and out, no place to keep dirty boots so they did not track through the house. The new home was a big improvement for them, like it was for me and my family. But all six of them lived in a five-bedroom house, and even on the best of occasions, it was difficult to get so many people on the same page. Regular deep cleaning was not on any agenda. Even on those rare occasions when Bud's mom yelled loudly and long enough to wake all the kids, extended family, and guests, get them all dressed, and get them motivated with threats and bribes to clean—it still looked messy.

This messy look was largely due to the state of the kitchen. No matter the previous efforts, the dirty sinks were always stacked full. Cooking one meal for so many people dirtied almost every pot, pan, and dish in the house. Bud's mom was a single mother with several kids, a huge immediate family, and a larger, uncountable extended family. Yeah, it got loud and profane, but that family loved each other, no matter what. And it was that family love that I wanted so desperately.

Given all of these circumstances, when Bud cooked us something to eat in the late night or early morning, he had to begin by first finding a frying pan clean enough to use. His signature dish, scrambled eggs with onions, required a frying pan. In all the years he made this dish, I do not ever remember him using a clean frying pan retrieved from the cabinet. If a pan was already on the stove, Bud would find a brown paper bag and give the black cast iron a vigorous scrubbing. Bud's mom, like mine, used only thick and heavy black cast-iron frying pans to fry foods. Bud's "cleaning" method also worked if the dirty skillet was in the sink, not fully submerged, and not too filled with dirty water. Then he would pour the dirty water back into the sink, concentrating it for later, and use a brown paper bag to finish cleaning the pan. Sometimes Bud took a few extra minutes finding something like tongs, which he would use to grab a more submerged pan so he did not have to reach into the dirty water. If the pan was absolutely filled with sink sludge, then Bud would begin by first taking the offending pan out the kitchen door to the rear of the backyard and emptying the crud into the nearby woods. When he brought the pan back inside, he would proceed to the paper-bag step. He never violated the grease seasoning of the skillet.

When the pan was clean enough, Bud would grab an open can of lard off the counter near the stove, where commodity cans of lard were stacked, and using a tablespoon as a shovel (I have also seen him use a butter knife for this step), he would put two huge splats of creamy white lard into the frying pan.

As he waited for the lard to begin its snap, sizzle, and pop dance, he would push the mess on the kitchen table aside to create a small workstation. He used a yellow onion from the mesh bag always kept in a certain spot on the kitchen counter—the onion spot. Bud's mom never bought the more expensive white onions. Using a kitchen knife recovered carefully from the sink, he would dice about a third of the yellow onion on the kitchen table, leaving tiny pieces in a small mound. Bud was the only person I knew who added onions to his eggs.

Sometimes other dirty tablespoons, butter knives, cups, or

plates were needed. This required us to form piles of sorted dirty dishes, and only what was required for the moment was washed. One late night, we ate our scrambled eggs off one plate—me with a fork, because I was the guest, and him with a spoon.

With the recovered kitchen knife, Bud would scrape the onion pile into his hand and dribble this into the smoking-hot pan. Once, Bud could not or would not find a kitchen knife in the murky sink and simply used his trusty fishing knife, first wiping the blade on his jeans. That time, there was a fishy taste to the onions.

After these onions hit the pan, Bud would search for eggs in the fridge, four to six eggs, or whatever was available. He'd let the door slam as he returned to the stove and cracked them against the black iron pan. He cracked the eggs with one hand as he poured them into the smoking-hot pan, tossing the shells to the side of the stove alongside an unused burner. Then Bud would take the spatula in his hand, wait a few moments, and use it like a whisk, breaking apart the eggs while they cooked. He whisked—or rather, he spatula-ed—the set parts of the eggs with the panache of a master chef.

Sometimes there were no fresh eggs, and so Bud used powdered commodity eggs to make breakfast. These powdered eggs are distributed in small paper envelopes with the instructions for use printed in English and Spanish. For people who might not read English or Spanish, like some of the old-time Menominees, the label showed pictures of the steps for preparation. These dehydrated eggs required only a little water and stirring, and then they were ready for use.

Powdered eggs on their own look a little thick and fuzzy, like pudgy scrambled eggs that need a haircut, and they have a stale taste. To be at all edible, they must be mixed with the proper amount of liquid. But Bud had a trick for correcting overwatered eggs. After the powdered eggs were mixed with water, and if they appeared runny, he would throw a handful of commot potato flakes on top and let the mixture sit for a minute. The potatoes soaked up the excess moisture. He would then fold this resulting pile of chunky potato flakes into the egg mix. He would spoon a portion of the egg and potato mix into the smoking-hot frying pan with the onions and cook it until it achieved the desired consistency. This made the eggs thicker and chunkier, almost like potato pancakes. He salted and peppered to taste and then served.

Bud's scrambled eggs, fresh or powdered, always looked homemade. They were a chunky pile with blackened bits of charred onions—not at all like those thin, smooth, and carefully folded eggs served in diners, with a dusting of dried parsley flakes. Bud's eggs tasted delicious. These egg techniques, like my friend Bud, were original.

Eggs were a standby on the reservation, almost always available. Mom made chicken eggs in two ways, hard or soft. Hard fried eggs had pierced yolks and a rubbery texture. They were cooked until the yolk was a solid yellow spot within a larger white spot with crusts, which was just the way my older brother liked them. Mom would then put that hard egg between two slices of buttered Wonder Bread to complete the egg sandwich. For me, she made soft eggs, which were actually over-medium sunny-side-up eggs. The runny, savory yolks were velvety soft, and I could dip toast into them. We never ate omelets, would never even consider them. The idea of chopped meat, vegetables, and cheese mixed with eggs was incomprehensible to us, and I know that my grandmother would have disapproved of them also. We ate bacon and eggs, regular things for breakfast. These were traditional on the Menominee Reservation and beyond, in diners in border towns around the reservation.

My mom also made wonderful egg salad. She used her trusty go-to: Kraft Miracle Whip cut with a dash, or rather a dribble, of pickle juice poured straight out of the bottle with some added cut-up bits of sweet pickles. This was the same recipe my mom used for potato salad, just with boiled sliced potatoes substituted for the boiled eggs. My mom had a much cleaner kitchen than Bud, of course.

Bud was a friend for many years. He never joined me in hanging out in the neighborhood, because he was a few years older than my gang. We went places together, he and I; we just did not hang out in the woods together. So, it was the rest of the gang, sans Bud, that hung out at the Beach, the Roots, and Warrington Hill. Other kids would pass us along the trail that ran past our spot, where Brooks Lane T-bones the highway. Lots of those kids sat in our spot, since it was a comfortable place with plenty of tall white pines for shade. But no one else hung out there the way we did.

Sometimes, though, we really were the hateful troublemakers that the old ladies claimed we were. We once showed how even eggs could be used to ill purpose.

It was a couple of weeks before Halloween, a dark and crisp night, and the smell of wood smoke hung in the air. The guy that gave voice to this bad idea was not one of our gang regulars. Jimmy B., a light-skinned guitar player from Mississippi, lived downtown across from my grandparents and was definitely an outsider, even though his great-grandfather had been a Menominee chief. His sister had a crush on me, and I tried to stay away from his house. This was the first and last time he hung with our gang. Once his plan was uttered, we all got on board with it. The goal? To egg passing cars. That is, we would buy some eggs and, as unfamiliar cars drove by, throw eggs at them.

In no way do I encourage anybody to behave similarly. Egging a car can result in serious property damage. If the egg mess is not washed away quickly, the egg may begin to eat away at the car's finish. Besides that, egging a car while it is in motion may cause the driver to lose control and crash. Of course, we were young teenagers, and none of this occurred to us at that moment.

Once committed to mayhem, we walked downtown to buy some eggs. We first had to throw off anyone following us, so we backtracked through the woods in the dark until we found the trail from Banana Island, past the Roots and the old hospital. We then walked down the dark street over to the wall by St. Joe's and turned left to Frank Skubitz's store, where we bought four dozen eggs. Frank was on duty, and he did not even glance up from the newspaper as he rang up our sale, as though six teenage males coming in at eight o'clock to buy four dozen eggs happens every night. I suppose that he only would have cared if we'd tried to buy booze.

We then, following the same route, returned to our prime perch overlooking the highway.

Once situated, before passing out any eggs, we decided on some rules. We all knew not to be throwing eggs at any Indian cars, because those Indian owners would find out who we were and come back and kick our asses. So, rule number one, our gang decided, was no egging any Indian cars, period. Generally, it was pretty easy to tell the difference between Indian and White-owned cars. Indian cars were old, loud, and rusty, while White-owned cars were new, quiet, and shiny. There were a few Indians who owned fancy cars, too, but among the six of us, we were positive that we could recognize all the local cars. After we settled on rule number one, that seemed to be enough.

As dangerous as this stunt was, it was fun. We nailed several White-owned cars as they drove past our curve and down the hill at the posted speed limit of thirty-five miles per hour, which made them easy targets. After being peppered with eggs, tiny white grenades coming out of the darkness, they sped off quickly—after all, it was nighttime and they were in hostile Indian Country. What probably scared these tourists even more was when we screamed like wild Indians as we threw the eggs.

After the second dozen eggs were gone, we decided to vary

our attack. Finding some empty beer cans in the ditch alongside the road, we arranged them like traffic cones, stacking them up, so that any oncoming cars would see them. We built a car trap. They had to slow down and make wide curves around them, and at that moment, we would pepper them with eggs. We were going to ambush a wagon train! That would be even more fun.

As it was nine thirty in the evening, we had to wait a few minutes between cars, Indian or otherwise. In this quiet darkness, our next target announced itself well before we saw it. We could hear a semitruck getting closer, miles away, downshifting, double-clutching, using that Jake Brake to reduce speed as he approached town center. Lazy drivers use their Jake Brakes to avoid using their legs and truck brakes. This practice is illegal in places with high population densities, as the Jake Brake is loud. As the semi rounded the curve, we could see it hauling a gasoline tanker. It slowly approached our ambush—but drove right over our beer cans, leaving a trail of flattened aluminum. Still, as the truck slowed down for the curve, we fired, hitting the front and side windows of the cab with our eggs. This driver must have expected trouble, though. He slammed on the brakes, opened his cab door, and began swearing at us as he climbed down out of his truck. There was a wooden club in his hand. To paraphrase, he was going to beat the crap—though he did not use that word—out of us. He was angry enough and certainly looked tough enough to do it. In fact, this guy was so big that I was fully prepared to run in the other direction, all the way back to Banana Island through the thick woods.

Jimmy B. yelled back at the dismounted driver, "Shut up or we'll throw a match at you!" To our collective surprise, as all of us were prepared to bolt into the dark forest, the driver turned around and climbed back into his rig, roaring off. He left a thick, black, belching diesel smoke wake in the ether. We were not ready to die for our art, and neither was that truck driver.

This kind of malicious behavior was not something our gang regularly engaged in—probably because we did not like paying for our destructive fun. Also, our parents always seemed to find out. My parents never found out about this car-egging event, and so I considered it successful. It was a one-time, big-deal thing, and a lot of Indian people who were not on the receiving end of a thrown egg thought it was funny. If any of our victims had called the local police, I suspect the gendarmes would have known exactly who it was. Things like this are hard to keep quiet, and copycats will certainly follow such a spectacular staging.

There were lots of other groups and gangs of kids in Keshena. Another gang hung out at the end of the Chapel Hill Trail near the intersection of Rabbit Ridge Road and the highway. There was a nice sitting spot right where the moraine trail overlooked the highway on one side and the deep Ice Age kettle on the other side. The guys who hung out there were our occasional allies, since we all had to live there.

A few days after Halloween that year, in early November, the weather kept changing from beautiful to miserable and back again. This was an Indian summer. On one of those beautiful, warm autumn days, our envious peer gang decided to try the egging game.

We heard about this misadventure later, secondhand, from an eyewitness. Mooch—one of my best friends—was walking in the Banana Island neighborhood on his way to visit family when we waved him over to talk with us. We all liked Mooch. He told us the latest news. He and a friend had been standing on Rabbit Ridge by the Chapel Hill Trail, just hanging out, and some guys from the other gang were nearby. They got up and walked down to Skubitz's Store. Then they returned ten minutes later with a brown paper sack filled with several dozen eggs. They made themselves comfortable and waited for a car to drive by to egg. This was just after lunch in broad daylight, on a beautiful warm Saturday. They did not wait long. A late-model convertible came by, driven by a White guy with a pretty White girl sitting next to him—they were outsiders and fair game.

The gang members each threw an egg at the car, hitting the hood, the seats, and the rear deck. Egg guts splattered all over. They laughed at the driver and threw another round of eggs. Then, someone hit the girl with an egg, square on the side of her head. All of a sudden, things got really serious.

"That hit would leave bruises," Mooch said. "It had to have hurt." We all agreed.

The man slammed on his brakes. He stopped short and jumped out of the car, over the car door. Who knew he would be so damn fast? He ran up the hill and chased the Menominee teens down the Chapel Hill Trail from near Rabbit Ridge all the way to downtown near the Third Station of the Cross Chapel. On the way there, that White guy caught one boy, beat him up, and then kept running until he caught up with the next boy. He continued until he had chased all of them down.

The fastest was the last one caught. The man finally caught him and beat the hell out of him only a few feet away from the Third Station of the Cross. This guy then walked all the way back to the pretty woman in the convertible, which was still blocking the outbound lane. The whole episode took ten minutes. Then, Mooch told us, they drove off.

After some discussion, we decided that she must have been his girlfriend, because no man would fight that hard for his wife. We all agreed among ourselves that, if we ever threw eggs at cars again, we would not target women.

When I was writing the book *Good Seeds* as an elder, one of the witnesses to that egging became the inspiration for an essay I wrote about climbing trees. He had always seemed fearless to me in an unassuming way. I once watched him climb a giant white pine, well over a hundred feet tall, by the intersection of Brooks

Lane and Morrin Street. His family was one of the last of the original families living in the Banana Island neighborhood. Their home was the most recent construction prior to the wave of low-income housing. Once that housing was built, disreputable and unsupervised kids like me became his playmates.

My uncle Bobby and aunt Nita were also original residents of this neighborhood, back when the only name for this loose clump of houses was the nearby Banana Island in the river. A grove of white pines was growing near their house, almost in their backyard. Three huge pines grew in this clump, each one close enough to the other at the base that the tops of their trunks arched outward to avoid one another. Most pine trees are easy to climb, because the limbs are regularly spaced, like the rungs of a ladder. It is just that white pines grow pretty tall. The first fifty feet are easy, but it gets harder the higher you get. These three trees were no exception—very tall with regularly spaced limbs.

Seated on the ground and leaning against a pine tree a hundred yards away, I watched this kid as he started climbing a huge pine tree at about ten o'clock in the morning. It took him almost two hours to get up to the top—the very tip of this tree—and back down to the bottom. I do not think that he knew I was watching him.

The last time I had seen this guy was probably when I was fourteen years old. Flash forward fifty years, and I was doing a reading from my first memoir at the College of the Menominee Nation. He was in the audience. We shared our memories of Banana Island, and he generously bought my book. His feat stays with me anytime I remember that part of the neighborhood.

Larded Baked Potatoes

In addition to his famous eggs, Bud also made baked potatoes for our late-night meals. Why not? They are easy and nutritious, and it does not take much to prep them or to clean up afterward—the perfect meal. Back then, we did not know that more than five hundred varieties of potatoes exist. Sometimes my uncle Jim Smith—the best fly fisherman in Wisconsin—would bring family members hundred-pound bags of potatoes grown on the commercial farm in Antigo where he worked.

Bud had his own trick to customize his late-night potatoes—his technique left the baked potatoes with a thick, crispy skin, just perfect for loading up with butter and eating as a side dish. His technique makes an impeccable boat for loaded baked potatoes.

Serves 2 to 4 people

4 large potatoes
1 handful of lard
Salt, pepper, and butter, to taste

Preheat the oven to 450 degrees. Gather the potatoes. Wash the potatoes, if you plan to eat the skins, by rinsing them under the kitchen sink tap. Using a clean knife, trim black spots, green spots, and roots. Let the potatoes dry for a few minutes. Using a fork or knife, pierce the dried potatoes a few times. Reach inside an open can of lard and fill your hand with lard. Lather each potato with lard and place them in the oven on the top rack. Bake for 40 minutes or until tender. Serve with salt, pepper, and butter to taste.

Alcohol and a Friend Named Clifford

The School View Addition housing development, our neighborhood's official name, was designed with only two road exits. Both followed previously existing dirt ruts, which were foot and wagon trails left from a previous era. Each paralleled the river. Sections of these were straightened, becoming official paved streets.

One of those trails became Morrin Street, the southernmost exit to the housing development. Its intersection with the state highway became a prime spot for people who wanted to hook a ride somewhere, to hitchhike. This T-bone crossroad sat at the top of a low rise, with numerous shade trees and plenty of friendly traffic, and people came to expect somebody to be standing here hitchhiking. It was easy to find an outbound ride, and even if you didn't, so what? Home was only a few blocks away. Even better, the local cops didn't hassle hitchhikers. Because at fifteen I was too young to own a car but old enough to want to see the outside world, this became a regular hitchhiking spot for me. Using my thumb, depending on the kindness of strangers, I got safely and quickly to and from many destinations, including Green Bay, Wausau, Madison, and other more distant places around Lake Michigan. Later, after I owned a car, I practiced good karma and picked up plenty of people.

The state highway also crossed the other foot trail, now called Brooks Lane, forming a T and becoming the northern exit from

Banana Island. A forested, hillside lot called Warrington Hill overlooked the highway at this intersection. Thick, soft grasses grew on the hill, and there were many towering white pines to lean against when sitting, talking, or thinking. An impregnable tangled mass of thorny red raspberries and stiff cane blackberries, as well as a grove of waist-high poison ivy, grew on the hill's sunny flank. Few people braved these natural fortress walls, which served to hide and protect the trail. But during those times when a person wanted to be hidden in plain sight, this was the place to go.

Kitty-corner across the street was a gas station. No, to be fair, it was really much more than that. It was a full-service station with two garage bays and mechanical lifts. Now it is a ghost station for ghost cars—ready whenever some ghost needs to buy cigarettes or use the restroom. That building is shuttered, darkened, and abandoned, like a preserved corpse from another epoch in some museum's anteroom.

Nonetheless, fifty years ago this place was filled with vibrant movement—with colors, sounds, and sweet memories. In those days, when a car pulled off the highway for gas, it ran over a thin rubber hose connected to an air pump that would ring a bell inside. That *ding-ding* signaled the service attendant, the "pump jockey." He was always male. Such attendants would stop whatever they were doing and run outside to the car. The first questions were always, "Fill her up?" or, "Ethel today?" Sometimes Uncle Buddy and I would pull into a full-service station just to buy a pack of smokes and disappoint the attendant.

This was full service, and you paid for it. Even the regular-grade gas was several cents a gallon more than the pump-it-yourself joints, which were still very rare back then. Self-service gas stations didn't become common until after the mid-1970s, as the amount of lead exposure permitted by the government was raised. Ethel, or premium-grade gas, was much more expensive than regular leaded gasoline. Regular cost less than thirty-six cents per gallon just about everywhere, but if you looked really hard you could find it even cheaper. For example, in the early 1970s, as an older teen, I routinely bought gasoline at a station someplace in Fort Howard for 22.9 cents per gallon. Two dollars' worth, about six gallons of regular, was my usual purchase, and since I had a Volkswagen Bug, it probably would have caught fire if I tried using premium gas in it, so I never bought any.

No matter the size of the purchase, the procedure remained the same. After asking those preliminary questions about quantity and grade, the attendant positioned the gas pump hose into the car and clicked the hose to automatic. In those days, access to the gas tank's filler neck was hidden. The opening to the gas tank filler neck on my stepfather's 1972 Chevy Impala was hidden behind the license plate. On a 1972 VW Bug, the gas tank filler neck was accessed only by opening the front hood. On some cars, like a Chevy Bel Air and some models of Cadillac, access to the gas tank was hidden behind one of the taillights.

Setting the hose nozzle to automatic allowed the pump attendant time to rush to one of the front sides of the car, where he pulled a shop rag out of one rear pocket and a small bottle of blue window cleaner from the other. Squeezing the bottle and squirting blue liquid across the windows, he then wiped the windows dry with the rag. Sometimes, you'd encounter a great pump jockey. They were the ones with T-shaped squeegees in their belts, like swords to vanquish dirty windows. Outside mirrors got a squirt and a wipe. Next, the attendant opened the hood or the engine compartment deck lid and checked the oil level in the motor. In those days, the engine in a VW was in the rear. The jockey would bring the dipstick to the driver's window to verify the oil level.

Among the other free services provided was an air pressure check for all four tires and the spare. If needed, the tires would be "aired up" on the spot. One time, I asked a service attendant to test my car battery. After getting a couple bucks' worth of gas, it wouldn't start. That had started happening to my car with increasing frequency. The only way to get it going was by push-starting it, which was easy enough to do, but it was annoying. Checking the battery required that we find it first. On the 1972 VW Bug, the battery was located under the rear passenger seat, which had to be completely removed from the car. After we placed the bench seat on the cement, the helpful gas station employee checked the battery. He was surprised to find that this German car was a six-volt system. After he put distilled water in the battery, it started right up, and off I drove. This service was free of charge.

The gas was always paid for at the pump, too. I would hand the payment out the car window, just like a fast-food drive-through. My car held just ten gallons, eight in the main tank with two more as reserve. Stepfather's Impala held twenty gallons. After handing the jockey a few bills, he would make that change on the spot from a clutch of folded grease-stained bills kept in one shirt pocket, while any needed quarters, dimes, nickels, and pennies came out of the chrome four-barrel money changer on his belt. Breaking a fifty or a one-hundred-dollar bill usually required a trip into the office.

It was during the night that this gas station came alive, when the outside neon branding lights supported by metal poles and the navigation lights surrounding the cement pump islands combined with the interior incandescent lights. When I was a fifteen-year-old, this stirred my overactive imagination. My buddies and I watched the gas station from Warrington Hill as people drove in and out until closing time. Packs of neighborhood children, including us, came in to buy candy and ice-cream bars in the early evening. The effects of the sugars and fats caused us to react like moths to an open flame. We made regular runs back and forth across the street for potato chips, candy bars, and soda. The station sold a particularly noxious brand of cherry soda pop called

Worms. I didn't like the taste but drank it anyway—it was for grossing others out. It was reminiscent of a very sweet cherry-flavored Pepsi, almost like a thin, bubbly cough syrup.

Sometimes we hung out with the owner while he worked on cars inside the station. All of us stood solemnly around the ailing patient as he performed a last-ditch operation to bring it back to life. I liked the owner, but my stepfather hated him for some reason. Still, this guy was always really nice to me. Later, he majorly fixed my VW Bug at least twice without charging me, so he was all right with me.

Warrington Hill is where we Banana Island denizens came to collect ourselves and decide what to do—as adults, for the rest of our lives, or just for that night. I was so wrong about what I thought I would do the rest of my life.

We so desperately wanted to be in control of ourselves that we tried many dumb things in unsuccessful attempts at hurrying adulthood along. Several of the older kids, some of whom we thought were real tough guys around town, talked about drinking and how adult they felt. We decided that we liked to drink, too, and highballs seemed innocent enough, or at least they looked innocent enough. Ultimately, we spent much more time *trying* to consume alcohol than actually consuming it. We thought that just having it available, at our side, would magically transform us into sophisticated adults. We liked the idea of being sophisticates who came home from work and had martinis. Attempting to buy alcohol was how I first came to hang out with my future best friend, Bud. We shared far-too-many-to-count adventures.

Once the gang collectively had decided to buy some booze, we began a logical, methodical process. We asked around the neighborhood, stopping by those homes that were known for *drinking*. We sauntered to the driveways or garages of likely scores and asked anyone there, often sitting in lawn chairs with drinks in hand, "Does anybody have any booze to sell us?" This didn't work, of course, although we were offered a few free drinks, which we politely declined.

On this reservation, nobody seemed to have a well-stocked liquor cabinet or a full wet bar for guests. Booze wasn't stored in anyone's pantry. It was bought, then it was consumed. It seemed to us that booze was a spontaneous magical thing—appearing one moment and disappearing the next—at least to those drinking adults around us.

We usually had better luck at our homes, right after supper when we asked our older brothers, cousins, or sisters to buy. Also, relatives didn't normally charge to buy booze, so our money went further.

If all else failed, waiting outside one of the local stores or taverns was a last option. This was dangerous—the kind of people who might buy us booze were often the very same people who might take our money away from us, and we knew it. Seldom do you meet upstanding people outside a bar. Hanging around a tavern at night was especially dangerous, and it was something that we hardly did. It was usually only done when one of us knew somebody already drinking inside. The next step was to get word to that person, via another patron, to come outside and talk to us. This method mostly worked, but it was spotty. We had to wait for somebody we knew, somebody who would do it for us.

One day, I was hanging around the neighborhood when this guy about my age came walking past my house. Bud and I would soon become good friends, but I only knew him slightly at the time. Taking a chance, I approached him and asked if he knew anybody who would buy me something to drink. "No problem," he answered. "I can probably get you some booze from my mom's boyfriend." I was taken aback—first upon finding out that his mother had a boyfriend, which meant she was having sex, and second, that Bud could ask the guy having sex with his mom, an adult, to buy some booze. He said that his mother's boyfriend,

Clifford, sometimes bought him beer or brandy. "I like to drink brandy and sour," Bud said, in a worldly, offhandedly adult manner. This is when I knew Bud would be my friend. Clifford, he continued, also charged him at least one pack of cigarettes, and usually it was a couple packs of cigarettes, but that was Clifford's family rate. All we had to do was wait and ask him ourselves. "But don't expect to get the family rate," he said.

Soon, a pattern developed. We would save our cash all week and, on the weekend, we would try to buy something to drink through Clifford. If we were lucky, we got a six-pack of beer. It worked out to be one or two bottles per person, and it cost us maybe three dollars per bottle. This was in 1969. Today, those would be twenty-dollar bottles. We didn't realize how much we were being cheated on this deal. Still, it was Clifford who would go to jail if we were caught and not us.

Whether or not boozy Clifford would help us depended on several factors, chief among which was timing—ours, his, and others'. Friday nights worked out better than Saturday nights to ask him to buy us booze, even though we would rather have had it on Saturday afternoons. Clifford spent all day Saturday drinking, from the moment he woke at noon until he fell asleep, a bottle next to his bed. Long story short, he was usually too drunk to do anything for us anytime on Saturday.

To be fair to Clifford, he worked hard at the Neopit sawmill all week long and had no dependents. His life was his own—he paid for his own drinks, and quite often for others', too. Our issue with the timing arose as we tried to work our scheme around Bud's mom's schedule. If we went over to Bud's house too early on Friday afternoon, like right after school, his mom would be home, sober and pissed off at the world, her normal Friday after-work mood. She would throw us "the hell out." That workweek bad mood preceded her weekend good mood by a couple of hours. If we arrived too late on a Friday night, after the good mood window had closed for the night, then Clifford would either already be gone for the night and drunk or at home, drunk, and crashed. On those occasions, we would be SOL, shit outa luck.

So timing was everything. Oh, Clifford was an agreeable, social drunk, not violent or mean. We knew lots of violent and mean people around town, and some of them were violent and mean whether sober or drunk. Clifford was a nice guy who liked being drunk. We learned, however, not to ask him to get us booze when he was already drunk. If he was already intoxicated, he sometimes took our money, forgot all about us, and went right on drinking by himself. The next day, he always apologized. So, we learned to time our arrival for around eight o'clock at night, after Bud's mom had already gone out for dinner and drinks after work and returned a bit drunk herself, while Clifford sat in a darkened living room, watching TV and nursing a bottle—maintaining his buzz—before he was completely wasted and couldn't walk. Then, one of us, usually Bud, would ask him loudly enough for his mother sitting at the kitchen table to hear. "Hey, Clifford, can you buy us something to drink? We'll get you a pack of cigs and a bottle for yourself." Around that magic time on Friday night, his mother could be counted on to be in a benevolent mood. She'd say, "Oh, go ahead, Clifford, and get these kids something to drink. Christ, maybe it'll get them out of this house for a while." Eventually, around ten o'clock, after days of planning, we would get maybe a two-dollar six-pack of beer delivered to Bud or to our Warrington Hill rendezvous in exchange for our twenty dollars. If we were lucky.

This was all happening soon after the Summer of Love in 1967, and twenty bucks was a lot of money. Clifford would slowly and dutifully write down whatever we wanted on a scrap piece of paper. Depending on where he went, they might not have what we wanted. He usually asked us if we had a second choice. Not that any of this did any good. We got what Clifford bought. Our bar was actually set pretty low, as we would settle for anything—except cheap wine. Clifford was a self-identified wino, so there was always a chance, a really good chance, that at the end of the night we would receive a pint bottle of Gallo's Dark Port, something that we prayed wouldn't ever happen. Pints of cheap wine, white or red, were a buck. This was never our first, second, or even third choice. It wasn't even our last choice. Sometimes, if he brought back port, we left our score with Clifford and just walked away. There was always a fair amount of uncertainty attached to our booze runs. Many times we were disappointed. Sometimes Clifford kept all that he bought. Who knows? Maybe this was good training for adulthood.

We didn't really like beer, either. As a last resort, our underage gang would drink shorties, those small, almost condensed bottles of beer. They were like glass grenades, no neck. We tossed many of them into the woods unopened. One apiece was plenty. Mostly, we drank Hamm's beer. I don't remember if it was because we found it relatively better tasting than other cheap beers or because it was more widely available on the reservation than other brands, or maybe we were just taken in by the Hamm's bear mascot. There were lots of television commercials for Hamm's on Wisconsin stations. In many of those commercials, the bear was dressed as an Indian. We knew the illustrator, Patrick Desjarlait, was an Ojibwa and a successful artist, so in our minds, Hamm's represented the success of a member of another northern tribe, in addition to being an agreeable beverage. You could share a bottle of beer with your friends without getting too drunk. We had less luck doing that with a bottle of vodka or cheap wine.

In the daylight hours, there were five places around our small town that sold beer, wine, and spirits. This is normal in any small Wisconsin town, whether the residents are White, Indian, or Black—there are lots of places to buy alcohol. In Wisconsin, beer is a right.

At night, just three places in our small town sold booze. Two were taverns. The War Bonnet Tavern was the farthest away, located at the very north end of town on the highway. The closest tavern, B&B's Bar, was about two blocks across the street from our hangout on Warrington Hill, on the ground floor of the old government and Catholic boarding school building. The third place to buy booze, Skubitz's Store, was a downtown convenience store that closed at ten o'clock.

I quickly discovered that the War Bonnet was off-limits to me, since a couple of my uncles hung out there. Oh sure, they would have bought me a couple of beers if I had walked in and asked them, but then I would have had to drink with them, and no hard drinks. My usual self-imposed limit was one bottle of beer or one highball anyway, but they would stop me from buying any kind of carryout, which was my reason to be there. Once, I spent a very cold evening hiding from my uncle Donny in the small aluminum tepee that sat in front of the War Bonnet while trying to find somebody to buy me some booze. It was ten degrees below zero, and there was too much standing snow to use a bike. That long walk back to Banana Island—by taking the Chapel Hill Trail by Rabbit Ridge, going around that spooky old graveyard behind the Catholic church, darting across the highway by the skating rink, and then walking down the trail past the Roots, past the Beach, and then through the woods, just to get home empty-handed—wasn't any kind of fun. The War Bonnet Tavern became off-limits because it was simply too far away for my comfort zone.

Skubitz's Store was also off-limits. The owner, Frank Skubitz, didn't care about state-issued identification cards, because he knew who was legally able to buy alcohol and who was not. His store had been there for thirty years, and he knew almost everybody on the reservation. His home on the west side of the river lay very close to the actual Banana Island. Frank certainly knew me because Uncle Billy, my older brother, and I used to sell him bullfrogs that we speared using long poles with trident-shaped, barbed, spear-point ends. He sold those frog legs to restaurants in Milwaukee. Besides that, my grandmother worked for Frank during most of his store's existence, so I would never ask him to sell me any booze. He wouldn't do it. Anyway, I was pretty sure that he would tell my grandma if I even tried.

That left B&B's Bar. The tavern had a prominent, well-lit Pabst Blue Ribbon sign on the front corner of the building that was visible from the highway. From one direction, it was the only light escaping from the dark forest gloom, like a far-off beacon on the horizon, beckoning to lost men. But it was a false signal. It was more like a beautiful mermaid that would turn into a grizzled sea cow moments before you crashed and died upon the rocky shoals, moments before you realized your folly.

This was no public house—this was a rez bar. This tavern, for several reasons, was our very last choice to buy booze. Still, despite my long list of worries, I also had fond memories of this old bar.

If it was after ten or so in the evening, Clifford, being already in his cups, would simply walk over and buy cheap wine at this tavern—a good deal for him, since he was related to the owners. Gallo brand dark port came in gallons, quarts, and pints. Clifford bought quarts for himself. It was the dosage he could live with. We would receive a pint for our troubles. A pint of fortified wine was more than enough to get the six of us boys crowded into Bud's room falling-down drunk. Then Clifford would laugh at us and drink what was left in the bottle. Drinking this kind of wine was our last choice for a fun evening. It didn't take too long before we lost interest in that kind of fun. Soon enough, our gang grew older and went about bigger and better things. We left Clifford behind in our rearview mirrors as we drove into the future.

Gray Squirrel Stew

You know that pesky squirrel that has been raiding your bird feeder all summer? Here is the ultimate revenge. This stew was a staple in my grandparents' kitchen. Singeing the squirrels over charcoal or a gas range fire before stewing them gives the stew an authentic tribal flavor. When eating, watch out for bones and bone splinters.

Serves 3 to 6 people

3 gray squirrels—in a pinch, red squirrels or flying squirrels may be substituted
½ cup flour, plus 1 tablespoon for thickening stew
Salt and pepper, to taste
2 quarts water
1 slice salt pork
1 stalk celery, roughly chopped
2 white onions, roughly chopped
3 medium potatoes, diced into large cubes
3 carrots, sliced into rounds

Skin the squirrels and remove the entrails. Wash the carcasses thoroughly. Singe squirrels over hot coals, then cut each into 6–8 pieces. Coat each piece with flour, and season with salt and pepper. Place the pieces into a medium-hot pan and fry until golden brown.

Place the cooked pieces of squirrel in a 4-quart kettle, then add 2 quarts of water. Add salt pork, celery, and onions. Cover the kettle. Bring to a boil, reduce heat, and simmer for 90 minutes. Add potatoes and carrots. Simmer until vegetables are tender but not mushy, maybe another 45 minutes. Be flexible. Thicken stew with 1 tablespoon of flour, simmer for 5 more minutes, and serve.

Supermarkets and the Summer of Love

I turned fourteen during the Summer of Love. It did not feel like love then, like those television flashbacks of the late 1960s, but now I understand that this was a revolution. Despite our earlier tribal lip service to Indigenous traditionalism in the 1950s, we Menominees had since acquired a wider sense of sophistication and begun acting more worldly, especially after School View was built. One aspect of this new consciousness was our diet.

Our actions really were revolutionary in ways that we did not realize then—we redistributed and concentrated wealth, in sync with America as it changed. Family-run grocery stores were early victims of that redistribution of wealth. We began to shop exclusively for our dinner table at one of the brand-new supermarkets in Shawano. The local Main Street IGA, near the post office, suddenly seemed old-fashioned and confining. My most striking memory is this: the new Super Value Store had double-wide automatic doors leading to a big, well-lit parking lot, while the IGA had a narrow, single-wide hand-pushed door leading to a small parking lot on the side of the building.

The clean, stylish supermarkets stocked everything imaginable for one-stop shopping. We no longer drove to the now-long-gone dairy by the old theater on North Main for glass, wide-mouth gallon bottles of unpasteurized whole milk. That milk was so rich that the top two or three inches of the bottle was thick, solidified cream that needed to be spooned out before the milk would pour. Stepfather ate this cream ladled over sliced peaches. Fifty years after my mother first began collecting those wide-mouth bottles, they are still being used by her children to store flour, pasta, and sugar. They sit stacked on shelves inside her pantry, in her house up by a place on the reservation known as Crow's Nest, still helping the family. But by 1969, our milk came in disposable cardboard milk containers, and thousands of quarts and half-gallons all stood at attention behind cold glass walls. Supermarket chains received that milk from distant, state-level distributors that bought the milk from local dairies, like the one we had once gone to, and sold it under their own brand. This was before bovine growth hormone became standardized.

The vegetable departments of the new supermarkets caused my family to stop growing our own vegetables. My family simply could not grow the 100- and 250-pound sacks of potatoes for any less than what they cost at the supermarkets. We no longer bought fresh produce from local truck farmers. We stopped buying meat from independent meat markets, and we no longer talked to local butchers. Local meat markets used to bid on prize-winning animals raised by youthful 4-H'ers and auctioned off at the county fair. Now, our meat came uniformly cut and dressed in clear plastic wrapping. Hull corn and wild rice became traditional, ceremonial, and ritual meals, no longer household staples.

My university-educated mother made sure that we tried foods from around the world, as part of our education. Wednesday night was Chinese night at our house, straight out of the two cans that constituted one La Choy Chow Mein dinner. The paired cans were wrapped in plastic together and sold as one item. The larger, bottom can was filled with dried chow mein noodles. A smaller can on top contained the actual meal—all of the wet parts. Mom poured the can of meat bits and soggy vegetables into a saucepan and heated it. This was years before microwaves were invented.

The contents of the next can, the dried noodles, were distributed across our seven plates before Mom poured the heated chow mein over them.

Soon, we became so sophisticated that we started to keep a bottle of soy sauce in the fridge for our Wednesday evening meal. After eating, we would watch *The Carol Burnett Show* on the television. For several years after these ideal moments at the family table, a can of La Choy Chow Mein was my favorite—that is, until I discovered the numerous mom-and-pop Asian joints in Madison. Still later, I learned how easy Asian cooking is, and I now own a wok. My mother, as she aged and became more conservative, continued to visit Chinese restaurants. She knew the menus of at least three different Chinese restaurants in Shawano, and her taste went far beyond chow mein or sweet-and-sour pork. This love of Asian food was one of the few lessons from my mother that stuck with me.

Because of my family's irregular schedules during the workweek, our separate meals were easy and quick. Frozen and dehydrated foods became dining mainstays. We had a stand-up freezer in the kitchen filled with colorful and probably dangerous packaged foods created by corporate food scientists in laboratories, not kitchens. They had a host of added food dyes and preservatives. One of my favorite invented foods was a pizza burger. I think that I was the only one in the family to eat these fast-cooking frozen beef or pork patties stuffed with cheese and Italian spices. Since they were so spicy and full of liquid, there was no need for ketchup. An equivalent—no, a distant relative—would be the Juicy Lucy, a cheese-stuffed hamburger found in the Twin Cities area.

I cannot remember ever eating a side dish with a pizza burger. It was a complete and quick meal—straight out of the freezer into a hot black iron skillet for just a few minutes on each side, then flipped onto two slices of Wonder Bread, and they were perfect.

Biting into the sandwich, through the pillow-soft white bread and into the chewy ground meat, released a mouthful of scalding liquid cheese and spices. Napkins were required to catch all the dribbles and to wipe up the satisfying grease stains.

The original Pizza-Burger was born the same year I was: 1953. It was trademarked by a drive-in located in Muskego, Wisconsin. I do not think we ate these original Pizza-Burgers, but rather some knockoff version. Supreme Meats of St. Francis, Wisconsin, has distributed frozen "pizza-burger patties" since 1954. It seems probable this was the brand that I ate so many years ago. Because my mom was brand conscious, she felt that the brand-name product was the best made. Finally, though, availability was the issue. If the brand-name product was available, she bought it. If not, we would be left with the imitations. My mother would buy large, white cardboard boxes filled with generic frozen "pizza-burger patties" at the Shawano Red Owl.

My White stepfather, another brand-conscious eater, liked only a few certain kinds of dry breakfast cereal. When he found that his brands came with added freeze-dried fruit inside, he was hooked. I honestly think he was in awe because he could not understand how fruit could be dried. He was not super tight with his cereal as he was with everything else that he claimed as his own. He did not seem to mind if we ate his Special K with dehydrated strawberries or his Corn Flakes with dehydrated banana slices. We just had to be sure that we did not empty the box. He would go crazy, ranting and raving, upon finding an empty cereal box. If you saw this kind of behavior in a movie, you would start to laugh.

My mother kept the food pantry well stocked, and as a fourteen-year-old, I monitored it closely. We always had cans of pork and beans on hand. Dried beans, pasta, and flour, distributed as commodity foods, made up the bulk of our pantry. My mom called this survival food. The Menominee had had some lean times in our past. Mom also bought a wide variety of soups, as well as cans of creamed corn, Spam, corned beef from Australia, and sardines—Mom liked the ones in mustard, I liked the ones with oil. Cans of kippers, another staple, could be found as I made my way through the pantry. I learned to love Campbell's clam chowder, the cream-based one, not the Manhattan, tomato-based style.

There were always certain staples around the house. In our case, being a water people, we ate fish. In those days, most grocers sold fresh-caught smoked lake fish, especially smoked chubs, which are about one foot long and delicious. Smoked chubs are generally the cheapest of the Lake Michigan commercial smoked fish, even cheaper than smoked carp. They have lots of bones and are oily fishes. They are what poor people, especially us poor Wisconsin Catholics living near Lake Michigan, ate on meatless Fridays. Back in the day, smoked chubs were referred to as "Catholic candy."

Friday was meatless because in the old days Catholics were forbidden to eat meat on Fridays. (Eventually, the Wisconsin Friday fish fry was established as a result.) If Catholics *did* eat meat on Friday, even if saintly in all other regards, they would go to purgatory instead of heaven. It did not matter how good and saintly you were, one hamburger and you went to purgatory for eternity. The Vatican has since reversed that doctrine, and presumably all those souls stuck in purgatory for eons have received a parole and have gone to heaven or hell on appeal. In my youth, though, the church was dead serious about Fish Friday.

Smoked carp, in pound-sized chunks of smoked boneless white flesh, was also widely available in Shawano. Mom made sure that we had plenty of smoked fish, and the only way to do so on her salary with five children was to buy the cheaper cuts. We ate a lot of cheap but tasty smoked chubs.

Once some years later, after I had my VW Bug, I stopped by one of the cliffs overlooking the bay of Green Bay. Looking down, I saw a huge carp swimming below me in the crystal-clear waters. It looked like a powered telephone pole. This carp must have been fifteen feet long. On other occasions, I can remember seeing pickup trucks driving through Green Bay filled with giant carp—tails hanging off the back, most of them heading for the dog food factory. As a fourteen-year-old, though, I had not yet seen these giant carp.

Stacked up along the back of our pantry's top shelf was my mother's stash of Jell-O and Jell-O pudding. My mom always bought the Jell-O brand of gelatin, never any generic brands, and never, ever any gourmet elitist sheet gelatin. Not only was she brand loyal, but she also counted herself among the people who ate Jell-O.

I do not know how many different hues the Jell-O company produces, but my mother must have purchased most of them. I remember the rich reds, yellows, and greens but not so much the flavors that went with them. Made according to the directions, Jell-O is sweet. While often considered informal, Jell-O can be dressed up easily enough and serve functions besides the obvious dessert. For example, Jell-O can be the base for a very pretty vegetable or fruit salad. However, at our house my mother always served it *au natural*. I liked the school cafeteria green Jell-O salad with carrot strips. Red Jell-O with fruit cocktail made by Aunt Lorraine was another of my favorites. One Christmas, she made red Jell-O with tiny marshmallows floating on the surface. She was the only one of my aunts who added anything to her Jell-O. Ultimately, however, for me, Jell-O gelatin was not as personally rewarding as its cousin, Jell-O pudding.

I enjoyed preparing and eating Jell-O instant pudding. To me, the cold, sweet creaminess of the puddings was so much better than the thin, cold juiciness of Jell-O gelatins. My family agreed, and my puddings became the stars of our few family meals during the week. It was so easy—simply stir in some milk and leave it to set. After preparing and eating several boxes of Jell-O puddings, I concluded that the bland, beige pudding colors could be improved. I began experimenting with food colors and learned that the color of a pudding could be manipulated without altering the flavor. My first batch of bright blue pudding was politely received by my family, and everybody had a taste—but only a taste. The outrageous color appealed to me, though. Soon our refrigerator became crowded with psychedelic Jell-O puddings. It did not take long before I was told to stop wasting food. To me they all tasted fine, and I had no more competition from my four siblings for dessert. I ate my fill.

My mother tried to instill traditions. On Thursday evenings in the summer, my mother would make a salad and a pizza for our family supper. She thought the healthy salad would neutralize the unhealthy pizza, adding roughage to an otherwise constipating supper. Her salads were almost always plain iceberg lettuce—chunks torn with her hands from an unwashed lettuce head. Her salad dressing was made from Kraft Miracle Whip, sometimes straight from the jar. If we were especially flush, she might layer some tomato slices on top. Perhaps my mom's mayo fixation was some cultural holdover from all the French blood that the tribal elders always talked about. We did not use mayo on French fries, though.

No, Mom did not serve a homemade pizza. She found, for our Thursday night dinner, a ready-made pizza kit in a box, about the size of a box of mac and cheese. The family really enjoyed these Thursday night suppers, compliments of Chef Boyardee. Sitting at a plate half full of dressed lettuce, with the other half taken up by a slice of pizza, each of us felt like we were eating something exotic, as though we were from the *cities*.

To make these pizzas, Mom would open the box and pour the ingredients on the counter. She would mix the small bag of flour with water and bring the foolproof store-bought dough to life. She spread the thin, sticky dough onto a pizza pan. I do not know where she got a pizza pan, but our pizzas were round. She then poured the can of pizza sauce over the dough, creating a red lake of sauce lapping at distant doughy shores. That was it. She placed the pizza in the oven with the care of an artisan.

My mom used cheese on these pizzas only one time. My youngest sister, the baby of the family, did not like the taste of the Parmesan cheese that came included in the Chef Boy-R-Dee package. So forever more, for as long as I lived in the Banana Island neighborhood, we ate pizzas without cheese on Thursday nights. I wonder if any other family members remember the incongruity of pizza in Wisconsin without cheese? We even lived in Chicago at times before Banana Island, and I remember eating real pizzas filled with exotic ingredients, including several kinds of cheese. Chicago pizza from my childhood was so good. One time, back in Banana Island as a teenager, I was getting ready to go camping and digging around our pantry when I found a cardboard box—it was filled with all those little cans of Parmesan cheese from our years of cheeseless pizza. I wonder whatever happened to all those cans when we finally moved out of Banana Island.

The best suppers were on the weekends, followed by family time spent together with some of us sitting on the couch and others sitting or sprawling on the floor, watching some television program as it got dark. Something interesting, like the movie of the week, could almost always be found on one of our three network broadcast television channels. We did not get a public television station until 1972. *Gilligan's Island, All in the Family, Good Times, The Jeffersons,* and *The Carol Burnett Show* were all family favorites. We spent many wonderful evenings with *Columbo* and his vital clues, as well as with *Night Stalker* and the monster of the week. Sometimes I also would watch *Bewitched.* I think maybe those gentle family bonding programs kept our family alive—or, at least, just shuffling along.

As my siblings and I got older, we began to forgo this family time together and chose to go out with friends instead. For me, by the time I turned fifteen, it was getting more pleasant to spend time sitting in the woods by myself than at home.

Happy Hour Smoked Chub, Small Plate–Style

In Door County recently, I happened upon a Styrofoam tray of smoked chubs from Lake Michigan. They brought back memories of my childhood Friday night dinners. That day, I could not wait for dinner but instead turned the chubs into appetizers, which I ate with a chilled pale ale.

8 ounces smoked chub, chilled
3 tablespoons mayonnaise
1 tablespoon apple cider vinegar
1 teaspoon sugar
1 teaspoon black pepper—or white pepper, if desired
2 large apples, cored and sliced
8 ounces crackers or crostini—choose mild white or whole wheat, savory crackers without added flavoring

Drain the chub, remove the skin, and break into bite-sized chunks. Pull out larger bones. Arrange on a serving plate. Mix mayonnaise, vinegar, sugar, and pepper into a dipping sauce and pour into a bowl. Serve sauce and chub with apples and crackers or crostini.

Pops Smith and the Teen Road Crew

For legal purposes and in order to have a mailing address, I was living with my family in the Banana Island neighborhood in the early 1970s. My older brother was living in the Fox Valley and learning to be a chef. I worked for the county highway department on a federal grant as I stared at my nineteenth birthday, waiting for the military draft to catch up with me. In my daily life, I alternated between the two emotional extremes of an approaching adulthood and a disappearing childhood. Box lunches for work were the extent of my culinary adventures.

After a hard day of construction labor, I went anywhere but home. I am not sure what my mother thought about my absence, as I did not want to bother her. Mom was busy working on a teaching degree at the University of Wisconsin–Green Bay. During one of my semesters in high school, Mom spent more time in the principal's office than I spent in class. The school and I had a mutual parting of ways. A GED issued from UW–Stevens Point completed my high school education at age sixteen. I was mostly ready for the next step, but not quite. This was before the popularization of the gap year.

My Banana Island buddies and I were transitioning from high school to college or work or the military. A couple of neighbors had already graduated to the morgue. A few others had gone to state prisons. In Indian Country, death and jail carry little stigma.

Lucky ones enlisted into the armed services. All three places—morgue, prison, and armed forces—were equal opportunity employers. Few Menominees waited around to be drafted. I was one of the exceptions.

Getting a job was easy in those days, but there were always strings attached. All jobs on the reservation were temporary jobs paid through federal and state grants. The purpose of the grants was to get people working, to get money percolating through the community. Follow-through or end-product was not considered the priority.

Several of my friends and I were hired to man and equip a general-purpose county work crew, paid for with federal funds. Our supervisor, and the guy responsible to the feds, was Pops Smith. This name is a pseudonym. I do not want to make him look foolish. He was a decent guy, and he, too, was living in extraordinary times. After you got to know him, to understand his rules, Pops had his positive qualities.

We quickly found out many things about him. Since he was well known in the community, many people had lots to say about him. Pops was from the South Branch area of the reservation. South Branch refers to the populated areas along the South Branch of the Oconto River. It is a land of shallow lakes, cedar swamps, and Catholic missions. These people lived a long way from any tribal services, and thus they were always at the end of the line. The area did not have any real towns or villages, although a few homes were collected together at the paved intersections and at the Catholic missions. My own opinion of the South Branch area was not very high. My grandmother's family, the Heaths, were the only exception to that rule, but still, I had never traveled much to that area.

The federal government issued Pops an enclosed pickup truck leased from the county highway department. For the first couple of mornings, we met at the county shop on the way to work and piled into Pops's truck. A couple of guys used their own vehicles to follow Pops, so not all of us had to cram into the pickup truck. That was a good thing, too. Pops never encountered a pothole that did not make him want to test his shock absorbers at full speed, and so we bounced around the back of that truck. After a couple of weeks, we would just appear at the job site without having to muster at the county shop. Pops was not malicious, or at least, not totally. He was medium hateful. Like many of his generation, force-fed a diet of Catholic guilt, he spent his free time at Alcoholics Anonymous twelve-step meetings. Pops was a dry drunk—that is, he acted like a drunken asshole, sans alcohol.

Considering how Pops got this particular job was always a source of entertainment for the crew and provided endless hours of fun. The truth of the matter was probably much simpler than our speculations. In Indian Country, there are no golf courses. Business is conducted through the good-ole-boy network at the local twelve-step program. No, tribal business is not openly discussed, but AA is the local program that provides the top management running most Indian reservations.

Pops was an old-school Menominee Reservation Indian, and he thought that his hatefulness was funny. He was tough as nails with a bad sense of humor honed while cutting and carrying cedar poles in the swamps of South Branch to earn money. Cedar poles are pretty heavy. We took note of that.

He liked to talk dirty, and it showed, as his pornographic lexicon was outstanding. Pops professionalized talking dirty. Morning break was a teaser, filled with suggestive remarks. During lunch, it escalated. Over an imaginary beer, Pops's monologues morphed from the merely suggestive into a graphic wish list, featuring the wives, girlfriends, sisters, and daughters of the crew. By the afternoon break, Pops—well into his imaginary cups and with blood pressure pounding—included husbands, boyfriends, brothers, and fathers as fictional witnesses to his warrior prowess.

We described these blue rants as hard-on attacks. These were regular occurrences—very annoying regular occurrences.

Our first job site was just beyond the brand-new Banana Island neighborhood among the soon-to-be-gone white pine forest. Only a few years earlier, this forest had been my playground, where cousin Jammer and I rode our bikes among the great trees.

After a series of accidents on the first day of work resulting from our horseplay, we were all issued shiny white construction helmets on the second day. Dropping a pine tree on top of your crewmate was all good clean fun until somebody got a concussion. We were told not to deface our bright safety helmets. By the end of the third day, our helmets were decorated with beer decals, doodles, antiwar messages, and X-rated art. We began to feel like we belonged to an elite club.

Two crew members already knew how to use chainsaws, and they were assigned trim duty within our crew after a quick tutorial by a couple of county shopworkers. Henceforth, whenever our crew had a need to cut wood, these were the two guys to do it. They would lop the branches off a tree after it was chopped down and before it was cut into eight-foot logs by the sawyers, who were independent contractors.

Felling trees is a specialized job. Sawyers are full-time loggers who are qualified through their experiences with chainsaws to cut down the towering pines. When a tree is felled, trimmed, and cut into logs, it is then ready to be picked up by a logging truck. These trucks carry and pick up loads of logs using built-in cranes. After the trucks carried the logs away, our crew sprang into action. We dragged those branches into huge piles. Pops, wearing his chrome helmet like General Patton, would pour coal oil on the woodpile and ignite it using a county shop blowtorch. The smoke would rise into the heavens, and our jobs would be done for the day. Those piles of wood brush burned for a week. We cleared the land of trees for several weeks, long enough for friendships to form.

Eventually, I was assigned a specific job within the crew. I was to drive a huge (to me), battered, six-yard dump truck. Every other truck in the county fleet was shiny and new except ours, a dull, dented, and faded orange truck that had been sitting in some back building. Thick cobwebs obscured the windows and filled the cab. This truck really was obsolete, and a mechanic had to start the truck for me the first time. He wheeled over a big battery charger, lifted up the sizable engine hood, and connected it to the truck's battery. Next, he spit some tobacco juice off to the side of the truck—it smeared down the fender—reached over, and sprayed alcohol from a can down into the carburetor. With only a few coughs, rumbles, and rolls, the monster came back to life.

I got the position of driver by default. I was the only one with a valid driver's license who could drive a manual transmission. My personal car—an orange Volkswagen Bug—had a much smaller four-speed transmission. The truck took a little getting used to before I was comfortable with it. It had six forward gears, plus a low/high-speed split axle, so a total of eighteen possible gears. I soon learned that many of those gears could be skipped.

This truck would not go over forty-five miles per hour, and even then, the ride was rough with scary noises. That day, the mechanic asked if I wanted the speed governor removed. I declined. The first time I backed up to a ten-foot cliff to dump chunks of concrete, I was frightened about going over backward, but I survived. The truck clung to the bank.

I received the same pay as everybody else in the crew, but there were some unforeseen perks that came with driving the truck. The main thing was that it was inside work—inside the cab, that is. It rained often enough on our work crew to be unpleasant. Being covered with dirt and grime was one thing, but add cold water, and it was a mess.

The biggest benefit was that I gave up my shovel. Being a driver meant that I was not normally expected to manually labor with the rest of the guys. Of course, they did not help me with truck stuff, either. The time that I drove backward in the county shop yard and wrecked a work shed by sliding into the side of it was a notable example. Nobody helped share the blame. Neither did any of the crew help me load bags of concrete, shovel several yards of sand, or load, carry, and unload all the crew's tools and supplies. So, it all worked out.

Another positive thing was that highway department vehicles, with their flashing orange lights, are everywhere. They are both seen and not seen at the same time. People ignore county vehicles in their haste to pull around them. Or swear at them as they wait for slow-moving workers to pull over. Perhaps you think about them when you pass a county truck sitting on the road with its lights flashing. Perhaps you suspect the driver might be sleeping. Sometimes, you would be right—they really might be sleeping, like I did on occasion.

The members of our work crew ran the gamut from near genius to near imbecile, from lucky to cursed. We were a cross-section of the new Menominee—the children of those Menominees moving back to the reservation from the diaspora. We were a bunch of regular guys but raised without reservation tribal behavioral guidelines, since we were the first generation to have survived the termination of the Menominee Tribe. Most of us had heard about pretermination times from elder siblings. Many of the later residents of School View in Keshena had no knowledge at all of pretermination times. What they learned about being Menominees, they learned in a low-income housing project where gang loyalty was based on prior affiliation with neighborhoods in Chicago, Milwaukee, and Minneapolis–St. Paul.

One guy on our crew, my buddy David, was also attending Saint Norbert's College in De Pere. We never talked about it, but he knew that his sister and I were developing a tentative relationship. Besides, two of his younger brothers had already come over to check me out in Keshena. They advised me to be nice to their sister. I did not need any threats to be nice to her, but now I knew I also had to be nice to her brothers.

Her brother David and I, on occasion, would park the truck downtown, turn on our flashers, put out our hazard cones, grab our pry bars, open a manhole cover, and then, using a ladder embedded in the concrete, crawl down under the street to smoke hash. That was a whole lot of effort. Sometimes we would just park along the highway. No one noticed, either way.

My crew buddy David had an excellent source for hashish. These were the days of Blonde Lebanese hash, Sony reel-to-reel eight-track stereo tape recorders, and Santana. The advent of cassette and VHS tapes was still a few years out. Turntables were the mainstay. Album covers made convenient rolling trays, with their rigid cardboard expanses. Double albums were the best.

David had some amazing skills—and, remember, he was still an adolescent. He could take a hit of hash off his pipe while standing, then while holding that hit in, do a deep-knee bend, which caused a fart. A slow deep-knee bend would produce a slow fart. A fast deep-knee bend would cause a fast fart. David could do this as many times in a row as we dared him, until we all fell down laughing, too stoned for effective communication.

I do not mean to imply that we were completely out of control on taxpayer money all the time, because we worked hard on Camp Four Hill. On the Menominee Reservation, Camp Four Hill was named after a nearby logging camp—the fourth camp on the Little West Branch on the Wolf. These logging camps were small, mobile towns with rail service. After an area was logged out, the town migrated to the next site. Although many reservation logs were removed by rail, at Camp Four, a mile upstream from the sawmill, it was much easier to move the harvested logs by river.

As we spent the summer reshaping a natural river levee into a more manicured form for state highway engineers, all of us learned a lot about each other, ourselves, and the natural world. Under normal circumstances, with no Vietnam-era drafts into the military services, none of us would have been hired for these positions, and even if hired, we would not have lasted. Most of us on the crew had problems with authority. This was the reason that many of us were unemployed in the first place. In fact, not liking authority, no matter how friendly the face of the boss, was probably the single strongest unifying characteristic of our crew.

Once our crew began the task of finishing the landscaping and drainage of Camp Four Hill, we began to employ teamwork. We each knew our respective jobs and put in a full day, according to anybody's standards. Somehow, we always met our daily quotas.

Our days in the forest were always interesting, with bear sightings and visits from occasional passersby. Sometimes we found old fishing gear. Uncle Buddy told me that as a teenager, he had snooped around the 1870s site of Logging Camp Four, near where it begins and Dutchman's Field ends. There, he found an iron pot—just like one of the giant cooking pots that cannibals might have used to cook up a dinner of Christian missionaries, he joked. It was big enough to hold five men. This must have been a major campsite. He thought there must be large refuse pits lying undiscovered. One time, and this really seems incredible, a modern logging crew found an abandoned set of railroad tracks, which they followed until they found a steam locomotive and its coal car rusting away in the pine forest. This was towed to the county shop, where the shop workers eventually restored them. They proudly displayed the restored locomotive until the county shop was moved.

Highway 47, our work assignment route, follows an ancient Indian trail network once used by trappers and traders. It heads northwest to Duluth, Minnesota, circles the western edge of Lake Superior, goes north into Canada, and then loops east on the north shore to the Dog River. Finally, it arrives at Thunder Bay, Ontario, where our distant relatives live. That is the overview of this major Great Lakes trail.

Before our work crew helped re-form Camp Four Hill, the road made an almost ninety-degree angle at the base of the hill. Our crew worked on the backside of the third version of this road. The first version of the road was created by the military, who simply widened an existing Indian trail. Over several years, this section of the road was widened to its present width and laid with gravel. When that gravel road was paved, it formed the third version of the road.

I remember when this highway was paved for the first time. My family lived in a log cabin about a hundred yards away. The road up the flank of Camp Four Hill was steep. Creating the third version of this section involved scraping several feet from the road's surface. Prior to this third attempt, many semitrucks and White tourists ended their trips to the bottom of the hill in the river. Numerous people were injured, and perhaps some even died here. More important to the Whites in the area, the distribution of consumer goods was impeded. Thus, the unstated goal of the grant employing our crew that summer was to improve the road. They hoped we would not screw it up, as most of the previous efforts had.

About a third of the crew were drinkers. The tribe had some experience with alcohol abusers. This addiction was somewhat understood and was considered relatively normal—aberrant, but not unknown. The tribe still maintains several programs to treat alcoholics. Another third of the crew were stoners. The tribe had no experience with this addiction and would soon head down a reactionary path paid for by Nixon. The remaining third of the crew were straight arrows. Not to say that those guys were normal. Maybe a couple. But deviation was a regular characteristic within members of this outcast Menominee band.

Anyway, none of us was exactly normal, not according to reservation standards and certainly not by outside White standards. One guy, a real nice guy, we called Wesley Norman Bates. The consensus was that he would someday snap and murder his mother. We imagined he would stuff her in his car and drive her around town. We suspected this because his mother drove to our job sites in her big car to deliver his lunch. He sat with her in the car and ate away from us. When our lunch breaks were over, he would rejoin the rest of us. He never commented on this, and we were all too polite to ask. She also dropped him off at the county shop in the morning and picked him up in the evening.

At some point that summer, we discovered that our supervisor wanted to try marijuana. One morning, we gave Pops a joint, and we goofed off instead of working as he sat motionless in the orange supervisor pickup truck until lunch. At lunchtime, we gathered around the truck to retrieve our lunches, but Pops had gotten the munchies. He had eaten several complete lunches and dug into all of them, removing any especially tempting morsels. He generously opened his wallet and paid for all the damaged meals. A couple of the guys drove into Neopit to grab some food. They returned with several six-packs of beer and sat down in the shade of a nearby tree, out of Pops's sight. We adopted the philosophy of live and let live. The drinkers did not say anything about us getting stoned all day, and we did not say anything about them drinking all day. We all did our work, and none of us complained.

Soon, this became our routine. We would slip our boss a couple of joints in the morning, and he stayed busy in the company truck. Once, I sneaked up behind the truck and peeked inside. Pops was sprawled lengthwise on the bench seat holding a powdered sugar doughnut, staring at the ceiling while listening to the radio, and singing along to a country-and-western song. His face was white with powdered sugar. This was how he passed his workdays thereafter.

The rest of us learned to leave our lunches in places other than the supervisor's vehicle, although we shared occasional treats with him. So the juicers and the hippies spent a mutually beneficial summer in harmony. Poor Pops Smith. He had to square all the government accounts at the end of the work project.

Bear Stew

Bear hunting on the reservation continues to provide a regular source of meat for some families, like my uncle Bobby and aunt Nita's. In an egalitarian tradition of our tribe, both women and men hunt bears, and my female cousins are experts. As we worked on the road crew in the summer of 1970, we reported our bear sightings to hunters.

Bear meat might be a little hard to obtain for the casual diner. I think that bison could be substituted in this recipe.

Serves about 6 people

32 ounces bear meat cut into 1-inch cubes (about 4 cups)
1 large onion, cut into large dice
4 large potatoes, cut into large dice
3 medium carrots, cut into large dice
2 stalks celery, cut into large dice
4 tablespoons cornstarch
Salt and pepper, to taste

Add meat and onion to a large frying pan, cover with water, and bring to a boil, then simmer on low heat for 3 hours or until tender. Put potatoes, carrots, and celery in a large stockpot and cover with water. After bear meat is tender, add it and its accompanying juices to the stockpot and simmer another 45 minutes or until vegetables are tender. Make a slurry with the cornstarch and 2–4 tablespoons water in a cup, add slowly to the stockpot, and simmer for another 5 minutes. Salt and pepper to taste.

Tuna Fish Sandwiches

My mom packed her classic tuna sandwiches for me every day of my Highway 47 work detail, and I never tired of them. Two sandwiches fueled me through the days of hard work. Canned fish, a convenience food, fits with the fishing tradition of the tribe. Fresh cooked fish never lasts long enough to withstand this adulteration of the flavors.

1 (4-ounce) can tuna
¼ cup mayonnaise
Chopped hard-boiled egg, pickle relish, minced onion, or diced celery (optional)
2 slices white bread

Mix tuna and mayonnaise in bowl. If desired, add chopped hard-boiled egg, pickle relish, minced onion, or diced celery to mixture. Spread on white bread. Slice diagonally for full effect.

A Jailhouse Home and Frank's Magical Breakout

Grandpa Moon never set me down to tell me the history of his Keshena house, which had once been a jail, nor about any of the spirits that lingered there. It was right on Highway 47, in the town. During all the years I lived there, I thought everything was normal—it was simply Grandpa and Grandma's house. Every house had ghosts, right? What little I came to know about this place, I learned through innuendos in several family stories over the years. The old tribal jail was a source of stories and spirits, and it even influenced some of our family cuisine.

To someone visiting Keshena for the first time, Grandpa and Grandma's house would not seem incongruous with the rest of the neighborhood, despite its late-nineteenth-century Gothic architecture. It was just another chess piece set upon a large checkerboard. There was no landmark building on this reservation in the early days, so nothing stands out. All of the parts of our town were built on the higher elevations and all during the same time period, using the same European design and regional building materials. This reflected how, in the late nineteenth century, the local Catholic church had controlled the Menominee Tribe and acted as administrators for distant federal authorities. On this reservation, there was no separation of church and state. This religion-based infrastructure was one manifestation of that fact.

In these days, the priests conducted all of their masses in Latin to people who hardly spoke English, which added to the eerie atmosphere. In my young mind, I thought of these buildings—church, school, courthouse, hospital, and supervisor's housing—as supernatural, as though they had been magically transplanted from some vintage black-and-white Frankenstein film onto our pine forest reservation. This was the kind of movie that I watched on Friday nights.

These buildings were too uniform, and they represented the outside, dominant White culture. They were certainly substantial, and being constructed on trailheads, they were physically in the way, so you couldn't help but see them. Their brick walls, arranged in a maze, formed a kind of cage.

All of these buildings had tall and narrow windows. Inside, blackout curtains that had hung since World War II served two purposes. They were designed to keep any inside light from leaking outside, since a leak could allow circling enemy bombers to locate and bomb reservation targets. They also kept any curious outsiders from looking in. Many things happened on this reservation that were kept away from prying eyes. We were Catholic, and therefore we had sins and shame.

All of the local Indian Agency administrative functions, including those of the jail and courts, were warehoused under one roof—the building that later became our family home. This square, two-story brick building was built near a moraine ridge at the beginning of its slope and next to a navigable stream. The building had three doors granting entry and egress. There was no door on the east side. Inside these four walls, almost all of the official interactions between the Great White Father and any individual Menominee tribal member occurred. The jail was meant to punish the local Menominees, but the members of other tribes were also welcome to stay.

When my family members took over this building, they defied

the architecture. The main entrance on the north side was a formal porch with white columns, a white banister, and a copper roof that sheltered double doors. Upon entering those doors, a small enclosed entryway led to another set of double doors and, just beyond, the second-floor foyer. During our family's tenure, we never used this door, the porch, or that inviting interior space trapped between the two sets of double doors. It was used to store things, such as boxes of Christmas decorations.

A second entrance on the west side of the building was originally designed as a side door providing access to and from the parking lot of grass and mud. Logs were laid in place of the concrete curb stops in the city's other paved lots. Those logs kept people from driving forward into the creek. The door from the parking lot opened at the ground level. We used this door as our front door. When people came visiting, this was where they entered.

About three feet above ground level on this side of the house, there was another small door, the coal door. It measured three feet by two feet, and it allowed coal to be unloaded directly off the back of a dump truck into a coal chute. As a child, I would watch the truck tilt its bed and funnel coal into a thick, lumpy black river through the door to the end of the chute, where it dropped inside and formed a black pyramid in the basement coal room. I was small enough to use that coal chute door several times to get into and out of the house. After lifting the metal door and working my way over the lip, I would tumble down into the pile of coal five feet below, until my grandma put a stop to that.

The family most often used the door at the back of the house, on the south side. It sat slightly below ground level and opened directly into the furnace room, which led through the pantry area and finally into the main stairway at the center of the house.

A wooden two-car garage sat on a concrete pad in the backyard. My grandparents used that garage as extra bedrooms. I often stayed there, as did Uncle Buddy. The rear wall of the garage sat five feet away from Keshena's creek, which never flooded during our residence there.

The jailhouse history of our house was always evident. The government had divided the interior space rather simply, with the courtroom and jail cells upstairs and all other government functions downstairs. When it was a jailhouse, the northwest corner of the basement was an office and communications nook shared by all of the local law enforcement agencies—the federal marshals, county sheriff, village constable, state game warden, and Indian Agency police. Once, a radio transmitter with tubes and a large microphone sat there on a large heavy table. Two heavy wooden chairs provided seating. An antenna on a three-legged tower sat on the copper-sheathed roof. It must have been ten feet tall. A phone line was added later.

After this building was converted into our family home in the 1950s, that office space became a large closet stuffed with cast-off clothing donated by well-meaning White people. I remember seeing dusty tuxedos on hangers and several dozen pairs of spats lined up against the wall. One side was taken up by wedding gowns. Everything smelled like moth balls.

Next to this office were a bathroom, another storage closet, a laundry room, and a shower room. A large conference room became our kitchen and dining room.

Fully half of the basement was taken up by the furnace room—filled with warm, dancing light—and the coal room, which was simply four brick walls filled with coal. The furnace was a great iron dinosaur of a boiler mounted to the floor in the center of the room. This was an artifact from a bygone industrial age, endangered but not yet extinct. It made noises as it burned—hisses, groans, and shrieks. Sometimes steam needed to be released in a frightening cloud. The sheer immensity of this machine always scared me. The firebox was big enough to hold several four-foot logs. Or, according to Uncle Buddy one late night, it was "big enough to hold a body." Steam pipes, wrapped in painted white asbestos insulation, funneled boiling water to heat radiators located in every room of the house and the stairway. This structure was built without any insulation back in the days when energy was cheap. The result? In the winter, the boiler needed to run constantly or the water and sewer pipes would quickly freeze.

Upstairs, the three jail cells became three bedrooms—two on the south side, one on the north. Each bedroom had a sink and a shiny metal mirror. There was also a full bathroom with a sink, toilet, and shower between the two south-side bedrooms. The courtroom, on the east side, became our living room. A roomy second-floor landing and foyer became my bedroom. Just off that foyer, also on the north side, was another bedroom, the largest of the three. This was Uncle Donny's bedroom.

Of the seven small windows on the ground floor, all of them were too small to crawl through, and I did try. They were about eight inches wide by two feet tall, more like firing slits than anything else. The second floor had eleven large windows, thirteen including the two in the foyer's double doors. When Grandpa bought the house, all of the windows, even the small ones in the basement, were covered by steel mesh plates. "We could withstand a siege," Uncle Buddy said when describing them. They also could restrain ghosts attempting to escape.

In the 1960s, after the coal boiler was retrofitted to burn wood, Grandpa converted the coal room into a woodworking room. Coal, he reasoned, was much too expensive at four dollars per ton, and cutting our own firewood was cheaper. Twenty years later, he told me that he still regretted that decision. In those days before insulation, we were never more than two inches of government-specified brick from the outside elements anywhere in the house. The foyer landing where I slept was always cold in the winter.

The jail part of our home was originally built to house Indians who violated any of the numerous local laws. An Indian reservation in Wisconsin may appear to be a relatively lawless place, but it is quite the opposite. There are many, many layers of law that include tribal law, church law, state law, and federal law. Sometimes, these laws work at cross-purposes. Any felons, whether they be real or falsely accused, could be handled by one or more of these agency representatives, including quasimilitary forces like the Indian Agency police. Just ask Tȟašúŋke Witkó (Crazy Horse) how effective this paramilitary force can be. He met his death at their hands.

This particular Indian Agency jail location oversaw serious infractions like insubordination to an American official (talking back to a White Man); destruction of federal property (cutting down a tree); and creation of a public nuisance (being intoxicated). This kind of lawbreaking occupied the local Indian Agency supervisors and a dedicated set of Washington, DC, bureaucrats up the chain of command.

One story Grandpa Moon often told involved a very traditional Menominee man, Frank, who was picked up for repeated public intoxication. When Grandpa first knew him, Frank was already middle-aged. I hope I get his name right: Frank Wishkano. It has been fifty-five years since I last heard that name spoken aloud. He still has relatives near Bear Trap Falls. He was related to us, but not closely. He was, as Grandpa described him, a shirt-tail relation. Frank, like all of our family in those days, was a member of the Keso' Band of the Menominee Tribe. "K" is an approximation for a glottal stop, sometimes replaced by a "W," which is my current surname, Weso. In English, *Keso'* means "Sun," which suggests the strength of One Who Stands Firm. When this band was forced to move to the new reservation in the late 1850s, they settled near several springs located in an area from just west of the Wolf River at Dead Man Spring to Perote, north along the edge of the reservation, east to the Bass Lake area, and south to Zoar.

Around Keshena, Frank was called a pagan Indian by local Christians (assimilated Natives). Early anthropologists used that term to describe non-Christian American Indians. This pejorative word in English meant a tribal member who chose to adhere to tribal lifeways, an unassimilated tribal member. The word was picked up by the Christian faction of the tribe, those endorsing Catholic assimilation. It began to be used as a derogatory term. Frank was, like most of my family, a pagan.

Grandpa admired him, as he lived without encumbrances or personal property. Grandpa told us grandchildren stories about Frank after evening meals. He carried his home and all of his possessions upon his back. He didn't wear his bedding as a backpack, but instead as a layer of clothing, so, our patriarch said, "He was free to come and go as he wished." When Frank grew tired after a long day, he would just lie down wherever he happened to be and sleep. Grandpa better described it this way: "Frank would just fall backward into a drift of snow to make camp." A flint, a knife, and plenty of furs made up the majority of his kit. Grandpa Moon, with his able wife, ran a household of between a dozen and thirty people, so he might have envied that freedom more than he said.

What really made Frank famous, or rather infamous, was his appetite. He could and did eat an entire deer at one meal. He did this not just once, as if he had won a competitive eating bout on the Travel Channel's *Man vs. Food*, but as a regular practice. That voracious appetite was the reason for his great unpopularity as a hunting companion, even though Frank was an expert at finding and killing game. He could consume the entire expedition's meat.

Besides being pagan, Frank was a social pariah. Keshena under Catholic rule became more and more genteel and a place filled with inflexible social hierarchies. Frank lived in the "lake country," a part of the reservation as far away from any Catholic institution as possible. The lake country was once an idyllic area filled with a chain of small sandy lakes. In those days, a canoer could paddle from the Wolf River through a chain of lakes all the way to Moshawquit Lake. At least one of those lakes, Blacksmith Lake, was spring-fed and deep, considered "bottomless" by elders. This place was once surrounded by giant white pines, but now they have all been drowned by a man-made reservoir, a resort area called Legend Lake. The dam has no purpose for flood control, crop irrigation, or the generation of electricity. The lake is now dying, with silt runoff choking it. This folly of the real estate developers, though, had not yet occurred during Frank's lifetime. Frank lived in the pristine landscape, alone most of the time. When he went to town, a whiskey run was his only indulgence. Such an excursion usually ended with Frank's perfunctory arrest as a public nuisance. He could count on a night in jail and a warm meal, something he looked forward to. His accumulative list of arrests all indicated intoxication.

Frank, like many Menominees and especially members of the Keso' Band, was also Potawatomi. These are closely related tribes. Members of both consider them to be the same tribe, although there is some variation of dialect and culture between the two. The name *Potawatomi* in English means "Fire Keepers." According to Grandpa Moon, "wherever two trails crossed, the Potawatomis kept a fire burning for travelers where they would be safe, fed, and warm." Early Catholic administrators built the Second Station of the Cross Chapel in Keshena near one such trail crossing. This disrupted the traditional lifeways by blocking travel.

The 1960s Legend Lake construction not only destroyed that chain of lakes, rice beds, and sturgeon runs, but it also drowned that ceremonial fire. This fire was kept alive by a lineage of Potawatomi medicine men since before any Euro-American history began on this continent. Many Potawatomis were accomplished sorcerers, while others were fearsome warriors. It has been documented that they would eat the still-beating hearts of their fallen enemies taken in battle.

As a pagan who may have eaten a few hearts, according to my grandpa's tales, Frank spent his days trapping small game for food and furs. He lived off the rabbits, porcupines, squirrels, deer, and fish he caught. Periodically, he paddled to town in his birchbark canoe to sell animal pelts, buy supplies, and, after taking care of business, enjoy a few drinks. There was a tavern and a sawmill in Keshena even before there was a town or a reservation.

On his last visit to town, Frank made some unfortunate comments about the local womenfolk. These were Catholic women, and since the federal government had given the Catholic dioceses de facto control of the Indian population, some descendants of Native leaders now served as agents of the local priest. Although Frank was arrested for his lewd comments, "intoxication" made a convenient excuse for jail time.

Previously, Frank had been allowed to sleep it off in jail and pay a small fine. He would be released the next day before the noon meal, as was standard practice. On this occasion, however, during court the following morning, the justice of the peace, hearing of his repeat-offender status, sentenced him to thirty days plus a hefty fine. Police escorted him the ten feet from the courtroom around the corner to a jail cell. He began to serve his jail sentence less than one minute after receiving it in what, thirty years later, would become Uncle Buddy's bedroom.

Frank made no complaint. After lunch on the first day of his sentence, he asked for a drumstick to help him sing his prayers. The justice of the peace, a man of faith, allowed this privilege on religious grounds, and a stout ironwood, or blue beech, branch was found and delivered to the new inmate. The stick had to be of hard wood so it wouldn't break after repeated drumming. Ironwood, an extremely dense wood, is consequently very hard, hence the name. By that first evening, Frank had prepared the stick both physically and ceremonially for its upcoming duties.

Right after the evening meal, the traditional Potawatomi man began singing a prayer, keeping time by beating upon the jail cell door with the drumstick.

At first it was almost a pleasant musical interlude. By the next morning, though, the jail had already received numerous complaints regarding the all-night prayer vigil. The singing and the tapping of wood upon metal, at full volume, drowned out all other sounds in town. Frank stayed awake all night singing and praying. It was now midmorning, and still he kept it up. Each song was repeated four times. But the justice of the peace was just as resolute. Frank could keep singing for another twenty-nine days. He couldn't care less.

The duty officer abandoned his post that afternoon after enduring almost six straight hours of prayer. Nobody bothered to bring Frank his evening meal, and still his song continued. Around midnight his singing faltered. For a few brief moments he couldn't sing. Yet he maintained his four-four cadence with the drumstick.

It was straight-up three in the morning when the drumbeat, and the hoarsely whispered accompaniment, finally stopped. After thirty hours of constant singing and drumming, nobody came rushing to the jail to ask the reason for the deafening silence. They simply nodded off. It would be another four hours before breakfast was to be served, before anybody even thought about the jail.

At seven o'clock, breakfast with hot coffee, contracted out to neighborhood women, was to be delivered to the jail, portioned out, and served to the guards and inmates. This time, though, with the guards still sound asleep, Frank's pagan singing made a good excuse for the Catholic ladies to take some time off. No harm done, they figured, as Frank was the only inmate, and he certainly wasn't going anywhere.

Finally, at the noon meal, the guards returned to eat, and Frank wasn't in his cell. The door to his empty cell was wide open with the lock clicked open. Thirty hours of rhythmic beating upon the iron lock with an ironwood branch had caused the lock mechanism to slip. Frank Wishkano's pagan prayers were answered, and he was far away in the depths of the scrub oak forest of lake country. No one went in pursuit.

The Catholic community got its wish. Frank was now a wanted man, so he never again returned to get drunk and make inappropriate comments to women.

I asked Grandpa if he ever saw Frank again. He told me another story, about the last time he saw Frank. This was some thirty years later, up by Weso Lake, when Grandpa was a state game warden. Hardly anyone ever went to the lake, maybe because the only road that led there was in such horrible condition. This meant that Weso Lake was only accessible in the winter when the road was frozen and could support traffic—unless you cared to walk half a mile or so.

Grandpa patrolled for any illegal activity, meaning unlicensed hunters or fishers. He checked every access point to every hunting or fishing spot on the reservation, in rotation. This was how, one early morning, he arrived at Weso Lake, not looking for anyone or anything in particular, just going down the list of places he needed to check.

Grandpa pulled into the small turnaround at the end of the drive, the only access point to the lake, and not seeing any other vehicles, he got ready to turn around and leave. To his amazement, an old man began to dig his way out of a pile of snow-dusted leaves, finally revealing himself in a flurry of excitement. The man stood, ignoring Grandpa Moon for the moment, and finished brushing the leaves off of himself. It was a very elderly Frank Wishkano.

After recovering from this unexpected moment, Grandpa

shared his coffee and lunch with Frank, catching him up on local events. "I had a real good visit with Frank. It was good to talk with him again," Grandpa said. "I was also town constable and the justice of the peace of Keshena then, too, but I never mentioned it to him." Grandpa was required to bring in any wanted criminals, but he ignored this duty. You do not arrest family.

Grandpa paused thoughtfully, then continued, "That was the last time that I saw him. He must have been in his late eighties, maybe even his late nineties by then." Grandpa did not tell me what the two old men talked about exactly, but Frank was the man I thought of every time Grandpa talked about the old Potawatomi elders. I don't know what eventually happened to him. Grandpa had finished his story by saying, "He must have died in the woods someplace. Somewhere that nobody ever goes, maybe some cedar swamp. No one ever found a body. He died as he lived, a free man."

Berry Lake and Suring, both small towns near the lake country area, were pretty wild and lawless in those days. Nobody ever called the police, as John Dillinger would learn in the late 1920s and early '30s.

Frank wasn't the only person to escape from the Indian Agency jail. A second, less successful escape from that same jail cell—Uncle Buddy's room—happened much later and left an open hole through the brick construction, just below the window. The hurried repair patch didn't match the original's quality. The hole was fixed with cement. The result was an even and orderly brickwork wall marred by a glaring man-size cement patch.

I know less about this breakout despite the scarred wall. I remember that a pair of drunken, disorderly brothers from the South Branch area were wanted for check forgery outside the reservation in Brown County. Their arrest was carried out without problems. A local town constable drove to their mom's house in South Branch and brought them in. The plan was to keep them at the Keshena jail until police detectives from Green Bay could come and get them. However, the brothers had other ideas. They turned a relatively minor forgery charge into an escape-from-lawful-custody charge by kicking their way through the brick wall to freedom. After jumping out of the building, they stole an Indian Agency car out of the parking lot. But instead of fleeing, they continued drinking and driving on and off the reservation.

Shawano police eventually caught them several days later. I heard that there was a gunfight, but I do not believe this. If there had actually been a gunfight with desperate, escaped Indians, the Shawano Police Department would still be bragging about it. In any event, their escape was unsuccessful, and it only resulted in more serious criminal charges for the pair.

Frank was not the only one of my relatives to serve time as an inmate in our future home. I heard this story just once, and even then, certain portions were censored to preserve her dignity. I know the gist of this story, though, and I am not embarrassed by her actions.

Grandma Jennie was famous for stating her opinions, readily sharing what was on her mind when asked and sometimes even when she wasn't asked. Grandma wasn't especially opinionated about many things. However, when she did have an opinion, she was not hesitant about voicing it. She may not have known who was president of the United States, for example, but upon tribal issues, she was knowledgeable, loud, and persistent.

Grandma attended most tribal meetings. In those days, women were expected to remain silent. At one such occasion, she was exceptionally animated. For the uninitiated, I should explain how these old-school tribal meetings functioned. In those days, the 1930s or so, tribal meetings were presided over by Indian Agency supervisors who took orders from Washington, DC. This agency predates the Bureau of Indian Affairs in organization but not intent. Since almost all meetings back then concerned the loss of some right or land, almost all meetings were contentious. Tribal meetings held in those days were an opportunity for the federal government to dictate tribal policy to tribal members.

The government's agenda proceeded according to Robert's Rules of Order. Those familiar with these archaic Euro-American-based rules could manage a meeting according to their will, meaning that certain subjects, things the government wished to avoid, were simply not addressed. The federal agents used the Rules of Order at meetings with attendees who weren't very good with English, and they always had logical reasons to stonewall certain subjects. These tactics inflamed my grandmother and other passionate tribal people.

During one particularly contentious meeting, my grandma and a few others kept raising off-topic issues that were of greater concern to the tribe than to Indian Agency supervisors. The presiding officials tried to silence Grandma. Finally, she was given an official warning by an Indian Agency administrator: "One more word out of you, Jennie Weso, and you will go to jail."

When she didn't stop, the sergeant-at-arms of the meeting turned my grandma over to the county sheriff, and he took her to the Indian jail on the very serious charge of insubordination—talking back to and ignoring the lawful commands of a White administrator. She was placed in the same jail cell that would eventually become Uncle Buddy's bedroom. That same jail cell had housed Frank, the South Branch brothers, and now my grandmother. She spent the night and was released in the morning, just before lunch. She must have felt pretty good when she and my grandpa bought that jail to turn it into their home. It had never silenced her. And the ghosts of many desperado inmates were never silenced either. I often saw their shadows in the halls at night.

Jailhouse Hash

Hash is a typical meal in the North Woods that uses leftovers, travels well in a wicker basket, and is filling. Frank would have enjoyed this meal during his visits to the jail.

Serves 4 people

2 tablespoons butter or lard
2 carrots, sliced
2 stalks celery, sliced
1 onion, chopped
2 cups leftover beef, cut into bite-sized pieces—other leftover meats, like pork or venison, may be substituted
2 cups leftover baked or boiled potatoes, cut into bite-sized pieces
½ cup frozen or fresh peas
1½ cups leftover gravy (or drippings with 1 tablespoon of cornstarch or flour)
Salt and pepper, to taste

Melt butter or lard in a frying pan over medium-high heat. Add carrots, celery, and onions, and sauté until cooked through. Add beef, potatotes, and peas. Heat through. In a separate pan, heat gravy or make gravy from drippings by adding a tablespoon of cornstarch or flour to the drippings. Pour gravy over hash, stir, and serve with salt and pepper.

Roast Rabbit

Frank probably roasted his rabbit meals without the complications of the fry pan. My grandmother, however, made this tasty comfort food from rabbits killed by either moi, since I was a good shot, or my uncles. The red meat is like chicken thighs, rich and tasty.

Serves 8 people

2 rabbits, dressed, cleaned, and quartered, making 8 pieces
1 cup white flour
4 tablespoons vegetable oil
2 large onions, roughly chopped
2 cups tomato juice—may substitute 1 (15½–ounce) can of diced tomatoes
½ cup of water
Salt and pepper, to taste

Heat oven to 350 degrees. Dredge pieces of rabbit in flour. Heat 2 tablespoons vegetable oil on high heat in a frying pan until very hot. Brown the rabbit pieces in the frying pan, adding more oil if needed. Place meat and drippings into roasting pan with onions, tomato juice, and water. Roast for 1 hour or until tender. Sprinkle with salt and pepper to taste.

Grandma Jennie Attacks Gorgeous George

It was not that Grandma was especially pugnacious. In those days, you had to be tough to survive—especially women. While she was known as somebody who would not take guff, she did not look for a fight. She just did not like to see somebody being taken advantage of by a bully. Nor did she give up. Once a person got on her list, that person was there forever.

One night, not that long after Grandma's death, Grandpa, Uncle Buddy, and I sat at the dinner table finishing our evening meal of sweet corn and meat loaf. Our bachelor dinner was nothing like her dinners had been, but the coffee was just as thick.

All of us were quiet in that awkward silence of grief when so much needs to be said but no one can begin. Finally, it was up to Grandpa to fill that empty space. He told us a story about the time Grandma had gotten kicked out of a professional wrestling match.

It is hard for me to think of my grandparents as young. "This was many years ago, when our marriage was still fresh," Grandpa began. "Babe," as he called my mother, "was a toddler, getting into things, while you, Buddy, were still an infant." He continued to describe how the family lived in an apartment in Wausau, one of the larger towns near the reservation. Living off-rez was not unusual for Indians, as housing and work are limited on the rez. The only nearby places were Wausau to the west, Green Bay to the east, Antigo to the north, and Shawano to the south. Compared to the reservation, Wausau was a big city that teemed with distractions.

In Wasau, my grandpa liked to watch professional wrestling. Pro wrestling was big business then, and it has only gotten bigger since. In the day, results of matches and highlights of bouts were reported in newspapers and on the radio, and later, in the 1950s, on the television. Weekly pro-wrestling studio bouts were broadcast out of Green Bay. The reservation was at the northwestern limits of their broadcast range, and Grandpa had a good set of rabbit ears as reception antennas. When I walked in front of the rabbit ears, the picture might turn to snow. Sometimes, I had to hold the rabbit ears in a certain direction to get any picture at all.

Some of those stars from the golden age of 1950s and '60s pro wrestling were scientific, Olympic, or Greco-Roman-style wrestlers with connections to Wisconsin. They practiced actual wrestling, without theatrics. Our favorite straight-style wrestlers were Jim and Bert Gagnon, a father-and-son team of Ojibwa wrestlers. The Gagnons used real wrestling moves in the ring, and when they pinned their opponents, it was for real. This was a "may the best man win" kind of wrestling, without a script.

As part of the Gagnon family's plan to bring wrestling to smaller markets—small cities without sports complexes—they presented wrestling cards at local high schools. This was not entirely philanthropic, as the Gagnons owned a wrestling school and needed a venue to showcase their stable of local wrestlers. Scientific wrestling was less popular than the high-flying theatrical wrestling, but we were loyal to the Ojibwa Gagnons.

The Gagnons were not the first promoters to bring wrestling entertainment to town. The sport was already popular, and Wausau attracted some of the stars. My grandparents had attended a wrestling match at the Wausau High School featuring Gorgeous George in the 1940s.

When George Raymond Wagner became Gorgeous George in 1941, he integrated theatrics into his bouts. He was popular nationwide. George was not popular because he was a hero, and he was not a great wrestler. He had one great talent: being an over-the-top villain. His theatrical conduct included wearing a cape and spraying the wrestling ring with perfume, supposedly Chanel No. 5, and he was finicky. He required that the referee wash his hands before patting George down for illegal weapons. His trademark entrance into the ring included flashy, effeminate mannerisms after assistants had laid a trail of rose petals at his feet. In our eyes, he was not overtly portraying a homosexual character, which would have been banned in this early era. He was role-playing an overly pretentious heterosexual liar and cheater. That was permissible in 1940s and 1950s America. In his bouts, Gorgeous George would use illegal maneuvers while his associates distracted the referee.

Wrestlers like Gorgeous George were not just stars, they were virtual family members. We grew up with them, as soon as there was such a thing as television. From the 1950s through the 1970s, at 10:30 p.m. on Saturday night, via the magic of our black-and-white television set, these men and their friends stopped over to the house and told us of their doings around town. Over bad jokes, we laughed with them and celebrated their victories. We cheered them on when they gallantly met evil men in the squared circle. We screamed murder when our heroes were unfairly beaten in the ring. We cried with them when they lost—especially because the real heroes only lost when the challengers used illegal means to win, like villainous Gorgeous George did. The wrestlers got us, my whole family, including my grandma, into feuds with people we did not even know. Wrestling was the perfect medium for Gorgeous George's gift for great spectacle.

That night after dinner, when Grandma's death was fresh, Grandpa continued his story about his wrestling match date with her. The show was in the high school gym. Cheap seats were in the bleachers on two sides of the ring. The more expensive seats were rows of folding chairs on the other two sides. "It was unbelievable—just like walking into any small-town high school," Grandpa said. "At first it didn't seem like a real star would appear in such a small town."

The card first listed the lesser-known wrestlers, according to convention, and the promoters saved the most popular bout until the end. Gorgeous George, the headliner, was one of the nation's highest-paid athletes in the 1950s. When he appeared in Wausau in the '40s, he got 50 percent of the gate. Having Gorgeous George on that wrestling card sold many advance tickets.

My grandparents had bought tickets for the "expensive" folding seats, according to Grandpa—two rows back from the ring, near one of the neutral corners.

Through all of the preliminary bouts, Grandma did not say much. Those guys were all no-name, scientific wrestlers. She seemed to enjoy the show, according to Grandpa, but she really did not say anything. All that changed once Gorgeous George began his lengthy entrance. She straightened in her seat and sat attentively.

First, the house lights dimmed to near darkness. Then a spotlight aimed at one of the gym's exits, perhaps leading to the biology lab. Next came loud, grand music, with brass fanfares. Lingering echoes filled the gym. Finally, the exit doors were opened by unseen hands. One of Gorgeous George's assistants began a slow, elaborate march, a funeral gait, toward the stage, all the while followed by the spotlight. While marching, this formally attired assistant reached into a basket that he held and pulled out handfuls of flower petals, scattering a trail as he kept time to the grandiose music.

After an eternity, this assistant reached a spot ten feet from the ring. That is when a brighter, bigger spotlight found Gorgeous

George standing in the exit doorway. While the audience's attention had been diverted, the main attraction had magically appeared. He wore a cape and was followed by a pretty blond woman holding the long train of the cape at waist level. She herself was decked out in a pair of knee-length, black leather, high-heeled boots, fishnet stockings, and a pair of tight black satin shorts. This was Gorgeous George's wife. She, of course, was another distraction.

Grandma stared. That woman, more than anything, got Grandma's hackles up. Her eyes filled with dislike for this Hollywood whore. How dare this woman come to town and expose herself in such a manner in front of Grandma Jennie's husband, and how dare any man let his wife parade around in such bawdy lingerie in front of strangers?

Grandpa assured us, "Grandma wasn't alone. As soon as the spotlight found Gorgeous George, the jeers, catcalls, and boos started." George milked the crowd's hate for all he could. He was a consummate showman and gave the crowd exactly what they wanted. They paid to see an arrogant bully exploit his pretty assistant, and that is exactly what the Wausau crowd got.

I do not think either of my grandparents really understood that this was a perfectly executed show-biz act. George's walk to the ring seemed to take an eternity. According to his reputation, this entrance would take longer than the actual bout. Why not? It did not cost anything, and it increased his appeal, hence his bottom line. Besides that, he did not even have to break a sweat.

His female assistant received many wolf whistles from unmarried men in the audience. She was a big part of the show and played her role to the hilt. A pretty girl could titillate the audience and, in the case of professional wrestling, could also serve to distract the referee. George and his wife were masters at this game. They made a lot of money with this formula—antagonize everybody, distract the referee, cheat using illegal holds and punches, and then, win. Wham, bam. They gave the crowd their money's worth.

This night was no exception. As the bout commenced, George spent the majority of time fleeing his opponent. This increased the audience's anger. When the referee warned him to start wrestling, his female assistant climbed onto the ring apron lip across from my grandparents. She bent provocatively over the ring ropes, displaying cleavage, and called to the referee. This caused him to turn around, distracting him from officiating, and it also gave the male audience a large slice of cheesecake. That is the moment when George let loose with a couple of sucker punches.

When the crowd noise finally caused the referee to turn around, George was innocently standing near his prostrate opponent. George did this a few more times, keeping his opponent down near the neutral corner closest to my grandparents. His wife kept distracting the referee, and George kept using more and more crippling moves.

Grandpa was busy watching the match. He noticed that Grandma was fidgeting and did not like the action, but he did not think too much about it.

Eventually, Grandma could not stand it any longer. She moved ringside and began screaming at the referee to turn around. She slapped the canvas floor with her hand to get his attention. That did not work. She yelled at the referee to quit talking to the scantily clad woman and see what George was doing. The referee continued to ignore her, but her behavior did get Grandpa's attention. He ran up next to her to calm her down.

The referee did not turn around, the blonde woman did not stop distracting him, and George did not stop choking his opponent. That is when Grandma took things into her own hands. George, who was pinning his opponent with his rear end pointed at the neutral corner, was only a couple feet away from Grandma.

Grandpa was close enough to see but not quick enough to stop Grandma from pulling a hat pin from her hat. This was a formal event, and a proper lady always wore a hat to formal events. She held the hat pin in her gloved hand like a dagger. She reached between the bottom rope and the canvas floor and stabbed Gorgeous George in the butt.

George screamed, and that finally attracted the referee's attention back to the match. George, now standing, kept screaming, rubbing his butt, and pointing directly at Grandma. The audience was silent. Two startled police officers appeared, seemingly out of nowhere, and restrained Grandma, one on either side. Grandpa watched them escort her out of the building.

He said he waited in his seat for a couple of minutes before following. The match had not restarted yet. He went outside and looked around the parking lot. At first, she was nowhere to be seen. He finally found her sitting in the car, waiting for him.

Neither of them ever said a word about this incident to each other or to anybody else until Grandpa told us the story at the kitchen table, after Grandma was safely buried six feet down. We enjoyed hearing about this side of my proper, Catholic grandmother.

Another of my boyhood wrestling heroes was ex–National Football League player "Chief" Wahoo McDaniel, a Choctaw-Chickasaw Indian. He came along in the late 1960s. Baseball and football seasons came and went, but pro wrestling was always in season on north-central Wisconsin television. Years-long story lines filled our imaginations. We were happy to find an Indian wrestling hero, even if he was from a distant tribe.

In 1961, Wahoo McDaniel began his professional wrestling career in Indiana after a professional career in the NFL. In those days, pro wrestling was bigger, with bigger paychecks, than NFL football.

There was no doubt that this guy was an Indian. He looked Indian. He even had a real Lakota headdress. Everybody on the reservation knew of him, partly because of his sheer longevity and perseverance. He wrestled in at least ten thousand professional matches. A big part of his fame came from his American Indian story line, which was accentuated with a feather headdress (unlike any authentic Chickasaw head gear), a prop tomahawk, and an Indian war dance. Chief Wahoo played this role to the hilt.

A big part of his television shtick—something meant to draw the fans in—was his ability to take a beating. "He took a beating better than anybody else," Uncle Buddy said. Week after week on the television, Wahoo would war-dance his way into the ring to adoring fans. After a few moves, his opponent would throw some illegal punches. Wahoo, acting kind of surprised, would just stand there and take the punch. The opponent would throw more punches into him, and then Wahoo would begin a stationary war dance. Every illegal punch just made him look meaner, crouch lower, and dance faster. Finally, after the opponent had spent all of his strength, the chief would straighten. He would lock his eyes on his opponent, grab him, and slam him to the mat. Once he started fighting, he would win the match in less than five minutes.

Afterward, within moments, a tuxedo-clad announcer would spend a few minutes talking with a sweaty Chief Wahoo about his upcoming matches in nearby cities. With friendly bluster, he would invite all of his fans to come watch.

This was how we spent our Saturday nights. The entire family sat around the television set watching wrestling on the local Green Bay station.

I had not thought about Chief Wahoo McDaniel for many long years, maybe even thirty years, when I was eastbound on I-88 heading for Lake Shore Drive in Chicago. My wife, Denise, was spending a summer residency in Chicago, and I had been holding down the fort, or family encampment, in Kansas. I was on a visit, first to see my wife and then my kin in Wisconsin. The hardest part of driving long distances is to keep yourself from getting bored and feeling dead. I like to look at license plates as I drive. I have seen Hawaiian plates on the streets of Antigo. Personalized license plates are the best, plates that really convey something about the owner. I read them, look at the vehicle, glimpse the driver, and imagine what that person's life might be like. One of my favorite plates was "OOBPRN" (Out of Bed Per the Registered Nurse, or ambulatory) on an early '70s Porsche 911. That was in Wisconsin. Cruising at a steady eighty-five miles per hour in a turbocharged AWD Subaru, one can get from Kansas City to Lake Shore Drive in just under seven hours, if need be.

Somewhere in the Illinois barrens, I came up behind a huge gold SUV. This was the first gold-colored anything cruising down the highway that I had ever seen, and it was also the biggest, a GMC Suburban. Intrigued, I decided to break my pace, pulling up behind him.

As I got close, I realized the plates read "WAHOO." No, it couldn't be.

I gave my Indian pony a little gas and pulled into the passing lane. The gleaming finish on that behemoth looked like real gold. That must have been an expensive, special-order paint job.

As I drove by, I got a real good look at the driver. Chief Wahoo must have seen me slow down, pull out, and give him the once-over. Maybe he thought I was a cop. But he must have been used to being recognized. At seventy miles per hour, we were parallel to each other and made eye contact. It really was Chief Wahoo McDaniel.

We looked at each other's faces, identifying each other as tribal. He smiled and waved. Wahoo must have done this thousands of times, but his smile and his wave seemed genuine, like he was honestly happy that the two of us Indians crossed paths so far from either of our homes. I kept glancing at him until the distance between us became too great for me to make him out clearly.

Those two minutes meant so much to me. It was like unexpectedly seeing a family member on television. He was one of my childhood heroes, and I feel so much richer for having been so close to him in such an unexpected manner. I wish that I could have told him about all those wonderful Saturday nights that he, my grandpa and grandma, and I spent together on the reservation, but maybe he already knew.

Roast Corn

The night before his once-in-a-lifetime battle with the Sioux and their allies, General George Custer dined on a meal of bison steaks, beans with molasses, and roast ears of corn. This dish can be made in an oven or on a grill, and it has also been traditionally made using a simple wood fire. Since all ovens and fires vary, the most important rule is to give the fire time to get hot and yourself enough time to bring it together.

Serves 1 person

2 ears corn, with husks
Large pot of water, or a bucket
Salt and pepper, to taste
Butter, to taste

Preheat oven to 425 degrees. If using a charcoal grill or wood fire, start the fire and let it get hot. Pull the husks back from the ears of corn, but leave them attached (they will become handles). Remove corn silk. Pull husks back over the ears of corn, then soak the ears in a pot of salted water for 30 to 60 minutes. Place ears, with husks still covering the cob, on the middle rack of the oven and bake for 15 to 20 minutes, or until done. The husks will be dried out completely. If cooking on a grill, place ears on the grill. If cooking on an open fire, place ears above fire, trying to avoid open flames.

After removing ears from the oven, grill, or fire, pull husks down, but not off, to use as handles for eating. Remove any remaining silk. Salt, pepper, and butter to taste. If drying corn for storage, do not add salt, pepper, or butter, and proceed to next step.

Using the husks, tie roasted corn into bundles of up to 5 ears. Place bundles in a sunny, well-ventilated space. Dry for up to 2 weeks.

Once dry, shell kernels from corn cobs. Place kernels in cloth bag for storage.

Seasoned Butter

My grandparents added salt, pepper, and butter to their ears of corn grudgingly. They liked the taste of the corn and did not think it needed enhancement. I like bold spices. Chili pepper and lime is a favorite flavor of mine. The lime moderates the heat of the chili pepper.

2 tablespoons cumin seeds
⅓ cup butter
1 tablespoon powdered chili pepper
1 lime

Toast cumin seeds in a hot frying pan for 90 seconds. Remove from heat. Crack seeds using the back of a spoon or the bottom of a saltshaker. Combine butter, cracked cumin seeds, and powdered chili pepper in a small mixing dish. Add zest and juice from one lime to mixing dish. Using a large fork or wooden spoon, mix all ingredients together. Use immediately or refrigerate for later.

The Crane Clan's Place on the Wolf River

Along the old Indian trade trail, which is now Wisconsin Highway 47, the base of Camp Four Hill makes a convenient spot to ford the Wolf River. This is north of Neopit. A mile upstream from the ford is a dangerous place on the river called Race Horse, an especially fast section of an already cantankerous torrent. As it nears the bottom of Camp Four Hill, with the current now spent, the river is not especially powerful. A person can stand upright on the inviting gravel and hard-packed sand bottom with little effort. The water level varies from ankle-deep to neck-deep. An occasional dark blue pothole can be six, possibly even eight feet deep. Trout use these potholes to hide from smaller prey and bigger predators. Many children from Zoar and Neopit come to play at this friendly place along the cold, clear river.

Just downstream, at the confluence with the Main Branch of the Wolf River, there is a pool of quicksand. From the highway, it looks like any other small, sandy beach—an inviting spot situated away from the thick shoreline brush. But it is not a beach. It is dangerous quicksand. One cannot reach this location without first climbing down a steep briar patch slope; if it were more accessible, there would be many more unfortunate encounters with it.

Hidden within this forest landscape by the Wolf River are several scattered bubbling springs, and these also are associated with pools of quicksand. A bubbling spring results when subterranean pressures force a jet of water to rise a few inches above the surface of a pool, like a continuous, cold water geyser. The underground water stream unceasingly erodes the granite bedrock, tearing away tiny bits of silica, or sand. When granite bedrock erodes into a roundish, fine-grained sand, it can collect into pools of floating sandy water.

Some quicksand pools are so small that just a human hand is in danger of disappearing for a moment beneath the surface. Other pools are much larger and less benign. The one located north of Neopit is large enough for at least one person to disappear into the depths. Below the clear surface of this spring lies a thick layer of quicksand. People can drink from the spring, which appears clear. Indeed, a cup has always hung from a nearby tree branch. The icy cold, mineral-dense water tastes crisp and satisfying. But reaching into the spring to fill that cup can be daunting. What looks like an inviting pool in the middle of a thick forest is actually quicksand—beautiful, yet dangerous, like a Venus flytrap. I once reached into this quicksand pool. My arm disappeared into the sand. I could see where it disappeared at a specific line, not a gradual gradient, and I became aware of a supernatural presence. I could feel unseen things—like urgently probing fingers that tugged and stroked my forearms and tips of my fingers. Of course, they were not really fingers. Nothing with fingers lives in the darkness of this watery hole, below a surface of opaque sand. But the experience was so unnerving that I never reached into it twice. A friend once described it as reaching into another dimension.

In some stories, the Neopit Mill Pond and Keshena Falls are said to be inhabited by supernatural giant eels—snakelike monsters that live below granite overhangs. These rock shelves lie barely visible under turbid spots in the river, always hidden from the daylight. When the Mill Pond was created by the widening of the small river, these eels were apparently disturbed from their mud dens beneath the granite. This was in the early 1800s.

Every year, one of these dangerous water serpents would visit each Menominee village. Perhaps the monsters were upset with what the Menominees were doing.

According to Grandpa Moon, the water emerging from those bubbling springs north of Neopit originates from Thunder Bay on Lake Superior. The water from those springs flows along a dynamic network of underground fractures in the shattered granite bedrock. Tons of rock are separated and forced apart by high-pressure jets of water, and the granite breaks in long parallel splits. This rocky aquifer lies just beneath the Great Lakes. Certain creatures use these fissures in the bedrock to travel from place to place. This is one explanation for how trout get into landlocked springs. Fingerling trout are pushed along by subterranean water pressure through long, oxygenated fissures until they reach a sunlit pool.

Springs are wellsprings of life on the reservation. People draw daily drink from them. Ceremonies take place at them. I have found brown, buttery-looking flint that originates in the Flint Hills of Kansas on the Menominee Reservation next to a bubbling spring. Maybe my ancestors, my family, traded for these stones that came from hundreds of miles away, or perhaps some Prairie Band Potawatomi relative brought these precious stones home on a visit.

My family originated in the same places that members of the Crane Clan lived. Perhaps my family, in those dim, old-time days, were also members of the Crane Clan and not the Bear Clan. This might explain why my branch of the family is Weso, not Wesho. It might also explain my family's long association with the Crane Clan, as we lived on their land. By the twentieth century, though, my family was and continues to be part of the Bear Clan.

While we walked around my mom's property one day, Uncle Buddy pointed out some important landscape features. He showed me where three child-sized graves lay in a row, each marked by a white pine. The grave plots pointed upstream to the northwest. Perhaps these were the last three children of a lost Crane Clan village. The natural levee of the grave site overlooks the confluence of spring and river, making this a beautiful but lonely spot to spend eternity.

The children were buried outside of the nearby Catholic cemetery, under no Christian cross—instead, they are remembered by white pines. The pines and graves seem to be a similar age. Those three young ones must have died in the same season. Influenza might be a good guess, given the age of the trees. During those years of Catholic domination, several of my relatives were denied spots in sanctified ground, so perhaps these children are my Crane Clan kin.

At the far end of the cemetery, outside the sanctified part, lies the grave of an old wizard named Charlie Dutchman. His grave is also out of directional alignment with the Catholic burials, as befits a shaman or wizard. There is a tree marking his spot, but not a white pine. His is hardwood, and he does have a stone.

According to Uncle Buddy, members of the Crane Clan lived around my mother's land, across the highway. He even showed me where wickiups and tepees once sat around the upper part of the glacial kettle holding a recently buried bubbling spring at the bottom. I could still see depressions in the earth when I was a boy in the 1950s. The electric company installed a high-voltage power line and roads crisscross relentlessly over parts of this ancient village, breaking its harmony.

The Menominee people built both bark dwellings and tepees. In the Menominee creation story, it is Beaver Woman, the first woman, who taught her people to build dome-shaped bark homes. Tepees of the old village sat around the spring. Uncle Buddy showed me tepee rings, bare spots on the ground where nothing grows because something once compacted the ground. We also found a darkened place where a long-term campfire had burned—like the kind the Potawatomi built. The tepee rings could be as old as the reservation, which dates from the 1850s, and perhaps even older, as this was traditional Menominee land for thousands of years. Uncle Buddy remembered as a child in the 1930s seeing some old people still living around the wet, sandy patch, next to the highway, although the spring itself had already been blocked for forty years. He said they always kept to themselves. They never talked to outsiders, even to other Menominees, as far as he knew. "They just got older until they all disappeared," he said. My wife remembers grave houses, simple wooden frames and roofs built around regular grave mounds, in this area in the early 1990s.

In the late 1800s, members of the United States Army filled this bubbling spring with boulders and gravel. This was the largest of the bubbling springs in the northern Wolf River valley, essential as a sacred water source, and it was an impediment to the army. The reason? An existing foot trail was not wide enough for a freight wagon. That trail, an unimproved part of the military road, narrowed as it went between the bubbling spring and the pool of quicksand. According to a local Antigo newspaper, a German trader almost lost an entire wagon of goods and a team of oxen when he drove across sand to avoid that spring. Disaster was apparently averted when the oxen were able to extract themselves from the watery pool of quicksand.

After neighboring White farmers' complaints to the Indian Service Office to do something, engineers from the US Army arrived in Neopit and quickly created an ecological disaster. They plugged the spring, treating it like seepage. This bubbling spring was more like a fire hose. The army workers who filled the sandy water with tons of gravel and boulders did not realize that water pressure would simply force another opening somewhere else.

A washout resulting from that blockage occurred as the water was forced sidewise, toward the river, and it flooded several acres, including a railroad line. The old tracks still lead into water and disappear. Ghostly stumps rise above the water's surface, supported by long, tenacious roots that reach under the water to the sand below. The topsy-turvy tree roots create weird wooden sculptures. Some de-barked limbs look like the legs of water spiders, beckoning passersby into their watery webs. They provide evidence of that past environmental disaster.

Before the army's interference, the stream from the spring's overflow was small enough for thousands of foot travelers to simply step across. The hydraulic pressure dissipated harmlessly as small water geysers. Its pool spilled over and flowed to the river. After the army's interference, a jet stream of water washed away everything. At first it began to wash away the soil that anchored trees. Then it washed away the Menominee-owned railroad bed. This spring still creates some surface seepage, which is now funneled under the road by a metal culvert. The highway is built directly on top of the spring.

In the mid-1990s, a hundred years after the army filled the original spring, a new spring emerged—part of the same system—just outside the nearby town of Zoar across from an old traditional Menominee burial ground with grave houses built above the ground. Water began to seep, then pool, and finally flow out of the ground to flood the graves. Then a large spring hole with a sandy bottom took form next to the highway. Local children described it as bottomless. The county highway department plugged the spring with tons of rock. Again, engineers redirected the water with brute force.

By the 1910s, most of the loggers' and rail barons' damage to the Menominee Tribe's land was complete. The giant white pine forest near the springs drowned, died, and fell. The soil washed away. And all this was exacerbated by a series of dams constructed on the Little West Branch of the Wolf River. Lumber companies used mixed-race logging crews to remove the white pines, and logging continues to be an important Menominee business. Because logs easily float, transportation costs were nil. The series of lakes created by the dams were seasonal, and when the dam ponds were released in the spring, carrying thousands of logs, this pent-up flow acted like an avalanche, pushing everything in front of it downstream to the Neopit sawmill. Numerous water-saturated logs still litter the bottom of the Mill Pond upstream to Camp Four Hill.

This is near where my family performs ceremonies. The state highway passes within a few short yards of this last vestige of the Crane Clan on the northeast. On the northwest side is an electric power line, while the third, southernmost side is a Catholic cemetery protected by a wire fence. I wonder what the priests erecting the fence thought they were keeping out. The Crane Clan and the bubbling spring, a spiritual center, might be gone, but so are the Catholics. The cemetery's crosses and statues of the Virgin Mary are now deteriorating as more people on the reservation revert to more traditional Menominee beliefs. So who has the stronger medicine?

Like most old cemeteries on the edges of towns elsewhere, the old Catholic graveyard has its share of stories. Some people claim to see strange lights dancing and circling over the lost spring and among the uppermost branches of the surrounding white pines, as though performing some long, silent ceremony. This spot in the woods is visible only from the cemetery. Although close to the highway, it is hidden from that view by numerous willow and birch trees.

I have never had the courage to walk to this spot at night when those lights are active, although I have seen them. I could not bring myself to explore them more closely when I lived near them as a young man. In those days, I was afraid to die.

On the town side of the Catholic cemetery, across the road from the spot known as Crow's Nest, once lived an elderly woman named PEmecewan Cook, known as Old Lady Cook (*PEmecewan* means “River that Flows Deeply and Gently”). She was a step-grandmother to my mother, who remembers how fondly she treated all the children. Grandpa Moon named my daughter PEmecewan in the hope she would enjoy a long life, like Old Lady Cook.

Crow’s Nest lies within a group of giant white pines on the bank of the Wolf River. It is bounded by the old railroad bed running to Camp Four. The sandy gravel river bottom is an ideal locale for trout. It is such a relaxing spot that people still come here to enjoy the scenic beauty. Crow’s Nest used to be a place for families to swim and play in the river. There even used to be a small concession stand in a wooden shack where sodas and chips were sold. It was run by relatives of Old Lady Cook. As long as the concession stand stood, Crow’s Nest was clean and safe. When the stand finally fell, Crow’s Nest was taken over by drinkers. Drunks often threw garbage into the water, including broken beer bottles. The danger of glass offshore stopped any further recreational use of this spot.

This was not the first spiritual haven ruined by drinkers. The late 1950s and early 1960s were marked by alcohol abuse and alcohol-related accidents. When I lived with my grandparents in Keshena, across from the store owned by Frank Skubitz, I often lay awake at night listening to tires skidding across the parking lot, radios blasting tinny country-and-western music, and the shrill laughter of women. This store was open until ten at night. The front door had a bell attached to the top that loudly chimed whenever the door opened. I listened for the sequence—car doors slamming, the doorbell chimes, a pause, then doorbell chimes again, car doors slamming again, and squealing tires. Thirsty people would race to get to the beer store before it closed.

Skubbitz’s Store opened at six in the morning, and my grandmother worked the opening shift. Sometimes she worked from opening until closing. It must have been uncomfortable for young adults to buy cheap wine and beer under my grandma's disapproving stare at six a.m. Over our evening meal, she would tell my grandpa in Menominee exactly whose kids were *drinking*. In the old days, they would have told the parents and grandparents about this behavior, and it would have stopped. That did not work anymore because the old ways of enforcing acceptable behavior were gone. The old grannies were disappearing. Disease, death, and diaspora were destroying family, band, and clan social structures while the federal government micromanaged the tribe. Without any social pressure, entire families engaged in self-destructive behavior, and there would always be a crowd waiting for the store to open to buy beer, seven days a week, in those days. I remember Grandma going to work on Christmas morning and finding several carloads of older kids waiting for the store to open.

Often in my youth, sounds out of the darkness woke me at night. I could look out my window and see carloads of kids pulling into the parking lot for an all-night stay. Once parked, they turned off their cars' engines without revving them. From the window of my bedroom, I could hear only the anonymous murmur of voices, slightly louder than the frogs and buzzing insects. There they waited unapologetically for dawn. Even the neighborhood dogs ignored these strangers after a few perfunctory barks. Amazingly, those carloads of inebriated young adults were never bothered by the police.

These were the days before the federalized tribal police, so most of the tribe's law enforcement came from the neighboring Shawano County sheriff's department. An occasional State Patrol officer also drove the roads, including the lake district on the southeast end of the reservation where most of the drinking parties occurred. Those White sheriff's deputies could have been more proactive and reduced the number of car accidents by stopping drunk drivers. Instead, they did nothing. In fact, they displayed the crash remains of fatal reservation accidents at the Skelly gas station, across from the Shawano Police Department. The wrecked Indian cars were displayed in public alongside the main street. The cannon sitting outside the police station pointed at those wrecks. Whether this was meant as a visual warning to the Native community or as a trophy display for the non-Indian community, I still do not know. I do know Grandma encouraged us to drink coffee and tea, not alcohol.

Sumac, Pine Needle, and Birchbark Twigs Tea

At first glance, this may look like a complicated blend of exotic ingredients. However, I think they are actually pretty widely available. This blend of tea tastes good and, according to the literature, is healthy as well. This tea can be made at camp in the forest, as its ingredients can be found fairly easy. It makes an astringent, sweet, flowery tea.

This tea requires dried staghorn sumac berries. Individual berries are called drupes. If you picked the sumac fresh and allowed it to dry, you might get properly dried sumac, but most likely not. In the fall and winter, dried berry clusters called sumac bobs may still be found on the plant. No luck? Try a fancy place to buy spices, like a Mediterranean food shop. One last option—sumac berries can be ordered online. Sumac is high in vitamin C. The antioxidants help to regulate blood sugar and to reduce cholesterol. It is an antifungal and an antimicrobial, which can help treat skin disorders.

Pine needles from the white pine are also high in vitamin C, and, for that reason alone, pine needles are a good option in places where citrus is unavailable. The needles are also high in vitamin A, which is good for vision. Being a natural antioxidant, pine needles promote cognitive functions.

Leaves from the paper birch are high in vitamin C, too. An infusion, or a tonic, is said to improve urinary tract health and fight skin rashes. Use the tips of the paper birch, the very ends of the branches, for this tea. Two good handfuls are plenty.

Makes 4 cups of tea

1 quart water
½ cup birchbark twigs
½ cup pine needles from the white pine
½ cup dried sumac berries
Maple sugar or syrup, to taste—you may substitute honey or white sugar

Bring water to a rolling boil. Add birchbark twigs and allow to boil for 5 minutes. Add pine needles and allow to boil for 5 minutes. Remove from heat and add sumac. Let steep for 5 minutes. Sweeten to taste with maple sugar or syrup.

Pan-Fried Trout

Catch trout in the Wolf River's deep pools or purchase whole trout in the grocery store. The best trout I ever ate was caught by my young daughter. We cleaned it, built a fire, and skewered it on a stick. After searing it for a few minutes on each side, we served it and it was delicious. Even farm-raised trout are good eating.

Serves 4 people

2 whole trout, cleaned (guts removed)
1 egg, beaten
1 tablespoon prepared mustard
1 tablespoon flour
1 tablespoon cornmeal
2 teaspoons salt
1 teaspoon pepper
¼ cup lard—oil or butter may be substituted

Wash and pat dry the trout. Mix the egg and mustard together in a small bowl. Mix flour, cornmeal, salt, and pepper together in a shallow dish. Coat trout in egg mixture, then roll in dry ingredients. Heat lard in a nonstick fry pan over medium-high heat until it sizzles. Place coated trout in fry pan for 2–3 minutes on each side, until the coating is crusty and the inside flesh is no longer transparent. Do not overcook.

Grandpa Moon and the Witch Bag

The original, precontact foot trail of the Menominee Reservation, which has now become Wisconsin Highway 47, winds to a low plateau called Dutchman's Field. This is a heavily glaciated landscape, filled with kettles and moraines, rivers, and lakes. Maples fill the forest. Sugar maple trees provide an important part of the Menominee food pyramid, which consists of meat, water, salt, and sweet—and maple sugar sweetening is an essential. The site's history of witchcraft is not readily apparent.

For many years, Grandpa Moon had a sugar bush camp midway up the northwest slope of Dutchman's Hill. Making sugar was a family activity. Everybody who worked at this family business, from the youngest to the oldest, received a share of the profits from the sales of syrup and candy. Occasionally, Grandma made our camp's coffee from the vat that held the maple sap, mingling the two flavors, and all of us had our share. How I miss that strong, North Woods concoction.

Dutchman's Tower, a forest fire tower, sits at the top of this sugar bush moraine. The Works Progress Administration of the 1930s built it during the economic depression. In my youth, I played on that hill, also called Fire Tower Hill, and explored the maple forested slopes from all sides, but I never ventured across the highway onto Dutchman's Field. I never knew why; I just did not.

One early spring, when I was small, my uncle Billy came home on leave from the army while we were at the sugar bush. That cold spring day, he stood at the bottom of the tower looking up. Then Billy urged me onto his back—"Come on, Tommy"—as he stooped down. I climbed on. My knees clenched his waist tightly, and my arms wound around his neck. He shifted my weight a moment, then climbed the tower frame, stepping up the outside steel beams.

Grandma saw us. Running to the tower base, she started yelling at Billy, "You get the hell down from there right now and bring that baby with you! What the hell is wrong with you, taking that little boy up that tower on your back? You better not drop that kid, or so help you God!"

He ignored her, and we kept going up and up. We climbed to the very top landing. Meanwhile, Uncle Donny had run up the tower steps, at Grandma's insistence, so he was at the top, ready to help pull us off the steel supports and onto the wooden steps. This was the first time I had ever gone up the tower, as my grandparents certainly would not ever climb a forest ranger tower. I marveled at the sights. I saw the bottom edges of clouds and crows in flight, and, below, I spotted a porcupine waddling into the forest. Uncle Billy, not my grandmother, was my hero on that occasion.

After my grandma got done with me, and then Uncle Billy, it was also the last time that I ever went up that tower. My grandparents kept us away from Dutchman's Field, and not just because of the danger of the tower.

Dutchman's Field has an eerie feel to it. Nothing in particular stands out, and to my knowledge, nobody actually died there. This glaciated floodplain and alpine meadow area is not like the rest of the reservation where the trees, smooth granite boulders, and gently flowing rivers make you feel welcome. I always felt that Dutchman's Field, which never seemed bright even when the sun burned away the mists, disapproved of me. And some people did die close to this spot.

Years later, when I was home from college, Uncle Buddy told me some stories that explained the dangerous feel of Dutchman's Field. We were sitting at Grandma's rectangular Formica-topped kitchen table one evening in the basement of the old Indian Agency jail where we lived. It was after supper, and we were sharing a bottle of cheap wine and smoking cigarettes while Grandpa attended an overnight peyote meeting. Grandma's ghost was standing by the stove, disapproving of Buddy and disappointed in me for drinking with him. I used to smoke cigarettes back then—either the cheapest or the ones with the most colorful package. Winston was Uncle Buddy's cigarette of choice. In those days, brand names of cigarettes seemed important to me. Smoking kept my mind off Grandma's eerie stare. Yes, on occasion I can see ghosts.

I am not sure why Buddy told me this story. Maybe it was to fill the time as we went through our cigarette ceremony, each of us tapping a package, coaxing cigarettes out of the opening at the top, selecting one, putting it to our lips, and carefully lighting it. Buddy's story was just a few comments meant to fill an auditory void, but it led me down a spiraling rabbit hole with him.

On this evening, Buddy confided that the only place that truly frightened him was Dutchman's Field. If he had to cross it, he said, he would break into a fast run through the foggy, lonely meadow that stretched about a quarter of a mile. I tried to get Uncle Buddy to explain himself. At first, he just said that the field on foggy evenings was unsettling. Walking into the cool, misty flatland felt uncomfortable, even scary. This admission came as a surprise to me because Buddy, a World War II vet, had always seemed fearless to me. After a couple more sips of the wine and a few more cigarettes, he finally told me his story.

When Uncle Buddy was a young, "cock-strong boy" (his term), the old ladies living around Zoar teased him with stories about Dutchman's Field. In the fog, they told Buddy, crazy sorcerers stalked people traveling alone, especially proud young men. They were most dangerous at dawn and at dusk. These were not human people. They were spirit people that sometimes emerged from pools along the rivers. They could drift between the trees like miniature rain clouds, leaving no footprints, just wet trails like slugs.

Buddy paused and squished his cigarette into the bottom of the ashtray until it was out. Then he field-stripped the butt, like he had done during his combat days. He separated the cotton-based filter from the paper and spidery shreds of leftover tobacco. Lastly, he tore the filter into tiny bits.

He continued, "These sorcerers, the old ladies said, murdered their victims by drowning them in the fog, and Dutchman's Field is usually foggy." He explained how fish eat all bodies of drowning victims in a particular order—the harder parts last. So drowned bodies were just heads, minus all the soft parts, and torsos, minus the genitalia, with the limbs detached. Such bodies had been found floating in area waters. Buddy said, "The eyes are always the first part to be eaten by fish. Next are the mouth, inner checks, and tongues." I am not sure why my uncle wanted me to know all these details, but they surely set the mood.

Buddy balled up another wad of paper, tobacco shreds, and a filter into fibers in the crusty bottom of the ashtray. He paused, and I remained silent. While this tale seemed outlandish, I knew that any story told by an old woman carried a lot of weight. After all, many of those old women on the reservation really were witches. The most common method of witching a victim was, and is, for an old lady to stand and silently point her index finger. At a young age, I learned that it is important for your personal well-being to not upset any old women. That was all that Uncle Buddy would say about the witching field that night.

Now, a half century has passed since Buddy told me his story. Unsurprisingly, it is not an alpine meadow anymore. A mature second-growth stand of white pine crowds this rich plain, but it still feels spooky—perhaps even spookier now because of the trees blocking the view.

As a child, I learned how witches call to each other in a secret language that mimics the sounds of turkeys. At dawn and at dusk in the forest, they call to each other. Sometimes, these witches can even take the form of turkeys. Grandpa said they do this to quickly get to a different perch in the forest. Turkeys are fast. Even today, people do not hunt or eat turkeys on the reservation because you might accidentally eat a witch. You may become a witch yourself, or you might get a mouthful of turkey stuck in your throat, choke, and fall over dead. For that reason, I have never explored Dutchman's Field or eaten wild turkey.

Charlie Dutchman was a real person, of mixed Menominee and German heritage. He was the subject of at least two anthropological reports and was always referred to as "Old Charlie Dutchman." He lived somewhere in that meadow that still bears his name. His being part *Deutsch*, or German, is how his nickname Dutchman came about.

I can remember the remains of a log building existing in Dutchman's Field way back in the early 1970s. Maybe this was his home? It would have been over one hundred years old. One bright, sunny, and warm spring day, at about one in the afternoon, I pulled into the dirt road leading through Dutchman's Field, thinking it might lead to Race Horse, a nice spot on the river to catch trout. The road, however, was overgrown with poplar saplings. It was impassable to my Volkswagen Bug. The dirt pathway ended at an old building—what had been a log building, but was then just a caved-in pile of old, square-trimmed logs. I did not stop to poke around. At the time, this area was being used by some area logger as his staging ground for logging operations. Several marked pine logs had been left in neat, multiton piles for later pickup. Logging trucks, log skidders, and other crew vehicles had opened the road to that point and no farther.

I do not know if Charlie Dutchman has any kin left in the area. If so, I sure do not mean any disrespect to his spirit. He was dead and buried long before I heard of him. Charlie is buried outside of the Catholic cemetery in Neopit. His grave lies in unsanctified ground, among the blackberry brambles, staghorn sumac, and white pine saplings. He was not recognized as a Catholic.

The old women used his name to frighten children, and I was indeed frightened. Perhaps he was an unrepentant, pagan member of the Crane Clan? He lived in Dutchman's Field about the same time that the bubbling spring by my mom's, one half mile away, was plugged by the Army Corps of Engineers. He may have had a mind to level a curse on the project.

Sometimes, while hunting or fishing in the general area of Dutchman's Field, I have heard strange animal calls that my older companions would identify as being the calls of witches. I was fairly sure that they were only teasing me, but I had eyes and ears. I had listened to my family talk about this place for as long as I could remember. If I was with one of my uncles, I was never afraid. But alone? This part of the reservation is creepy. Uncle Buddy's story about drowning victims found downriver from Dutchman's Field did not inspire confidence.

Years after Grandpa Moon told me the following story, I searched out the spot where my own family's part of the story took place. It was easy to find. Nothing, no plants whatsoever, grew within a small circle near the old railroad bed. It was just a sandy, gravelly spot on the river, unnatural in its roundness. A weasel skeleton lying in the center of that circle on top of several carefully arranged river stones could have been coincidental. Or not. This was the 1990s, not ancient history.

Of course, there's no way I'm the only one who knows this story, as it is impossible to keep secrets on the reservation. We have several Forest County Potawatomi relatives from Wabeno who used to visit my mom's place, and who knows what they know? But this is the story from my family.

Grandpa Moon began his tale at an evening meal in the family kitchen, in the old jailhouse, near the confluence of Keshena Creek and the Wolf River, a quarter mile downstream from the first Menominee village of 1854. I had been working on Camp Four Hill for the highway department, saving money for college. This was in 1979, soon after Grandma died, and her absence still hurt. It was a couple years after the collapse of Uncle Buddy's marriage to the only woman he had ever really loved. The three of us—Grandpa, Buddy, and I—lived a mostly happy life together.

Uncle Buddy did most of the housekeeping. He did all the cooking and almost all the drinking. For dinner, he often made Swiss steak like my mom's, except his was spicy with hot peppers. He served this with fresh dinner rolls and greasy pan drippings poured over mashed potatoes, with green beans on the side. Buddy's cooking was different from my grandmother's, my aunt's, and my mother's. He aggressively spiced our meals, even game like venison and porcupine. Spice remains exotic on the reservation. Aside from salt and pepper, little else is typically used. Richness in a dish is usually achieved through fat, not spice, as in chili, for example. On the reservation and surrounding areas, chili is made with added lard for depth of flavor. The added calories also help us survive the cold and the hard labor of logging.

With my grandpa, I helped collect firewood and keep the yard clean. Sometimes I enjoyed a bottle of Boone's Farm wine. After pedaling thirty miles or more to work and back on my ten-speed bike, I was able to put a bottle to my lips, clamp the tip of the bottle's neck between my lips, tilt my head back, and drink the entire contents in a couple of large gulps. I was younger then. Dinner wine was not even available in our part of Wisconsin. On the other hand, I did like the Acapulco Gold marijuana making the rounds in Green Bay.

The three of us bachelors were like any other family. After our evening meal, we sat and talked at Grandma's kitchen table. It was times like this that I felt as if Grandma had never really left. It seemed like she was sitting across from me holding a Pall Mall cigarette in her right hand with an elbow resting on the table and a cup of coffee in front of her, smiling at me, like always. Maybe she was, again, quietly whispering something in Potawatomi to Grandpa so that Buddy and I could not understand what she was saying.

Our subjects usually varied. Buddy would talk about science facts and treasure hunting, if sober. When a little drunk, he talked about the Bible, especially the most unbelievable parts, like the one that began, "There were giants in the earth in those days. . . ." I often asked questions about certain philosophical conjectures. As a cryptozoologist, Uncle Buddy was ahead of his time in his knowledge of giants and Bigfoot.

Grandpa usually listened quietly, but I could tell he was mentally reviewing items in his private thoughts. One evening, without trying to trigger any awkward memories, I asked about our family history. Grandpa looked deeply at me, as though sizing me up. Then we both looked at Buddy, who was smiling knowingly. It was as if they had been waiting for me to ask, to take my place in the lineage of family storytellers. As Grandpa Moon began, I instantly recognized every place he described. I also instinctively knew some of his story, although I was hearing it for the first time.

He began his story over the last bites of potatoes and before his coffee. In his story, Grandpa was a young man, in his early teens, and still known by his Menominee name, Kesōq. He was not yet comfortable in English as his fourth language (after Menominee, Potawatomi, and French). He sat at the south end of Grandma's rectangular kitchen table, and Uncle Buddy sat at the north end, so they were looking at each other. I sat on Grandpa's left, on the west side of the table, so he had to turn to look at me before he told me this story. I faced the side of the table where Grandma would be sitting, on the east, if she were still with us, to complete the four directions. I could smell her, but my eyes kept missing her, like she was too quick for me to focus on. All four of us, nonetheless, were present.

"Tommy," Grandpa Moon began, "I don't know how much Indian history you know, but this story begins back in 1608, when the northern tribes held an intertribal conference in Saskatchewan, in that place called Rivers That Flow Quickly, in both Cree and Menominee." I knew that the Menominee language was even closer to Cree than it was to our sister tribe's language, Potawatomi.

I did not know about any of this 1608 meeting, but I nodded anyway. Grandpa continued, "All of the northern tribes attended. The purpose of the conference was to stop the White Man." All were desperate to think of a way to stop them from destroying the world.

He paused a moment, then resumed. "Tommy, it was the only way to keep the White Man from eating the land." I knew the 1600s was already past the time in history when military confrontations could be decided by courage, rather than steel. Native Americans had missed their opportunity to push the European settlers back into the sea when they had greater numbers.

Grandpa continued to explain how Euro-American technological innovations and the strategy of divide-and-conquer diplomacy had made it much less likely that Native people would retain their independence. True flintlocks, emerging in the early 1600s, were better than the matchlock rifles previously used by the early settlers. The faster reloading rate and reliable accuracy of true flintlocks vastly increased the odds in favor of gun owners in any conflicts against those using bows and arrows. Although arrows from bows could still be discharged faster in combat than bullets from rifles, that gap was narrowing fast. Moreover, the number of rifles—and colonists carrying those rifles—was increasing faster than the tribespeople's ability to repopulate.

Another problem was that tribes could manufacture wooden bows and arrows but not iron rifles. Even when tribes recovered the occasional rifle in battle, their inability to produce ammunition was another hurdle to its use. Native Americans had no mines, smelts, or large-scale forges. Ultimately, they lacked the technological infrastructure to create the weapons that this war required.

After a lot of deliberation at the conference, my grandfather explained, the tribes decided that the only possible solution to Euro-American colonization lay in using a different kind of weapon. The tribes decided to use magic against the White Man's "medicine" or power. The tribes decided to summon the greatest and most powerful sorcerers, wizards, and witches from all of the northern tribes. They were tasked with creating something—a spell, a medicine bundle, a witch bag—that would stop the White Man once and for all. With so many sorcerers from so many tribes, surely they would be unbeatable.

Grandpa turned to look at me directly. He swallowed coffee, then said, "These wizards finished their task, but the medicine bag they created was so evil that none of the councils of the northern tribes would agree to use this weapon. Once it started, there would be no end to this bad medicine. All of those different spells, the best and the worst magic, and all of those prayers tied up inside that medicine bundle would not only destroy the White Man, but it would turn on those wielding its power, too. This medicine bundle was stronger than any single medicine man or woman. It would bring chaos. It would eat our world, destroy our tribe, and change how things should be. Then, this bag would digest all that it ate and shit, giving birth to many little evils."

And so, my grandpa explained, it was never used. It was judged to be too terrible. Grandpa Moon ended the story there. I went to bed haunted by the idea of all those sorcerers and their powerful energies.

Several nights later, Grandpa Moon continued his story. In this part of the telling, Grandpa was a young teen (he was born in 1904). One morning, he was walking from Zoar to check his mail at the post office in Neopit. This was about fifteen years after the 1905 timber blowdown, back when Neopit was a sugar bush camp located along the river. As Grandpa walked along, he marveled at the landscape, which was bare from the effects of the cyclone. The entire forest and all the homes were gone.

In those days, a twenty-mile walk was not remarkable, and so this five-mile walk was not either. Grandpa had just started to pass through Dutchman's Field, and when he got about halfway, to the spot where Camp Four Hill was visible, he saw a bright light about the size of a large beach ball in front of him. He said it bounced up and down over the road, about ten feet in the air. It did not seem affected by the wind. The ball of light blocked him from going any farther.

Although he was terrified, he thought himself protected from evil spirits in the broad daylight. So he decided to investigate a little. The orb had a shiny, uniformly bright and glossy finish. "The only thing that I could think was that this must be ball lightning, something I'd heard of," he said. "This might be dangerous, but it was a natural danger."

As he slowly edged closer to the ball, it bounced gently up and down in the center of the road. When he approached to within twenty feet, the ball began a slow retreat with every downward arc, always keeping about twenty feet away from him. He followed the ball of light toward Camp Four Hill, and it stayed a uniform distance ahead of him.

This was happening about one mile from the spot on the trail at the crest of Camp Four Hill where the army plugged the bubbling spring. Grandpa Moon kept walking toward Neopit, and the ball of light led him on, setting the pace. He passed my mom's property and the Catholic cemetery. The ball of light continued until Grandpa was standing in front of PEmecewan Cook's house, near the river on the old foot trail. The new railroad tracks crossed there, at Crow's Nest.

Then the ball took one extra big bounce that sent it to treetop level, and it descended into PEmecewan's chimney without making a sound.

"I didn't know what to do," Grandpa said. "I knew that an old woman lived there, that she was related to me, a distant grand-aunt. I thought she might be in danger. The ball of light might start her house on fire. So I started toward her home to help. Just as I got within arm's length, her front door opened. She stepped out of the house onto the trail and said, in Potawatomi, 'I knew that you would come, Kesōq. I sent a messenger to bring you to me. I need to talk with you. I need your help.' "

Grandpa told how she stepped aside and motioned him into her one-room pine house. "Come into my home and have a cup of tea with me," she said. "It is a powerful medicine that I made with a dried plant that is found only in Texas. I get it from an old Kickapoo fellow who comes around. The tea is just about ready to drink. It will give you strength to do what I ask. Afterward, we will talk."

She seated him at a rickety table with a steaming cup of her homemade tea. Grandpa remembered there was a small bed along one wall and an open fireplace along another. There was no fire in the fireplace and no sign of the ball lightning.

Grandpa paused in his storytelling, swirled his coffee a moment, drank, and continued, "She handed me a beaten-up tin cup, the kind that the old-timers used to drink coffee from. I was not wanting to drink her brew, but being too smart to outright refuse any command from a witch, I slowly drank the thick, steaming, bitter drink. I struggled to keep my stomach from heaving and my mind from racing. I felt like screaming."

Then she told Grandpa that a medicine bundle lay hidden underneath the floorboards of this house. Grandpa turned to me and said, "This is the same bundle that I have been telling you about."

After what seemed like hours, she stood, left her chair, walked a few feet to the fireplace, and pulled up the end of a board. She reached into that dark space and pulled out a leather pouch. She undid the leather ties and tipped the bag, spilling the contents into her other hand. In her palm was another, smaller leather pouch—a witch bag.

Grandpa said, "I never touched the inner bag, the witch bag. It was just a small, off-color leather pouch. It wasn't deer hide, not bearskin or ermine, but something else familiar. It was decorated on one side with thin beaded symbols that looked Cree. There was nothing that special about it, although the bag was greenish. There were also some dark stains on it, like mold. It was well made. The seams were straight and hidden by folds of leather. There were no other markings." Grandpa explained that she showed him this bag just twice. This was the first time. She then placed the witch bag back inside the other pouch.

The outer pouch was decorated with a Menominee quillwork design on its other side. The old woman told him, "I don't like to touch the witch bag itself. That's why it is kept inside this other pouch, the one that I made." She paused, then said, "This medicine bag is hungry and needs to be fed. It has been nibbling. I can't stop it." She placed the two bags, one inside the other, on her lap and finished the history of the witch bag. Grandpa said, "It seemed to be listening as she talked."

Grandpa cleared his throat. Then he explained, "She told me everything about the northern sorcerers' magic, just as I've told you, Tommy." Uncle Buddy had said nothing as Grandpa talked.

The pile of shredded cigarette remains in his ashtray had grown as he'd smoked and listened.

Grandpa resumed the old woman's tale. "I've had this here for a few years, since it was given to me by an old man, a relative of ours, one of Red Cloud's band," she told him. "His time was near, and this medicine bag brought his time much closer. He told me its story and gave it to me for safekeeping. This is powerful bad medicine, gathered from all over the country—plants, roots, stones, spells. The incantations are what make it effective. There is not just one prayer or curse. There are hundreds of variations, uncountable layers of evil intent. Soon, there will be nobody left who can safely keep this medicine bag. I don't like to touch that bag, even inside the other bag. It feels wet and squishy, like a handful of raw cow's liver. Sometimes the bag bleeds, or maybe it throws up." She gestured at the stains. "It gets wet, like it's getting excited."

Old Lady Cook paused a moment and said, "I don't care what happens to the White Man. They are evil, uncaring. They strut about and wear indifference like some kind of badge of honor. But still, this medicine bundle cannot be used on them. Our people and the Whites had already mixed together too much when this bag was created in the 1600s. Now this would turn on us and attack us, too. This was why this medicine bundle was never used in the first place. The witch bag cannot tell the difference between us and them. To this witch bag, we and everyone that we love are its food.

"It has been sleeping for two hundred years, but lately it begins to stir, to twitch. You can feel it, if you wish, but I don't advise that you do. For now, it's not quite sleeping, only resting, but growing and gathering strength and getting ready to feast, and then to reproduce."

Grandpa was terrified as she described this power. The woman continued, "We don't want it to wake up. It needs to be disposed of before I pass from this world to the next, before it is too late for our people. I am close to my time, Kesōq. I can feel my spirit leaking out of my body from a lifetime of small cuts. I am like an inner tube that runs over a nail, and soon I will be flat—all my spirit will be gone. I need your help to do this, today, right now. There needs to be four of us, and I choose you, Nephew, to help me, even if you are young. Don't be afraid. That tea will give you the power to do what must be done. Just remember, do only what I tell you to do, and only when I tell you. If we fail, if our ceremony doesn't work, don't touch that witch bag. If you do, it will get your scent and follow you home. As long as I live, that bag and I remain tied. It will stay with me. You should be safe, but we four—you, me, and our two companions down the trail—are already in danger." She put a shawl upon her shoulders and walked out the door without looking back. Grandpa said he felt he had no choice but to follow her.

Grandpa Moon and Old Lady Cook walked a couple hundred yards down the tracks toward Camp Four Hill, not speaking and stopping only when they reached a spot across the road from the Catholic cemetery. In the midst of the many bramble bushes and poison ivy plants, there was a small fire made of maple wood.

Grandpa told me, "I could smell it burning—maple, the tree of life—in front of an altar made of sand in the shape of a crescent moon." He described how an old man of mixed Menominee descent, with a metal pot drum, sat on a blanket behind the fire. Another Menominee old man, somewhat younger than the first, kept the fire. He was kneeling behind the man with the drum and holding a feather fan. As Old Lady Cook and Grandpa circled the fire counterclockwise four times, Old Lady Cook praying and Grandpa following, the fire keeper added a pinch of cedar to the fire, releasing a fragrant puff of smoke. She sat cross-legged, opposite the fire keeper. "I sat down between them, also cross-legged," Grandpa said. "I noticed that while there were four of us, one side of the fire was left empty."

She set both bags on the ground between the fire and the altar, closed her eyes, and recited an ancient prayer, from the old days before the White Man. Suddenly, the older man started to drum and sing in Menominee, verses in fours, everything repeated four times. He passed four things to the fire keeper who passed those things to me, then returned to the fire.

"Four times I was passed a feathered staff and a bag of dried herbs," said Grandpa, "and I passed them to Old Lady Cook. She passed them back to me, and I passed them back to the first man. As these things were passed four times around the circle, the fire keeper raised puffs of cedar smoke to the four directions with his feathered fan—four times."

Uncle Buddy coughed, and suddenly, the spell was broken. We were back home in Keshena sitting at Grandma's old kitchen table with its sharp aluminum edges. As long as I could remember, that table—which had withstood countless celebrations, deaths, and regular family meals—had rested in our basement kitchen.

Grandpa was still at the head of the table, with Uncle Buddy at the foot and me on the side where I have always sat. The empty side across from me, the fourth side, was still Grandma's.

Uncle Buddy got up and poured us all another cup of coffee. I sat with Grandpa, not saying anything, just sipping my coffee. I could hear a neighborhood dog howling from the direction of Chapel Hill, toward Rabbit Ridge. Uncle Buddy had made our coffee that morning, and it had spent the day on the back burner. By this time in the evening, it was thick, hot, and bitter.

Buddy put Grandma's beat-up aluminum percolator back on the stove, and he walked out of the kitchen and into the furnace room. The aluminum coffee maker had replaced Grandma's huge, blue porcelain-coated steel one, the one she used every day to make coffee for the family and for any guests or passersby. Grandpa called it the "meeting coffee maker." Now it was used only for Native American Church meetings.

I heard the door of the huge wood-fired boiler opening with its recognizable clack as Buddy turned the handle, then the mechanical scratch as the fifty-pound iron door was dragged open. After a few seconds, it made the same clang as it shut. Buddy was finished preparing the night's fire. His footsteps preceded his actual appearance back at the table.

He began cleaning up the table and offered both me and Grandpa more fruit cobbler. Uncle Buddy made lots of cobblers, and he was good at it. He often used commodity canned fruits as the base. None of the three of us received commodity foods, but we had a good store from nieces and nephews, who often gave us a share. When Uncle Buddy was drinking, really drinking, he would make cobblers at three or four in the morning for himself and his guests. Sometimes, when the neighborhood drunks came to party, they would bring cans of commodity fruits as a trade for whatever spirits Buddy was drinking that night. The wooden pantry made by Uncle Donny in the space under the stairs, the one that Grandma and my aunts had once filled with her put-up foods, was now filled with government commodity foods.

As I finished the last scoop of fruit cobbler, using it to cool a mouthful of coffee so I did not have to speak, I used the time to think. The spell of Grandpa's storytelling had already been broken, and I would have to wait to hear the end of the story another time.

Grandpa went upstairs to watch some television. Buddy stayed downstairs, had a snort of vodka, and wrote letters expressing his opinion to the editor of the Shawano paper on his portable typewriter. I went outside and walked up Chapel Hill to the abandoned Third Station of the Cross, a Catholic chapel, where I smoked a joint. At the time, I did not appreciate the perfection of our life together. That was about to change for all of us. I would leave for a small college in Kansas, and a few short months after that, Grandpa Moon would die of an arterial aneurysm in a Green

Bay parking lot. Still later, Uncle Buddy would be murdered at this same kitchen table.

We always started the day with a cup of Uncle Buddy's intense coffee. Grandma's or Aunt Lorraine's coffee would get bitter by the end of the day, but Buddy's started out bitter. He never measured the ingredients for coffee; amateurs measured. Buddy just threw several handfuls of ground coffee into the basket at the top of the percolator and filled the pot about three-quarters full. I do not think he ever washed that peculator, either. Drinkers needed a generous pour of condensed milk and a heaping spoonful of sugar to make this coffee painless. We never brought up how bad Buddy's coffee was, as we were grateful to have somebody looking out for us, cleaning up, and making us coffee in the morning. Besides, Uncle Buddy had a really nasty temper. So we just bit our tongues about his coffee.

He was often the first one awake, sometimes spending the whole night drinking and not sleeping at all. In our time of bachelorhood, though, he was the first downstairs to the kitchen in the morning. Grandpa was usually the second to reach the kitchen table. I was almost always the third and last at the table, as I spent the longest in the shower. The day when Grandpa finished telling me his story was no exception.

That morning, Buddy used a spatula to place two over-easy eggs on his plate while asking me how I wanted my eggs. Without asking, he reached over and poured me a big cup of coffee. There were already some pork sausages on his plate, retrieved from a serving platter of sausages in the middle of the table. We always bought Oscar Mayer pork sausages, which came tightly packed in a foam package. The identical sausage rows looked like a sausage ammo clip for a sausage machine gun.

That morning, I grabbed toast from the pile on the table and placed a few of the sausages on one slice, using another slice to make a sandwich. Grandpa cleared his throat, which got our attention. This was out of character. Mornings were usually reserved for conversations about the coming day's events and things that needed to be done.

Grandpa held one of Grandma's mismatched china cups. Brownish liquid filled the circle channels of the porcelain saucer left on the table. His hand was motionless, frozen in anticipation of the story he was about to tell. The cup of coffee hung between table and mouth as Grandpa ended his narrative: "Tommy, we tried to defuse that witch bag. We thought, at first, that we were successful. We tried every spell the old man and the old lady knew. We tried to soften it, to change it—but we just did not have the right tools, the right prayers, the right medicine to hold it, to stop it, to finish it. Maybe we wounded it. But whatever was in that bag escaped into the woods." And so he ended the story.

In the silence afterward, we tried to finish our meal, as though this were a normal breakfast of cooked pork sausage, fried eggs, and toasted white bread with butter. Firewood had to be located in the forest, collected, and stacked alongside our redbrick home, because it gets cold in Wisconsin. Groceries needed to be bought in Shawano at the Super Value Store, brought home, and placed in the pantry, because we would get hungry. Our mail really needed to be collected from the post office in Keshena, as we were expecting some government checks. Trips to the tribal courthouse had to be made. On that afternoon, Grandpa and Buddy needed to drive the pickup truck to the sawmill in Neopit to fill it up with gas, check the oil, and gossip with relatives working there.

I needed to think about what I just learned, to spend some time digesting the story of how the world is doomed. I did my normal thing, jumped on my ten-speed and biked past Legend Lake on the long way over to Shawano Lake. In less than three months' time, at the end of that crazy summer, I would be on a plane moving a thousand miles away to finish college and to begin a new life.

Looking back, my thoughts return to that moment of balance among Grandpa and Buddy and my younger self. No matter what the future held, we still had the coming season. We still had our ceremonies to attend. We still had hope at that moment, no matter how things would eventually turn out.

Uncle Buddy's Commot Fruit Cobbler

Grandma and my aunts always made pies from the cherries, blueberries, and apples the family picked in Door County or around the reservation. Uncle Buddy did not spend time making crusts. He perfected the one-step cobbler topping that could be poured over any canned, sweetened fruit, usually peaches, apples, or blueberries.

Serves 6 to 8 people, unless they are hungry

16 ounces canned, sweetened fruit—either home-canned or store-bought
1 cup flour
1 cup sugar
1 teaspoon salt
1 teaspoon baking powder
½ teaspoon baking soda
½ teaspoon nutmeg
1 cup melted shortening—may substitute butter or lard
⅔ cup milk

Preheat oven to 350 degrees. Grease a pie pan or 9 × 9-inch square pan. Pour in the canned fruit. Mix the dry ingredients, including sugar, together in a medium bowl. Make a well in the center of the dry ingredients. Add the melted shortening and milk to the well. Stir wet ingredients until blended. Then stir wet and dry ingredients together to make a lumpy batter. Pour the batter over the fruit. Bake for 45 minutes.

Roast Porcupine

Porcupine is considered a survival food. Its meat is fatty, unlike most wild game. The animal is abundant and relatively easy to dispatch. Skinning and cleaning it, however, is difficult. A chef preparing porcupine has to contend with thousands of sharp quills.

Serves 10 people

1 porcupine
1 cup salt
1 teaspoon baking soda
3 onions, roughly chopped
4 slices thick bacon
6 jalapeño peppers, seeded and diced
2 teaspoons black pepper
Salt and pepper, to taste

Once skinned and cleaned, chop the porcupine carcass into a few manageable portions. Place pieces in a large kettle, cover with water, add salt, and soak overnight. Drain and rinse the porcupine pieces. Return the porcupine to the kettle, cover with water, add baking soda, and boil for 20 minutes. Drain, rinse, and return pieces to kettle again. Add 1 roughly chopped onion and enough water to cover. Boil for another 10 minutes.

Preheat oven to 350 degrees. Drain meat and cut into smaller pieces. Place pieces into roasting pan and lay bacon slices and the remaining 2 roughly chopped onions on top. Top with jalapeño peppers and black pepper. Place roasting pan in oven. While cooking, check to make sure enough water is in the pan to keep it from drying out. Roast until tender, about 90 minutes. Salt and pepper to taste.

A World War II Invasion and Grandpa Moon

A few weeks after Grandma's death, Grandpa Moon told me a story. Our grief was still so thick in the air that it was hard for the two of us to breathe. We were seated at the kitchen table, poking at a dismal meal of funeral leftovers including reheated coffee, soggy sandwiches, purple Jell-O, and a beige cake. In all those years I'd spent with my grandparents—Monroe and Jennie—that 1950s kitchen table had always been there in the background. Grandpa and Grandma bought it while living in Wausau a few years after the start of their marriage. I remember sitting next to it as a small child in a highchair when we lived in the Zoar house. For the past two weeks, family and friends had sat at that table drinking coffee and eating funeral sandwiches stacked on a platter. Unlike in the rest of the house, laughter was permitted in the kitchen. Grandma would have wanted that. After all, good memories bring laughter.

All those mourners, even members of the family, had since gone home to pockets of light and sound, leaving me and Grandpa alone to sit in silence, to cope for ourselves. For our first meal, at five o'clock, Grandpa had opened the refrigerator door and rummaged among the plastic containers. This was still thirty years before the microwave oven would become common and a week before Uncle Buddy moved back home to take care of us.

I was sitting at my place at the table, openly weeping for the loss of my grandma. Her spot was in front of me, on the long side of the table. While sitting there, and looking beyond me, she could keep her eye on the main entrance to the house.

That first meal by ourselves, we just pushed food from one side of our plates to the other. We were still using the paper plates left over from the funeral. Grandpa, at the head of the table, was not crying. He did not cry, ever. Oh, he might have secretly cried on the inside where only he and the Great Mystery could see, but not on the outside. Never. He already had buried brothers, sisters, sons, nephews, nieces—it is a curse of old age. But he never cried on the outside.

He and Grandma were real Indians from the old days. Grandma was the one who made all of the family life-and-death decisions: who will live, who will die. This is a matriarchal power. Within our family, the clan mother had final say, and now our family had no direction. "Now what will we do?" I asked. Grandpa made the clan medicine. He knew what to do.

I am not exactly sure what prompted Grandpa to tell this story, maybe something about our cold meal, maybe something about being afraid. Maybe it was just that Grandpa was thinking about interesting times.

His story began a few days after the Japanese bombing of Pearl Harbor, twelve years before my birth. "People were afraid, Tommy," he said. "There was no news, just a few reports of horrible losses of men. The navy was gone. People were afraid. There was no news, good or bad, just rumors. Japanese were hiding behind every tree, waiting. I was a justice of the peace for the reservation in those days, and I was responsible."

Zoar was near the intersection of a couple ancient trails. Only a few families, maybe a hundred people, lived in the area. Zoar had no electricity or telephones in those days, but Neopit, just down the road a few miles, had both. So most of the news came via word of mouth, and people on the rez were expecting an invasion by the Japanese.

We were living in a house built in the middle of Zoar by an evangelical minister. The town is surrounded by thousands of acres of second-growth forest, and our house was next to a large open field where ceremonies still occur. The house is now long gone, but the open field in the center of town is not. There is a small playground and a baseball field there. The house once sat near the pitcher's mound.

I remember that house being tall and narrow, just a white-washed enclosed space. Once as a small child, I thought I could fly down the steep three-story stairs of that clapboard home. Needless to say, I only fell and hurt myself.

We kept horses in that field surrounding our home. I must have ridden them because there are photographs of me on top of them with cowboy hat and toy guns. They were working horses, and Grandpa used them to drag logs out of the forest in his small logging business. Sitting at the kitchen table in Keshena, Zoar seemed like a distant memory to me.

Grandpa continued, "Dusk was approaching, and we were just about to eat our evening meal. It was already dark, maybe five o'clock, and your grandma had lit a kerosene lamp and placed it on the table. The table was set, but most of the meal was still on the woodstove. There was a tapping on the window, and we both looked up. It was one of the neighbor men. 'Moon,' he said, 'the Japanese army is here. There are many of them. They started to arrive by truck an hour ago, just as it was getting dark. All our men are gathered at the edge of town, waiting in the woods. We need you to come.'"

Grandpa followed the men through the darkened village into the woods. The sound of heavy machinery—tanks, cannons, trucks—soon became overwhelming. More army men were coming to the central, open area of Zoar. They silently counted hundreds, maybe thousands of armed men in uniforms. "In the dark we couldn't see what kind of uniforms these men wore,"

Grandpa said. "Occasionally, we heard some words in English, but not enough to tell if they spoke primarily English." In those days, many people on the rez and neighboring German or Polish towns did not speak English anyway. Some of the Menominee men did think that these soldiers were Americans, but that could have been exactly what the Japanese wanted them to think.

"These invading men did not seem to talk to each other very much," Grandpa continued. "There was no laughter. We knew that this army was not invading us, a handful of Indians, and they certainly were not sent to protect the reservation. So what were they doing?" The port of Green Bay was just east of Shawano and the old military road, Highway 29, ran directly to it. There had been wars fought over the port in earlier centuries, when Green Bay was a prize. This army could be there in under two hours. Grandpa went on to say that several of the men with him decided that this was a Japanese vanguard preparing to invade Green Bay, just like they had invaded Pearl Harbor.

It was up to the Menominee force to stop them.

"I didn't know what to think or do," Grandpa said. "We all had guns, but to start shooting would have been suicide. There were just too many of them."

The Menominees numbered about thirty, including a half dozen old grandpas and a dozen teens. Most of the town's women and children were already hiding along the river. Young scouts returned with information that this army stretched about five miles along the road to the west, both north and south of Zoar. Grandpa described to me how the army men were camped along the road and in a few small fields, including what is now the Native American Church Cemetery in Zoar. They were even camped in Dutchman's Field, which is haunted. They stayed on the north side of Camp Four Hill, not cresting the heights, so Neopit was safe. The hill created a natural barrier.

The foreign men set up tents and cooked food. They served

their meal and ate it silently. The Menominees could smell coffee, but no one knew whether the Japanese drank coffee. Some old men argued that the group must be the invading Japanese army, because White Men were always talking and these men were too quiet.

Several young Menominee men kept watch on the army from the forest, while the very youngest were sent out in all directions as runners to warn the people in neighboring towns of a possible invasion. They were told to direct people to form small groups, hide along the rivers, have their men keep watch, and wait for more news. They should also take guns but not use them unless they were shot at first.

The invading army set up guards along the road. Maybe they knew our people were in the woods watching, or maybe they did not. "All night long in the cold snow," Grandpa said, "we watched them. The invading army also kept watch. Guards were posted. We waited, unsure of what to do."

It snowed a little during the night. In the still-dark morning, men emerged from pup tents and stomped their feet, and clouds of steam from their coffee mixed with clouds of cigarette smoke. The army men murmured among themselves as they lined up to use the latrines, but hidden in the woods, behind trees and under the snow, the Menominees could not tell what language they spoke.

Finally, the army men packed up all of their equipment and stuffed it back into their trucks as the first light arrived. Grandpa said, "With the light, we could see that these were Americans. Many were blond. What we thought was pidgin English was a northern American accent. These funny-talking White Men were from Minnesota."

The troops mounted the vehicles and began their long journey south and east on the old military road past Neopit and to Japan and elsewhere. These army men must have known that we were watching them. Before the last truck left, two men unloaded ten cases of oranges and left them on the side of the road.

Grandpa almost smiled as he said, "That Christmas in Zoar, we had oranges to eat. We never heard about those men again."

After Grandpa finished his story, we went to bed in our house that had changed completely since the death of our matriarch. My tears had slowed, and I slept deeply. The next day, Grandpa fixed eggs for breakfast. In the storeroom, he pulled out onions and potatoes for our evening meal. I looked forward to one of the family favorites, baked onions, which must date back to a precontact method of slow baking at the edges of a campfire, an original technique for cooking comfort food.

Baked Onions

Onions are an inexpensive cold-weather crop that stores well. This old-timey recipe is ridiculously easy and yet produces surprisingly tasty results. Baked onions are sweet with a slightly harsh onion flavor. Remember that ovens and cooking times vary. It is not complicated. Just put some onions into the oven to bake—and voilá!

1 onion per person
Salt, pepper, and butter, to taste

Preheat oven to 350 degrees. Place onions on middle rack with skin on. Bake onions until fork-tender, probably 45–55 minutes depending on onion size and precise oven temperature. To serve, cut off root ends with a sharp knife. Grab onion tops and squeeze until insides pop out. Discard skins. Serve onions topped with salt, pepper, and butter.

Young Love, Taverns, and Chartreuse

Without hyperbole, 1972 was one hell of a year. The state of Wisconsin had just lowered the age of majority from twenty-one to eighteen. Under this new law, an eighteen-year-old like myself was able to buy alcoholic beverages and vote in all elections.

Previous to this new law, wine, spirits, and beer had been available only to those twenty-one and older. The Vietnam War changed everything. If teenagers were being drafted to go to war and face possible death, the US government apparently believed they should be able to legally buy beer at home and, as an afterthought, vote for those politicians who were sending them off to war in the first place.

Prior to 1972, anybody younger than twenty-one was forbidden from accessing any kind of alcoholic beverage, except for "near beer" and apple beer. Apple beer was hard cider and therefore presented a loophole, even though it had alcohol content. It was one of the local cash crops in northeastern Wisconsin, was unregulated, and sold in all local grocery stores. However, under the new law, hard cider was now unavailable to anyone younger than eighteen.

Also prior to that new law, anyone eighteen or older could patronize certain taverns called beer taverns and buy near beer. This beer, which contained just 3.2 percent alcohol, was considered benign. Wine, spirits, and beer with a higher alcohol content

(4.5 percent and above) were available only to those above the age of twenty-one. Under the new law, eighteen-year-olds could buy any form of alcohol that they wished, eliminating all demand in Wisconsin for near beer and an entire class of tavern.

After I turned eighteen, I used to go from the reservation to a small Italian restaurant in downtown Green Bay near the Fox River. This was on South Washington Street. In those days, the production of each handmade pizza became a spectacle as the chef tossed the dough high in the air to make the crust. This process stretches the dough, allowing the chef to give it a uniform thickness without mashing it and creating a dry, crumbly crust. There would be a significant wait time between the order and the delivery of the handcrafted pizza. This being Wisconsin, it was expected that one would fill this time by drinking beer. I must confess, however, that I did not like the taste of beer. In those days, we northern Wisconsinites did not pair our beer with knockwurst or other appropriate cuisine. We drank it to achieve intoxication, taste be damned. Peer pressure, price, and brand loyalty were the factors that affected our beer consumption.

So, I drank beer while waiting for my cheese and sausage pizza. Several times at this Italian restaurant, I ordered and drank a whole pitcher of draft beer, even though this always took far longer than the management might have preferred. Served cold, the beer was warm by the time I got to the bottom. Besides that, a pitcher of beer got me too drunk. The pizza helped cut the effects of the alcohol.

After a while, I quit ordering pitchers of beer and instead began to order a longneck bottle of Pabst Blue Ribbon beer as my favorite drink. One bottle of PBR, made in Milwaukee, cost about a third of what a pitcher of lesser-known draft beer would cost, so I saved money, and that one bottle gave me a pleasant buzz without getting me rip-roaring drunk. Although flavored malt beverages were increasingly available in Green Bay–area taverns, specifically those aimed at younger drinkers, this Italian restaurant did not carry them. These easy-to-consume flavored malt beverages were generally artificially flavored and higher in alcohol content than regular beer. They also cost more than regular bottles of beer and came packaged in smaller cans and bottles, but they were a lot cooler. They were malt beer—something special.

One evening, sitting in that Italian restaurant, I had an epiphany. I ordered my usual longneck bottle of PBR and a bottle of Golden SunDrop Cola. I half-filled the accompanying highball glass, sans ice, with soda, then filled the remainder of the glass with beer. This concoction—with its lower alcohol content—made a delicious beer alternative. SunDrop was not developed in Wisconsin, but it was bottled there, and it sold well. This yellow-orange, citrus-flavored, highly caffeinated soda was originally developed in Missouri. I felt very sophisticated holding a glass of my unique mix in the dark wooden booth. I practiced looking nonchalant while holding my glass. It was a struggle, but I was leaving childhood and learning to have the tastes and identity of an adult.

Some of my struggles had nothing to do with class or ethnicity. I was hopelessly in love with a White girl from Shawano named Jane. Our school set the stage for this to happen with its strict policy of alphabetic seating. Indeed, any time students were summoned to the office, it was by alphabetical order. Our last names, this dark-haired girl's and mine, were separated by only two consonants. All the way through high school, I sat near her—to her left, to her right, in front of her, and in back of her, all within whispering distance. First thing in the morning, I followed her from our lockers, which were next to each other (she gave me her combination in case she forgot it), down the hallway to our homeroom. After morning announcements, we often walked to our first class together, swept along crowded hallways. Occasionally, these circumstances forced us into welcome but agonizingly brief skin contact.

The last semester we spent together in Shawano Senior High School was a long series of life-changing moments that ended with my early exit from public schools. It was like Bob Dylan said, there was "revolution in the air." I should have told Jane how I felt about her, but I never did.

One academic year later, one of my best friends from the Camp Four Hill work team was with Jane. They were an official item—David and that dark-haired girl from Shawano that I let slip through my fingers. I missed our high school days together, and now she was back in my life, but still at a distance.

One day, I found myself sitting with Jane in her second-floor apartment overlooking the bay of Green Bay. I had gone to visit my friend David, and he was not there. It was a warm, humid day. We were passing a joint and listening to her favorite album, the one by Yes with "I've Seen All Good People."

I was wearing my best pair of beaten-up jeans and a tee. Jane was wearing a short yellow sundress. Her bare shoulders were tanned like her long legs. She looked good in yellow, as it set off her dark hair. A large, floppy yellow hat, like the kind Janis Joplin wore, lay on the table. Neither of us wore shoes. Jane had sexy feet, with long toes, and her toenails were painted the same bright red as her fingernails and lips. We sat close enough that her long bare leg rubbed against my blue jeans. It took a lot of effort for me to keep my leg from shaking. She smelled like flowers.

A black light seemed to be providing the space with more than three dimensions. Jane leaned over and touched my hand—stroking my palm and then my fingers, from bottom to tip—while passing the glowing joint. I turned and fell into her deep brown eyes. Staring back into my eyes, she told me that she had always liked me in school and knew that I liked her. She said she had a crush on me in middle school. These were things that I had wanted to hear from her for years. *Jeez,* I thought, *why didn't I know this a month ago*? Now she was my best friend's girl.

We were sitting on a fold-out couch in her living room. The couch remained folded up. I had honor in those days and would not backstab my buddy, no matter the prize.

After finishing the joint, Jane stubbed it out in the ashtray, got up, and walked to the cupboard. She returned to the couch with a bottle of green Chartreuse. She sat back down and crossed her legs, and we drank the syrupy green fire on ice out of mismatched bar glasses pirated from area taverns.

In those days, liberating glassware was not that difficult. It was just not a good idea to try it at some mom-and-pop place where they counted the glasses. You'd walk into a large bar, order a couple of drinks—highballs for tall glasses, old-fashioneds for short glasses—drink them, put one under your coat, and walk out the door. Then you'd return the next day and repeat. Glasses were easy, dishes much harder, and shot glasses almost impossible to steal. This was how my friends and I furnished our apartments.

Thereafter, Chartreuse became my drink, because it brought back memories of Jane, the dark-haired girl from Shawano. The first time our group of friends had Chartreuse on the rocks was at a night club on Main Street. It was called My Brother's Place. The neighborhood was seedy and dark, and the tavern was brightly lit on the outside, but not so much on the inside. A few rookie Packers-player wannabes and other hangers-on sometimes decorated the place. One guy sold five-dollar bags of souvenir turf from Lambeau Field to any tourists. Occasionally, a would-be gangster could be found here, too. When our Chartreuse drinks arrived, they came in tall, square shot glasses with smaller squares of ice floating inside.

Chartreuse is deceptive. At first, it seems mild and benign, full of flowers. In fact, it is a bright green liquor made from 130 different herbs. But it is as strong as moonshine at 110 proof, or 55 percent alcohol. Even back then it was expensive because it is imported from France. It instantly became our group's drink.

So on that rainy afternoon, Jane and I sipped our Chartreuse and listened to a quiet song. We sat on the couch with my arm around her shoulder, my hand on her bare flesh, and my eyes on her crossed legs. Suddenly, she turned to face me and asked, "Why did you never ask me out for a date? I would have said yes. I knew that you wanted me. You want me now—I can tell."

I paused. In the movie of my mind, I pulled Jane close and kissed her. I should have taken her hand, stared into her dark brown eyes, and told her that I loved her—that I would still love her fifty years from now. I should have told her that I would get a job in Shawano and work there for the rest of my life, buy us a ranch house, get a station wagon. I should have asked her to marry me.

She was giving me one last chance to take her into my arms before losing her. Like a complete moron, I let her slip through my fingers. I mumbled, "I don't know why."

But I did know why. I lacked any sense of self-worth because I had a crummy homelife and a crazy White stepfather. His violent outbursts had so far kept anyone in the family from achieving any success.

Jane read my mind. "My mother is crazy too," she whispered into my ear. "You know that. You met her. She is majorly controlling. I stay in Green Bay to get away from her. If I didn't, I wouldn't have a life."

I did know Jane's mother. She worked in the courthouse and did not like me, period. Just after turning sixteen, I needed some papers signed by somebody from her office. She had a "Thank you for not smoking" sign on her desk. I had a pencil and a few minutes, so I turned it into a "Thank you for pot smoking" sign. Boy, she sure got upset. Another time, while I was in her office to get some other damn paper signed, she kept me waiting in the outer office until a cop showed up. Before anything else, she told me in front of the cop, "Leave my daughter the hell alone." This was a preemptive strike in case I ever wanted to date her daughter. Then she shoved a sheaf of legal papers into my hands. The cop looked at her, then at me, and said, "Get the hell out of here."

With this comment about her mother, Jane was reaching out to me, metaphorically, one final time. But I did nothing, and soon she disappeared into the turbulent seas of my memory.

Fifty-five years later, in a much different place, I met a woman who had been in our senior class. She knew Jane but not me. She told me that Jane had gotten into some legal trouble after I left the Shawano area. She'd spent a few months in custody, then a few more on probation.

Things went downhill for Jane upon her release. She was still rebellious after her incarceration, so her family had her committed to another kind of institution for her own good. By that time, the state of Wisconsin had reversed its decision and reinstated the age of majority at twenty-one.

I can still see Jane and Green Bay. I remember the places where I drank Chartreuse and ate local fish—walleye and smelt. She and I fell out of touch soon after that day in her apartment. Me? I landed in Kansas for a couple of years, eventually returning to live in Madison. Fifty-plus years have passed, and I still think about Jane, about what kind of life we might have made together. She had such a long, difficult road to travel. I wish my very dear friend well.

Pan-Fried Smelt or Other Small Fish

One fall, a couple of weeks after the tourist season ended, I was sitting in a tavern in Door County's Baileys Harbor, just up the road from Green Bay, listening to local fishermen talk about smelt. They had been there awhile, as the empty beer bottles in front of them attested. The younger one said the easiest way to catch smelt was to stretch pantyhose around a coat hanger, walk along the shore, and scoop them up. His companion, a grizzled old-timer, said his preferred method of fishing was to simply wade in the shallows, scoop the smelt out with his hands, and put them on the shore. He added that the easiest method for cleaning them was to bite off the heads. The entrails apparently came off with the heads. I presume he spit the heads out. But his younger friend chuckled, so I am not sure of the biting-the-heads-off method. This story may be apocryphal.

Cleaning these little fish is time consuming, even if you are just biting off their heads. If they are cleaned in the traditional way, removing the heads is optional. Tourists remove the heads with a knife, not teeth. The entire smelt, including the bones, can be eaten. If the fish is served with the head attached, eat the head. Bass and other pan fish must be deboned.

1–2 quarts small fish, cleaned
1 cup flour
2 cups vegetable oil, or enough to cover two-thirds of the fish
Salt and pepper, to taste

Clean the fish by first placing it on a board. With one hand, hold the fish; with the other, make a shallow cut from the anal vent up to the head. Cut the back of the neck, through the spine, just below the head. Grab the head, twist, and pull. The entrails should follow. Rinse the entire fish, using your thumb to scrape any hard-to-remove entrails. After cleaning, let fish dry.

Dredge fish in flour. Heat vegetable oil in a frying pan. Gently place the fish in the pan, careful not to splash the hot grease. Cook fish for 2 minutes per side. Serve with salt and pepper to taste.

Bikes, Frybread, and Grasshopper Tacos

When I was in my early twenties and bored as an inhabitant of small-town America, I moved from the northern woods of the Menominee Reservation to Madison to attend college and then stayed on. For most of the next twenty-five years, I lived in a variety of small apartments throughout the metropolitan area. This counts for one lifetime in anybody's book. It was the true beginning of my foodie adventures, starting with Latin cuisine—specifically, tacos.

The area's geography favors dairy cattle and farm produce like corn, beans, tomatoes, and lettuce. Madison lies at the pointy southern end of a fertile green triangle that extends north on Wisconsin Highway 151 to Green Bay near the Fox River; west along Wisconsin Highway 29, past Shawano to Wausau; and back south to Madison on Wisconsin Highway 51, which overlays the ancient Ontonagon foot trail. This area includes parts of the Wisconsin River valley as well as parts of the Wolf River valley. If this sounds like a tortuously slow road system, it is. In Wisconsin—a geographic region crowded with lakes, marshes, and rivers—a direct route from point A to point B never exists. This is also true for the city of Madison.

In the early 1970s, "downtown Madison" consisted of just State Street. The University of Wisconsin's Library Mall anchored the southwestern end of the street, and the Capitol anchored the northeastern end. In between were gas stations, a few taverns, a liquor store, a bakery, and a couple of porn shops—I mean, adult novelty stores. Also, a taco joint. A few miles away, a convenience store across the street from the Town of Madison Police Department on Fish Hatchery Road sold beer twenty-four hours a day, seven days a week, 365 days a year. This was real beer, too—not the 3.2 stuff sold when I was a kid. I biked to this oasis regularly.

In those days, the metro area of Madison was nothing like the sleek, safe, upscale shopping area of today. According to an early article in the *Isthmus* newspaper, State Street was "filled with gas stations and Mexican restaurants." Although I wouldn't have described State Street that way, as I don't remember any actual Mexican restaurants, this statement contains some truth—there were a few places to find Mexican food. Perhaps because of my love for my mother's tacos, I sought them out in Madison. My favorite place was a walk-up window on State that served a soft-shell taco made right in front of you. Perhaps this was the Mexican restaurant the early *Isthmus* article was referencing. This was no franchise.

The tacos came wrapped in foil, and the chef passed them to diners through the walk-up window opening, each one for a buck. The food and the vibe of the place were Southern California cool. Acid rock from a local radio station was usually blasting from big speakers hanging from the ceiling. The long-haired guys behind the counter always seemed agreeable, as though they might be stoned. Since State Street was open only to buses, the only way to approach the restaurant was by bus, bike, or foot. There was a glass door next to the walk-up window and some interior seating in a long narrow dining room, but I never went inside.

Near the restaurant was a hippie bakery where people from all over the Midwest came to buy loaves of whole wheat and apricot pit bread. Raw apricot pits are toxic, but they are naturally high in a substance called amygdalin, which is a raw form of laetrile.

Laetrile has been touted as a cancer-fighting drug, but the FDA banned it because of its toxicity. This bakery made the bread using apricot pits and naturally occurring amygdalin instead of the synthetic laetrile, so they were technically legal. You had to ask at the counter for that particular bread. Many cancer patients being treated at University of Wisconsin hospitals came there to buy both bread and hope. It was the very last stop for some of those customers who lost their fight.

The owner-baker was a stoner guy with the first artificially bright red hair I had ever seen. In the 1970s, his picture was in the newspaper when he occasionally ran for public office. It was rumored that he sold things other than bread, like sheets of shiny paper with hundreds of teeny tiny pictures of Disney's Pluto the Dog, upon request. Perhaps those pictures were soaked in another illegal substance—lysergic acid diethylamide, or LSD.

This owner-baker next to the Mexican food shop was a friendly guy who enjoyed talking. In our conversations, he always seemed sincere about the bread. It wasn't sold as a cure, but as part of an anticancer therapy. He considered his bakery to be providing a needed service, seeing that it was the only source for what he called an alternative option. He also made some killer sugar cookies. So, I often walked my bike from the bakery over to the taco window.

If I may digress, again, my bicycle was an important part of my identity at this time. Filling up my 1968 Plymouth Satellite Road Runner, a two-door hardtop with a 318-cubic-inch engine and three-speed automatic transmission, had become prohibitively expensive. My maroon behemoth held twenty gallons, and I thought the fifty-five-cents-a-gallon price of gas was really steep, although not as bad as the sixty-plus-cents-a-gallon on the highway.

About this same time, ten-speed bicycles became ubiquitous and cheap. Travel across town was much quicker by bike than by car because of paralyzing car traffic and scarce parking. Needing no insurance, gasoline, or even regular maintenance, a ten-speed bike offered independence. It cost hardly anything to make the scene on State Street. All you had to do was pedal.

Once I saw an advertisement in a local throw-away paper for Billy Beer at "ROCK BOTTOM PRICES," so I pedaled the seven miles from Park Street to Monona. Entering the warehouse-like store, I saw several huge pallets stacked full of Billy Beer sitting near the front of the store. This was the beer promoted by Jimmy Carter's younger brother. It lasted for only one year, from 1977 to 1978, and it was rank. Billy Beer was being discounted and sold at ninety-nine cents a six-pack. Even at that price, I felt overcharged. Maybe the trip was for nothing, but I still enjoyed the adventure.

This freedom of movement, this getting to know every bump, dip, and hill of an area, must have been akin to the feeling early Indians had when riding their first horses. I was a first bicycle Indian, one of the first to choose bike over car, before it was touted as a green alternative form of transportation. I often rode up or down State Street a couple times a day, stealthily avoiding the blue-coat patrols. In those not-so-innocent times, much like these much meaner times, my Algonquian profile attracted unwelcome attention.

Biking altered where, what, and how I ate. Plus, I was an undergrad at UW–Madison—swelled head and all—and my new status required new foods.

After patronizing the bakery, on a typical day, I would walk my pony to the taco stand and order with my surplus change. My request then kick-started an assembly process conducted, every day, by just one hippie. He was a well-oiled machine. He first took a large corn tortilla from a stack and placed it on a sheet of aluminum foil. The tortilla and foil were then placed inside the bottom plate of a steamer. This unwieldy cast-iron contraption was coated with a patina of an indeterminate age. When closed, the lid of the steamer resembled a tortilla press—who knows, maybe it was made by the same factory that makes real tortilla presses. There was a foot pedal that controlled a steam vent in the base of the steamer. It always took the hippie, who sat on a stool, *three* leg pumps, resulting in three blasts of steam, to finish the taco shell.

Next, the steaming tortilla received a scoop of taco meat. One scoop exactly. This taco meat was cheap, finely ground beef and spices simmered for hours (possibly days) to form a greasy, reddish brown substance. Either this recipe for taco meat is universally known or there is a factory somewhere that produces tons of the stuff and sells it everywhere. Think Taco Bell, Taco John's, or any taco joint that you have ever visited. I have eaten this identical taco meat, maybe even coming from the same cow, in many Midwestern places. However, I've never had this generic-tasting taco meat on the East or West Coasts. Obviously then, this particular taco cow species is unable to climb the Alleghenies or the Sierra Nevada. It's not bad tasting, this taco meat, and it's been the norm for the past fifty years.

The next step was adding a spoonful of diced white onion, ladled out with a white plastic teaspoon. The precisely cut bits of white onions floated upon the silky surface of the meat. Then, the attendant took a pair of tongs and grasped a heap of shredded iceberg lettuce. He spread the strands evenly across the onions and meat. Iceberg lettuce is the defining vegetable base of most fast-food tacos sold in America today. Even back then, shredded lettuce was being used in place of the more authentic cilantro as the tacos' leafy green ingredient. The Madison restaurant worker always included a generous helping of lettuce on the tacos—it added great bulk and perceived value. In those days, lettuce cost a quarter a head. An urban legend of the day claimed that a head of lettuce could get a person high. Who knows? In the cold climate, the grease of the meat sauce congealed on the bottom edges of the lettuce and helped to keep the taco drip-free.

The last vegetable to be added was diced tomatoes. The juice of the tomatoes mixed with the grease and helped to bind the taco. Tomatoes are a relatively recent taco adaptation, coming out of Southern California where tomatoes are usually plentiful. The Madison taco place always used fresh tomatoes, which must have been difficult and pricey to acquire in wintry Wisconsin in those days, unless they had a greenhouse. The colors of the Mexican flag—white, green, and red—are represented by the taco's white onions, green lettuce, and red tomatoes.

The last ingredient to complete the taco was the cheese. In most of America—excluding the East and West Coasts and maybe the Southwest—taco cheese is almost always shredded yellow cheddar, possibly with a handful of Monterey Jack mixed in. Instead of being used as a flavor accent, cheese is used in modern tacos as a necessary ingredient. The cheese overwhelms the other ingredients. I have eaten very authentic tacos that use no cheese at all. Other times, I've eaten tacos made with feta cheese—yum. The joint in Madison always used shredded cheddar, something abundant and local in Wisconsin.

Finally, the taco joint hippie rolled and compressed the taco—using the sheet of aluminum foil as one uses a bamboo sheet to make sushi—to transform the pile of ingredients into a delicious treat. It was presented in a simple brown paper bag. I exchanged cash for the taco through the sliding glass panel in the window. I didn't even have to get off my bike.

The shop had one vegetarian option: a bean taco. It was also a buck. A companion of mine once ordered a taco without the meat and without the beans. The clerk just shrugged and made the taco with lettuce, onions, tomatoes, and an eighth-ounce of shredded cheese on a corn tortilla. It was still a dollar. I had a bite of the meatless, beanless taco (the third option), and it really didn't taste much different from the meat taco. Yes, the meat added another dimension of flavor, but not as much as one might think. Since there was no difference in price between the three kinds of tacos, the meat taco was the better bargain on my budget.

My favorite spots to eat a couple tacos were the Memorial Union Terrace, with a priceless view of Lake Mendota—I saw Iggy Pop do a couple of sets there, once—or at the Capitol Square, watching government officials at play. These were great tacos because they were simple, honest, and healthy. Such a restaurant was never a destination for adventure, but it was always a stop on the way to some adventure.

Sometimes the best new stuff is the old stuff in new wrappings. A taco is a prime example—an Indigenous Southwestern soul food that has lasted through many reincarnations. From ancient times until my childhood—the time period known by anthropologists as the ethnographic present, or an idealized "traditional past"—the taco has been a simple sandwich. Just assemble a round corn flatbread and a filling, and then fold the bread to hold the ingredients inside. The tortilla needs to be thick and pliable enough to fold. Once it is folded, it becomes a container ready for stuffing. Fresh and frozen tortillas require extra preparation because they must be cooked. Dried, right out of the cellophane wrapper, and boxed tortillas are good to go immediately, although they do taste a little dry, like eating a mummy.

Hominy corn, made from dent or field corn, is the main ingredient composing the tortilla shell, and it has been an Indigenous mainstay for a couple thousand years, at least. Tortillas aren't made with dried sweet corn or with cornmeal, a meal made from dried field corn ground to a coarse or relatively coarse consistency. Neither are tortillas made from corn flour, a cornmeal ground to a finer consistency. Instead, tortillas are made with hominy—ground, dried corn kernels that have been soaked in water and a bit of slaked lime. Bags of this masa harina can be found in most supermarkets. This is a pretreated corn flour that has been processed with a lime solution to loosen hulls from the kernels. It makes a softer, more pliable dough that is gluten-free. Lime also reacts with niacin, making the vitamin more accessible for use by the digestive tract.

Before contact with Europeans, the Menominees did not make tortillas with their multicolored corn. Instead, they collected the ash from a fire exclusively made from maple wood, the tree of life. The ash, mixed with water, served as the source of lye, or calcium hydroxide. The women added dried corn kernels to this water and lye mixture, and through a process of alternately soaking and boiling, the outer layer or hull of the corn kernels loosened. The women rubbed the corn to complete the process of removing the kernels' thin husks and then rinsed the kernels to remove all traces of the caustic natural lye. Once the outer layer was removed, the inner parts of the kernel swelled, perhaps doubling or tripling the original size of the kernel. Finally, the processed "hull corn" kernels were "put up," or dried.

Hull corn is known among most Algonquin tribes, which are related American and Canadian tribes located on the northern edge of where corn can grow, and farther north as well, wherever birch trees grow. Hull corn, as Algonquins know it, or hominy, as Mexican people know it, is a wet form of popcorn. That familiar can of hominy at the supermarket is a commercial version of this Algonquin favorite. In European cuisines, dried corn kernels are added to hot oil and made to pop. In Indigenous cultures, dried corn kernels are added to lye and boiled. One method uses thermal means, while the other uses chemical means.

Preserved hull corn, either dried or canned, can be added to a pot of boiled pork hocks to make hull-corn soup. My grandma made hull-corn soup for the family using multicolored hull corn—red, yellow, orange, and brown kernels—a couple of times a month from late summer, through the winter, and into late spring. She kept several quart jars of preserved hull corn under the stairs leading down to the basement, in the pantry that Uncle

Donny built. Grandma also kept burlap bags—pantyhose also worked well—filled with ground, dried hull corn mixed in a fifty-fifty ratio with dried, ground venison. She hung these bundles from hooks on the wall in the coal room. This corn and venison mix was a wonderful snack on cold winter afternoons. A delicious variation can be made with the addition of dried currants, cranberries, or blueberries. My tribe's use of corn involved no tortillas, which were exotic to me in my early Madison days.

In times past, tortillas were hand-formed, and each one was unique. But now, cooks place rounds of dough on a metal press and flatten them into discs of uniform thickness. This standardization in the 1970s was part of the process of the McDonaldization of America. Chain restaurants turned the tortilla from a chewy, savory piece of corn flatbread into a giant, fried Frito corn chip that disintegrates into several pieces after the first bite.

The filling within the folded flatbread, whether handmade or store-bought, can be anything, because the taco is perfect for spontaneous meals. Most home cooks use beans, red meat, poultry, and fish, but other ingredients such as iguanas, insects, avocados, chili peppers, and cacti are also possible.

In my search for authenticity, I once ate a taco with a mound of warm, crispy grasshoppers in a tortilla shell. These particular grasshoppers had been grilled on a large, flat, black iron skillet, about the size of a manhole cover. They were prepared at an open-air market over an open fire of mesquite. These were gourmet grasshoppers, seasoned only by a fast kiss of salt and chilis. My friend had placed them in a plastic bag the day after they were made in a small town in Zacatecas, Mexico, and hand-carried them on the airplane for me. She knew I was a foodie and was interested in authentic Indigenous foods. If she hadn't taken such pains delivering them—and telling me about it—I would have declined the delicacy.

First, I nuked those critters to get them hot and to kill any tape worm parasites. After I folded the tortilla shell onto itself, the grasshoppers weren't even visible. I don't remember the grasshoppers tasting *bad*, but I do remember that the legs kept getting caught in my teeth, so afterward my teeth needed a good floss and brush. Grasshopper legs aren't like chicken legs, with bits of meat hanging from the bone. They taste exactly like you'd imagine—like biting into some indigestible bit of bug. Definitely a little more salt, a bigger squeeze of fresh lime juice, and a longer pour of tequila would have helped with the texture. And I don't mean to disrespect the humble grasshopper. They are a valuable source of oil in a subsistence diet. Oils and fats are hard to find in nature without dairy cow butterfat and olive presses.

Unlike a pile of crunchy grasshoppers, a slice of breaded and deep-fried avocado on a tortilla shell makes a delicious taco, rich and savory. Fresh fish, pulled pork marinated in red jalapeño peppers, chicken in chocolaty mole sauce—the variations are endless.

A Mexican taco, at its essence, is simple—just ground meat, something vegetal like cilantro or onions, a squeeze of fresh lime, and pepper sauce on a tortilla. This authentic Southwestern taco has become the nouveau cuisine taco of the 2000s in many trendy Anglo restaurants.

Sometime in the early 1960s, fast-food restaurants appropriated the taco. Bulging, cheese-festooned tacos began to appear in gorgeous glossy pictures on the brightly lit menu walls of Mexican restaurants. Tacos gained in popularity across the United States as inexpensive and quick meals. Tacos and burritos can also tolerate heat lamps admirably, a great asset. Fast-food Mexican restaurants joined drive-in hamburger restaurants as American highway icons. Fast-food places, which emerged in Southern California, grew alongside the thriving new car culture.

Tacos of the American Southwest became accessible to all manner of people through these first chain restaurants. It's how my mom first learned about them. And as these nuevo-Mexican restaurant franchises began to increase in popularity, the taco became standardized. Their use of universal, cheap ingredients created standard expectations of what a taco should look like. Taco shells were redesigned to not drip or break apart. They were molded and dried to create a solid V that resonated with a satisfying crunch when chewed.

Fast-food tacos require many hands to assemble from quantities of prepared ingredients—otherwise, they become slow-food tacos. Therefore, they are still labor intensive. It takes a trained franchise restaurant crew to construct them in a timely manner, usually from a line of stainless steel bins filled with ingredients from a detailed corporate recipe. The mechanization of this process divides the employees into tiers. Some take the order. Others do the preparation work—slicing and dicing raw ingredients. Others heat the cooked ingredients, and still others perform the marriage of ingredients with tortilla shells. The result is an endless line of identical looking and tasting tacos made by a bevy of faceless workers in an antiseptically clean environment. They are profitable.

My family joined this culinary revolution before I moved to Madison. In the late 1960s, Mom spent weekdays commuting back and forth from Keshena on the Menominee Indian Reservation to the northwest part of Green Bay, where she was working on a teaching degree at the university. At some point she must have visited a Mexican fast-food joint and discovered that she liked tacos. She found a way to duplicate this menu item at home. Her homemade version was so labor intensive and time consuming that she cooked Mexican style only on special occasions when several family members, especially my sister Mary, were available to help. Otherwise, making tacos was just too much of a drain.

We never ate tacos in any season other than spring and summer, when fresh lettuce, onions, and tomatoes fit our food budget.

The endeavor was always on a Saturday afternoon when all seven of us were home.

These were happy times. During those bright, puffy-cloud afternoons of the Wisconsin summer, my mother and eldest sister transformed the kitchen table into a landing pad for dozens of plates and orbiting plastic tubs filled with dissected vegetables. The largest plastic tubs held thin slices of iceberg lettuce. We didn't rip and tear at a head of iceberg. We respectfully trimmed green watery slices off the sides using the wavy-bladed bread knife. A medium-sized bowl held the shredded Mexican-style cheese. Mom bought bags of this expensive grated cheese blend instead of slicing her own much-cheaper block of cheddar or free commodity cheese. My mom was trying to give us authenticity—to give us a taste of the real world, something not available anywhere on the reservation. And the directions on the side of the taco kit box said very clearly, in English, to use shredded *Mexican* cheese. It is also true that using shredded cheese from the store is a lot easier than shredding cheese at home by hand. Still, had the box said to grate some commodity cheese, then for authenticity's sake, I'm sure Mom would have done that instead.

From my mom's perspective, I suspect, the most important thing about our taco dinners was that they involved the entire family, bringing us together in their time-consuming preparation. We always entered and exited our home through the kitchen, never using the front door that opened onto the living room, so we couldn't help but take part. Many hands worked to toss ingredients together in the whirlwind assembly line creating identical tacos.

From the chaos came my mom's handcrafted tacos. She made tacos because she loved us. They were certainly not the traditional Menominee foods that she had grown up eating, garnered from the freshwater springs in the woods surrounding Zoar and the Bass Lake area. Neither were we a traditional Menominee family, not anymore, as we had survived too many years on the outside to be reservation traditionals.

Indian tacos made from frybread did not exist then. Maybe I simply didn't notice them, but I don't think that I ever heard of an Indian taco until the 1980s. I was in my midthirties and attending an intertribal powwow in Milwaukee when my mom, then a teacher at the Indian School in the old lighthouse on Lake Michigan, asked if I wanted one. Nowadays, Indian tacos can be found at most powwows across the United States. Although frybread and white flour have been around for perhaps two hundred years as "traditional" Native foods, the Indian taco has not. Nevertheless, its universal appearance among diverse North American tribes, maybe in the 1970s, makes it seem like a tradition, even if it's barely fifty years old.

There is a huge difference between regular tacos, served on corn shells, and Indian tacos, served on frybread, even though the fillings are similar. The big difference is the use of large, doughy, white flour tortillas for Indian tacos, which are deep-fried in boiling lard. The flat, unleavened corn tortilla is fashioned from hominy meal and grilled.

As with all American Indian dishes, there are just two ways to make Indian tacos: the first way is to make them exactly the same way that they have always been made; Indians are nothing if not traditional about food. The second way to make Indian tacos—that is, to make any changes to the original method—is the wrong way to make Indian tacos. So, stick with tradition.

Across Indian Country, Indian taco fillings include shredded lettuce, sliced onions, taco meat (ground beef with chili seasonings), beans, tomatoes, taco sauce, and shredded cheddar cheese. I'm sure that in the history of powwows and Indian tacos, some unauthorized commodity flour (perhaps Gold Medal instead of Blue Bird) or cheese has probably made its way into the serving line, but I avert my eyes. The powwow assembly lines resemble our family's. Onto a plate-sized piece of frybread, cooks deposit a scoop of seasoned hamburger. Then, beans to float upon the meat lake. To this, powwow cooks add tomatoes, lettuce, onions, and cheese. Taco sauce and hot peppers are popular additions, available on the counter. Depending on the popularity of the venue, exotic ingredients like sour cream and guacamole might also be options.

This Indian taco meal is presented like a tostado and not folded like a taco. Such a feast is a large, unwieldy meal. It isn't easy to keep one's plate drip-free while eating. You must sit down and concentrate with a knife, fork, and many napkins. A further problem is the difficulty of balancing an Indian taco on a flimsy paper plate. Even worse, sometimes the oil from an exceptionally greasy piece of frybread will leak through the plate. Then it becomes a race to find an empty table before the plate disintegrates. My own best technique is to eat the toppings and leave the frybread till last. Then it is possible to pick up the greasy, soggy piece of frybread and eat it in one hand, keeping the other hand grease-free. Some people use a knife to cut the frybread into bite-size pieces as they work their way through the meal. They have patience.

Any piece of lard-soaked frybread has lots of calories, upward of seven hundred. In addition, as any piece of frybread is physically larger than a standard tortilla shell, all that added acreage requires more toppings than a standard commercial taco, also increasing the calorie count. Indian tacos are deadly—and delicious. Who can resist warm bread topped with savory deliciousness?

I don't remember ever seeing my full-blood Menominee grandfather eat a piece of frybread. I mean, he must have. It was ubiquitous and around at many meals when he was still alive. But frybread takes a lot of work. The cook has to prepare the dough by mixing flour, salt, baking soda (or yeast), and water. Some tribes insist that Blue Bird flour is essential. After mixing, the cook pats the dough into discs, which look more like small pizzas than tortillas. Then, the last stage is deep frying the dough patties in dangerously hot lard in a large, deep vessel. When they rise to the surface and begin to turn golden brown, they are done. After being pulled out and drained, they are ready to eat.

Most North American Indians recognize frybread as an Indian soul food. The reason is simple. Those amber waves of grain, or wheat fields, and the modern-day Indian reservation system were established about the same time. Until the mid-1800s, wheat flour and rising agents were not generally available in the Americas as the land was occupied by Indians. White flour became a commodity food given to American Indians in the mid- to late 1800s, after Russian wheat with its high gluten content began to be grown on the Great Plains. Once emptied of Indians, the American plains made great wheat country. Mixed with water and fried in lard, wheat could be turned into frybread—a short-term survival food. Frybread has too much fat to be a daily part of a healthy diet. Nonetheless, many Indians eat it daily. Wheat flour and American cheese still form the basis of government commodity surplus foods for American Indians.

Apart from North American Indian tribes, just about everybody else on the planet uses corn flour to make taco tortillas. That thin circle of dough requires just a quick turn on a griddle or a steamer to cook. Frybread is never quick, but it is filling and aromatic. Most important, it brings families and friends together around the table.

Grasshopper Tacos

This is more a Mexican dish than something found often in North America. Grasshoppers are high in protein and fat—both important elements for survival. Friends gave me roasted grasshoppers when they returned from a trip to Vera Cruz state in Mexico. I froze the grasshoppers that I did not eat right away. In the central states of the United States, field grasshopper populations peak in September, so this might be a good time to harvest specimens for this dish.

Prepare the grasshoppers by twisting off their heads. The entrails should come out with the heads. The entrails are edible, but they may have parasites. Next, remove the wings and legs. Spread the grasshopper bodies on a cookie sheet and roast at a low temperature (180–200 degrees) until they are dried out and crunchy, about 30 minutes. Grasshoppers can be roasted with salt and lime juice for a stand-alone snack.

Serves 2 to 4 people

1 (12-ounce) can refried beans, or homemade refried beans
6 taco shells
1 cup roasted grasshoppers
2 teaspoons salt
Jalisco hot pepper sauce

Spread beans on taco shells. Salt grasshoppers and divide them among the taco shells. Set tacos on a cookie sheet or taco holder and heat in a 300-degree oven for 15 minutes. Serve with hot sauce and beer.

Frozen Mescal Worms

For a short spell around 1973, my cousin Jammer was going to college, while I was doing my best to remain underground. We were sharing an apartment over the once-elegant movie theater, the large expansive one located on Grand Avenue. It had fallen on hard times. No, it was not playing pornography—not in Wausau, Wisconsin, near the Menominee Reservation. But it had seen better days. It was losing revenue to the new multiscreen palace out in the suburbs. The theater was undergoing a major restoration, but the bills still needed to be paid, so movies were being run in the midst of demolition and construction. We watched many discounted horror flicks that summer surrounded by plaster dust and plastic drapes. The especially cheesy *Amityville Horror* still scares me. Besides discovering the horror genre of film, Jammer and I also discovered that mescal has a worm in each bottle.

Wausau is a small city in north-central Wisconsin. It is on a major north-south highway that overlies the Superior Trail, an Indigenous foot trail that follows the east bank of the Wisconsin River. Sawmills and paper mills continue to influence the local economy. The community is filled with industrious people who take great pride in their German heritage. Beer, sausage, and cheese are iconic markers.

As part of that social inheritance, a tavern offering food service directly across the street from our front windows opened for business at seven in the morning, every day. A sandwich board sign, like a painter's easel, in front of the double doors announced the early-morning opening time. Every morning at 6:45, the German owner brought that sign outside. It sat there in the rain, in the snow, and in the Wisconsin River valley heat until the 1:45 a.m. closing time.

I never visited the place at seven in the morning, and indeed, I never actually set foot inside the bar at all. This was one of the places that our uncle Donny warned Jammer and me about, saying that we should stay the hell out of that joint. Some hard-drinking men hung out there. Since we were more interested in meeting like-minded females than in drinking, this place never registered on our radar. Sometimes we thought Uncle Donny just did not want us to hang out at bars.

From our lofty front window, I watched bar regulars arrive within five minutes of the door's first opening. I believe that most of these early-morning customers were nearby factory workers who had just finished overnight shifts and were stopping in on their way home. These were not dedicated early-morning drinkers. Perhaps they worked at one of the nearby dairies and were tired of drinking milk the entire night.

The building that housed the tavern was old, probably part of the original downtown, which predated even the ornate Grand Theater, where we were living.

Old-time Wisconsin Germans are orderly, disciplined, and the bearers of grand food and alcohol traditions. Their taverns were public houses where you could get breakfast, lunch, or supper. They were places where beer, sodas, coffee, fried eggs, grilled pork chops, and wieners with sauerkraut were on the menu nineteen hours a day. In addition to this bill of fare, the menu staple in this north-central part of the state is a cold glass of Leinenkugel's draft beer accompanied by an even colder shot of peppermint schnapps. This local Wisconsin beer is brewed only ninety miles west of Wausau in the Chippewa River valley. Beers made in Milwaukee, to the southeast, include all of the usual suspects: Miller, Pabst, and Schlitz. But any beer purist living in Wausau would obviously choose Uncle Leinie's, the local nickname for the Leinenkugel brewery. This affectionate nickname partially springs from the company's corporate largesse, especially when it comes to community events. I was once a participant at one of them.

Five years before I lived in Wausau with Jammer, I was hitch-hiking in Chippewa Falls on the Fourth of July weekend. It was getting late in the afternoon, and I had to find a place to bed down. I had a full backpack with sleeping bag and tent, so that was no problem. I just needed daylight to find a spot to set up the tent. My ride was heading due east while I was going north, and so I jumped off about twenty miles south of Chippewa Falls.

A couple of young men picked me up. The driver owned a Fathom blue 1970 Chevy SS Chevelle. From the middle of the tiny back seat, I saw a home-installed Hurst linkage manual gear-shift mounted on the floor right in front of me. He wanted to show it off. The car left a trail of smoke and rubber as he speed-shifted through the gears. He then reached into his ashtray and pulled out a joint, which he lit using the car's cigarette lighter. Passing me the joint, he said his name was Dave. I told him that I was heading north to Lake Superior and needed a place to camp. He knew the perfect spot—a public campground near the fairgrounds. It was an island in the Wisconsin River. But first, we were heading to the local Fourth of July celebration at the fairgrounds, and my hosts were loaded for bear.

I did not quite believe them when they told me their plan. "Every Fourth of July," Dave told me, "Leinenkugel's brings a truckload of beer and gives it away. After tapping the keg, you provide your own glass and they fill it up for you. You can have as much beer as you want." That sounded too good to be true. Sensing that disbelief, Dave and his friend insisted that I accompany them. "Seriously, you can have as much beer as you want," Dave said. "Most people bring those dinky, plastic sixteen-ounce cups. Last year, we saw a couple of guys bring steel milk pails. The brewery guys did not bat an eye. They filled them up, and those guys took their full buckets of beer over to some shade, sat down, and drank them."

Looking around me, I saw three five-gallon plastic buckets on the floor in the back seat. The driver caught my eye in the mirror: "Yup, we're going to fill these buckets with beer and then spend the night drinking them. We'll show you." I was hooked.

We arrived at the fairgrounds complex around seven that evening, still daylight in the northern midsummer. My new friends drove me over to the campground parking lot and helped me set up my tent. That took about ten minutes. Then we jumped back into the Chevy, and Dave drove to the main lot, making wide, fast S-curves, spraying gravel with his oversize rear tires, and finally parking near the fairgrounds entrance. We got out, each grabbed a plastic bucket, and walked directly to the beer giveaway.

There were only a few people milling about. Following my hosts' lead, I plopped cross-legged to the ground. The three of us sat facing one another and waited about an hour until they began serving beer.

It was everything they said. On our first walk-through, we were given nine gallons of beer among the three of us. But, not to worry, within a few minutes several other acquaintances showed up to help us drink all that beer. When we began to fear an end to our feast, we poured the rest of our beer into one bucket, and two of us went back for more. By that point, I was ready to go back to my tent, more than ready, but I helped with the beer run at least twice more. Dave and his gang had planned well.

Finally, I went back to my tent and spent a comfortable night. After waking up, I stumbled my way to the showers, then walked out onto the midway looking for a cup of coffee. I found one and continued my walk, eventually reaching the place where Leinenkugel's had distributed the free beer. The entire lawn had been cleaned up. I might have imagined the whole thing. I headed back to the concession stand for another boring cup of coffee.

When I lived in Wausau with Jammer several years later, our mornings were pretty boring, too. I made coffee for one, or occasionally two, first thing in the morning. I used to smoke cigarettes in those days, and so I would carry a cup of coffee with me downstairs to Grand Avenue where I would stand, smoke, and greet the rising sun. Grand Avenue is, well, grand—a lovely locale to people watch. I would nod to certain patrons of the bar across the street as they came into view. Beer lowers social barriers.

Jammer had his own morning routine—no routine. He did not smoke or drink coffee, tea, or cola. Each morning, he put on some clothes, and boom, there he was. In all our years together, two lifetimes at least, I always thought that was the strangest thing about him.

Jammer used to enjoy big parties. He was going to college to become a radio disc jockey. These were the days of cassette tapes. Soon after he arrived in Wausau, he slipped into providing deejay services at birthday parties and weddings. This is common enough today, but back then, there were few deejays. With thousands of dollars of equipment and his collection of just about every song released on vinyl, plus his snappy repartee, Jammer was in big demand. I occasionally assisted. We did some partying.

Trips to acquire liquor for parties and other personal use became a new routine. I do not think that we ever walked to a liquor store while living in Wausau. We drove. Liquor stores in Wisconsin are a bit like convenience stores everywhere else. I have even purchased canisters of nitrous oxide gas at a liquor store to charge my whipped cream dispenser. If a Wisconsin liquor store does not have it, you do not need it.

On our booze runs, we always drove across the Wisconsin

River on the bridge next to the old train station, the one that appears in the Wausau Insurance commercials. That old train station was then a Chinese restaurant. We used to stop there for a drink called a Volcano. It was something big that waitresses lit on fire before serving. As soon as we figured out that the fire was burning up the alcohol, we asked them to not light it on fire, and they obliged.

Due to the confusing layout of one-way streets in downtown Wausau, we often found it more convenient to drive by this Chinese restaurant on the way out of town. Actually, we regularly got lost and invariably ended up on the wrong side of the river. Turning around at the first stoplight to avoid the crowds of Lutherans at nearby churches, we found the liquor store that we adopted as our own. The Chinese joint was just down the street to the right.

Fortified by a volcanic drink, our favorite way out of town and back to the reservation was to drive past the Frank Lloyd Wright house on Highland Park Boulevard almost at the top of the big hill overlooking the Wisconsin River. At night during the holidays, this was a stunning view.

Anyway, that is how we came to settle upon this particular liquor store. It was the most convenient liquor store on the west side of the river. Also, it was well lit, had walls made of clear glass on three sides, and had a big parking lot. Compared to all of the places on the reservation that sold booze—hell, anything in Shawano, too—this store was bigger. Its stock was incredibly varied, in many colors, sizes, and shapes. It felt like Disneyland to us young fellas.

One evening at this liquor store, after great discussion over the relative merits of booze in general, Jammer and I eventually settled on buying Monte Alban Mezcal. This stuff was some of the cheapest booze in the store. It was not as if we had sophisticated palates. But mescal's reputation tempted our youthful machismo, and besides, there was a worm in each bottle. How could two late-adolescent boys resist?

Even after we had each drunk a half of the bottle, even after teasing, daring, double-daring, and finally shaming, neither one of us would eat the mescal worm. That is a nasty, evil-looking invertebrate. Eventually, we decided to place the worm in a Ziploc bag and toss it in the freezer. The alcoholic stupor resulting from downing half a bottle of mescal felt kind of like that worm in the bottle looked—not altogether pleasant.

I am embarrassed to say that it did not take long for us to have a bag full of mescal worms aging in the freezer. The owner of the liquor store got used to us hanging around, and we had long conversations. Jammer was like that. You could not help liking him. We told the liquor store owner about our bag of frozen mescal worms at home. He explained how the worms were psychedelic, that they would get us high. What an inside tip.

One evening, while watching *Barnaby Jones*, who we knew as Jed from the *Beverly Hillbillies*, after dares and double-dares, we decided to try those mescal worms. We got the bag of worms engorged with tequila from the freezer, and as they began to thaw, we roughly divided the cold, wet pile into two smaller cold, wet piles. We put the solid worm part of our respective piles into our cups and poured half the slushy liquid part on top. We were ready.

I drank the liquid part of my pile first, then let the solid worm part drip and pour into my mouth. I thought tasting the booze first would make it easier to eat the mass of worms. I was wrong.

Jammer ate his worms first, then washed them down with the boozy juice, thinking that would make them go down easier. He was wrong, too.

We learned a couple things that night. First, these worms are not psychedelic, and they do not get you high. A handful of those worms *will* get you drunk, though, because they are soaked in alcohol and have absorbed a healthy dose. Second, the worms were crunchy with a thick, soft, pus-like, tequila-tasting filling. You might not notice this grossness if you ate only one worm, but it was very apparent after eating a handful. Third, those bad-tasting worms have hard, indigestible parts that get stuck in your teeth.

I wonder if that liquor store owner has stopped laughing at us yet?

Nan-Na-We-Sek

Milkweed grows along the roadsides of Wausau, along the way back to the reservation, and also along the river. Jammer and I passed many stands of luscious, budded milkweed on our trips back and forth between those places.

Milkweed is delicious, but its sticky white sap is poisonous. Some species, including spider milkweed and whorled milkweed, are toxic. Common milkweed varieties are edible, as long as the buds are boiled and thoroughly rinsed—sometimes as many as seven times—until they no longer taste bitter.

Milkweed should be picked before the buds have blossomed into flowers. Some people prefer smaller buds, others like them larger. Mature milkweed leaves, pods, stems, and seeds should always be avoided. Once cooked, a milkweed bud is visually reminiscent of a broccoli rosette. However, the flavor is sweeter and maybe a little more cabbage-y.

Milkweed buds
Water
Salt, pepper, and butter, to taste

Clean and rinse milkweed buds thoroughly—sometimes ants live inside. Parboil milkweed buds. Place buds into a stockpot and add enough water to cover them. Bring the pot to a boil. Remove from heat, drain, rinse with cold water, and repeat. Now taste a bud. If bitter, repeat the blanching and rinsing as many times as needed. If sweet, then it is good and ready to eat or to add as an ingredient to something else. Serve milkweed buds with salt, pepper, and butter to taste.

Macaroni and Cheese with Tuna and Milkweed Buds

Jammer and I found many fast-food shortcuts when attempting to make traditional foraged dietary items. For this recipe, purchase the best box of mac and cheese that you can find. This may take some experimentation. Sometimes the best mac and cheese is the most expensive brand. In other cases, it is the cheapest stuff.

Make the contents according to the instructions. As you experiment with brands, try experimenting with the required ingredients, as well. For example, you do not actually need the oil, fat, or milk. Yes, they make it taste better. They can also be added later. So, make the mac and cheese according to the directions and your personal preferences.

Serves 5 to 6 people

1 (6-ounce) box of macaroni and cheese
3 tablespoons milk
1 (4-ounce) can tuna—I use tuna packed with water
1 cup cooked milkweed buds (see important information about the toxicity of milkweed in the *Nan-Na-We-Sek* recipe on the previous page)
1 small bag plain potato chips

Cook macaroni and cheese according to directions (boil the macaroni until tender and drain, add the cheese packet from the box, and then add the milk). Place in a large baking pan. Add drained tuna, stir, then add milkweed buds and fold them in. Top with a handful of crushed potato chips. Place in a 350 degree oven for 5 minutes to crust up.

Third Station of the Cross, Mary, and the Elephant

Grandpa and Grandma's house sat about three hundred feet downstream from the original village established by Chief Keshena. Back then, there were only a few people living in Keshena. Those few were isolated by millions of acres of unbroken pine forest. The parcel of land chosen by the Indian Service for the official building that became my grandparents' house was at the intersection of an ancient trail network with a spring-fed creek that flows into *Muk-wan-wish ta-quon,* or Bear's Head River. Whites renamed it the Wolf River. Using this river, it is possible to travel by canoe from the Chain of Lakes area near the Michigan border with Wisconsin, south past Shawano, then east by Oshkosh, and finally north from Lake Winnebago into Green Bay on Lake Michigan. It takes six to eight weeks for a log to make this journey. Paddlers can go much faster.

The foot trail near my grandparents' house follows a gentle incline that provides easy access to the creek for water traffic. I lived along this trail with my grandparents when I was young and unaware of its history. At that time, I was also unaware of a neighbor who I would one day meet and the story about her I would hear as an adult.

The part of the trail near our house was isolated because it followed the crest of a steep moraine and the lip of a river levee many feet above the Wolf River. This is where the federal government built its administrative center, high above floodwaters. In the old days, canoes were parked here, a hundred feet upstream from the confluence of the river and the creek, while the owners went about their chores. It was an easy walk from the moraine, Rabbit Ridge, to this official building. This part of the trail has been called the Chapel Hill Trail since the Catholics arrived in the nineteenth century. The trail divides here. One network leads northwest past Neopit and around the western shore of Lake Superior. The other leads northeast toward the town of Wabeno, continuing around the southern edge of the Great Lakes. This is a major throughway of the original network of trails.

Without the help of the local Catholic diocese and its considerable political and economic power, the tribe would have been disbanded well before 1900. Menominee habitat—those lands where the rivers empty into the Great Lakes—became much too valuable for the United States government and its majority population to waste on Indians. The Menominee could have been terminated in the nineteenth century, a fate suffered by so many of my Indigenous relatives. The tribe and I are indebted to the Catholic Church, ironically, for its help in the establishment of the Menominee Reservation. Without the Catholics, the tribe would have disappeared. I would have never existed in the twentieth century and beyond. Still, nothing in life is free.

All the Church asked in return from the tribal members was for them to accept some basic European ideas, like the concept of sin. It was at this moment that the rainbow world of the Menominee became black and white. According to Grandpa Moon, who never set foot inside any church during his lifetime, "In the entire history of the White Man, there was only one good one, out of the whole bunch. And what did the rest of them do when they found out about him? They nailed him to a tree!" Our family had mixed feelings about the Church.

The first reservation church, Saint Joseph's, was founded almost as soon as the Menominee Tribe became situated on the banks of the Wolf River, in the 1850s. Priests arrived as missionaries and never left. When I was a boy, there were fourteen stations of the cross inside the sanctuary, depicted by painted panels along the walls—seven on one side, seven on the other. But those images were lifeless and mere ornament. Latin-inspired art had little impact on tribal members. Something more was needed, the Catholics agreed—something that excited the congregation. The priests had an answer: build three chapels and march the entire congregation of Indians on their own trail in a colorful procession to encourage devout worshipers to relive those last moments of Christ. Along that old foot trail, the highway that connected the area to the Great Lakes, the local Catholic diocese built three room-size chapels that they called stations of the cross, one each for the Father, the Son, and the Holy Ghost. Walking that path from the first to the last station represented the passion of Jesus as he walked along the path to his crucifixion. This allowed for an impressive parade along an important Menominee trail.

There was another reason, an unspoken one, for the location of these chapels and the government building. Together, church and state erased Menominee and neighboring Potawatomi history by appropriating this trail. Now that the Catholics owned this ancient Native pathway, the Indians were no longer able to travel from one place to another. Henceforth, the Menominee became fixed to one spot. As a result, they no longer followed the seasons in their foraging. They no longer spread like the *manomin*, or wild rice, dropped into the clear rushing waters. Any time a Menominee tried to walk the old way, they were confronted with this new Catholic iconography, which blocked off the trail that had once provided access to the forest and lakes.

When I was in Catholic school, the annual Good Friday procession mustered, grade by grade, at the church. There we formed a long column. Priests smeared our foreheads with ash, and a few lucky kids got to clutch palm fronds. Then we marched from station to station, about a mile, in a long line. This took a couple of hours. The processional speed was determined by the elderly priest leading the column.

Good Friday became a public, one-day holiday on the reservation, with picnics, cook-outs, and family gatherings. This formal event marked the beginning of a three-day weekend culminating with the Easter Sunday service at St. Joseph's Church. Once a year, we Menominees were all practicing Catholics. A few worshipers, I was told, bore evidence of stigmata, but I never saw any flagellation or self-torture to celebrate the crucifixion.

The First Station of the Cross, called the Father, sat on a hill directly across from a marsh where descendants of Chief Keshena's band could see it from their homes. The Second Station of the Cross, the Son, was built where several ancient foot trails intersected. The Third Station of the Cross, the Holy Ghost, was built along the crest of the river levee and moraine where the trail meets a navigable stream. In later times, this third chapel overlooked my grandparents' and neighbors' houses.

Everybody connected to St. Joe's was expected to make this spiritual procession. Kids on their deathbeds arose and made that walk. Not making this walk, we were told, would tarnish your soul, and the best that you could hope for after your death would be an eternity of purgatory. We were encouraged to act like those children on their deathbeds were left with one spiritual goal: to march in the Good Friday procession as a way to gain favor with God. Even schoolyard bullies—teenage delinquents, future tribal cops, and altar boys in training—made this procession obediently. We were accompanied on our march by a few of the more devout parents. None of them was directly related to me, as my family were all pagans. The officers on this march included all the Catholic sisters, brothers, and priests on duty at St. Joseph's.

The most elderly priest led our group, and the nuns walked along the sides of the column, setting the cadence. After the lead priest came the brothers, who unlocked the chapels and performed other last-minute tasks. As soon as the march moved toward the next chapel, a brother locked things up and brought up the rear.

Everybody wore their Sunday best. I wore a white shirt with a black clip-on bow tie, black trousers, and a pair of black leather shoes with white socks. The shirt required cuff links. Uncle Donny let me use a pair of his. Nuns and brothers wore simple black-and-white robes. The junior priests also wore simple black robes, but theirs were more ornate than the brothers'. The elder priest leading the procession and giving the public prayers wore brilliantly colored silk robes.

As the procession neared each chapel, or station of the cross, the doors opened to reveal an altar covered with rich velvet material. Religious banners hanging from the walls hid the whitewashed lumber of the small, poorly constructed buildings. Gold candles burned in two gold candleholders, one at each end of the altar. A large gold crucifix filled the center back wall, and Jesus gleamed atop it. A smaller gold crucifix was displayed at the very center of each altar. Only the priest and his immediate entourage were holy enough to enter. The rest of us watched from a distance, outside the chapel walls.

The elder priest would then recite an incantation in Latin while gesturing toward the woods. Perhaps he was exorcising the pagan spirits from the place. The crowd said "Amen," and then we could see the priest extinguish the candles with his snuffer, a gold staff with a cone at its end. The cone fit over the candle, starving the flame of oxygen and extinguishing the fire. Real Catholics never blew out a candle. After this short ritual, the procession would march to the next station. All this ceremony occurred on a northern Wisconsin Indian reservation in the 1960s, and I was there.

The last chapel, the Third Station of the Cross, representing the Holy Ghost, was built so close to Grandma and Grandpa's house that Jesus was our second closest neighbor. Without trying, I could see the chapel from the living room window.

After the congregation's final prayer, we were dismissed to go about our day. Many families drove up into the lake country for picnics. While all three of those chapels are now long gone, the ancient foot trails through the forest that they were built on still exist. That was not the Catholics' plan, of course. It was supposed to be the other way around.

The Catholic Church used these chapels only one day each year. The other 364 days of the year, they mostly were used by emotionally, mentally, and physically dangerous people—drunks, druggies, and other hoodlums. It was not all craziness, though. In the summertime, during daylight hours, children often played on the trail, and couples walked hand-in-hand along it. Many wildflowers bloomed on the sunny slopes. In the early summer, milkweed, or *nan-na-we-sek*, and wild asparagus spears were plentiful. We lived within a hundred yards of that chapel, at the base of the long winding moraine, but we never entered it.

No, that is not quite true. There was one time, and only one. When I was about ten years old, on the Saturday morning following a Good Friday procession, I was sent outside to play after eating breakfast. Being curious about the previous day's activities, I walked those three hundred feet up to the Third Station of the Cross.

I was shocked at the signs of violence. The doors had been forcibly opened. The padlock hasp protecting the chapel from vandalism was ripped off the wood doors. One of the doors was torn from its hinges and lay on the ground. The whitewashed chapel was wide open. It was horrible to see, and yet I could not stop looking. This was the first time that I had ever been inside. I stepped in and violated some papal edict—a sin of commission, having done something wrong. Tempting an even more immediate retribution from God, I walked behind what was left of the altar. It was only a simple box made from lumber, but I had never seen it without its velvet covering. On this morning, it was just a broken pile of wood. Somebody had even used pieces of the altar to build a small fire. Maybe the vandals had been cold. The inside floor was littered with bits of broken beer bottles. I stepped on flattened cigarette butts and torn matchbooks. All of this destruction was shameful, but the thing that most frightened me—no, it made me feel much worse than that—was that somebody had smeared fecal material inside. It was not dog shit. It looked and smelled human. It was on all of the inside walls and even on the ceiling, as if the perpetrator had tossed it upward trying to make stalactites. Somebody had taken the time to strategically place stripes of fecal matter in angular patterns.

I was careful to not touch anything as I tiptoed my way out, leaving no tracks, no evidence of my passing. I wiped the bottom of my shoes on the clean dirt outside on the trail and committed another sin, a sin of omission, because I never told anybody about what I had seen until now.

Although this vandalism was an egregious violation of the space, there were always lesser litterings around the chapels of broken beer and wine bottles. Sometimes, I found unbroken empties on the trail, which I would collect and return to the store for candy. Each bottle had a two-cent deposit. As I walked by the chapels, on any day other than Good Friday, I often noticed that the outside walls had been crudely painted with sexual images. The brothers from St. Joe's must have spent hours cleaning, painting, and raking up a year's worth of mess to prepare for the ceremony.

One warm spring morning, when I was much younger, about the age of seven, while on my regular bottle-collecting run, I interrupted an undressed couple on a blanket. I did not actually walk up to them. That would have been embarrassing for all of us. But, after hearing a young woman giggling, I began to try finding the source of the sound. Soon I could smell perfume. I crawled and crouched my way over to spy on the couple, who were hidden within a thick grove of brush on the slope. I did not actually see their bodies, as they were really well hidden. At age seven, I had never been around people having sex before.

Being a good Catholic, and a bratty smart-ass kid as well, I ruined their moment of intimacy. I crawled within feet and yelled, "Hey, what are you doing?" I told them that they were committing a sin. "You better stop coveting that woman!" I said. "You're both going to hell." I knew the girl, who was from Rabbit Ridge, and her mom. "Eww, I'm going to tell your ma that you're pregnant," I yelled.

The naked man got up and chased me through the woods. He yelled exactly what he planned to do to my neck, but I was faster—and wearing pants and shoes. I did not let the guy give up, either. I was having too much fun. A couple of times, when he was about to give up the chase, I sat down just out of his range and taunted him. "Hey, sucker!" Truly, I could be a hateful, horrible little kid.

This old trail was a shortcut from Rabbit Ridge to downtown, so on an ordinary day, it got lots of foot traffic. On weekday mornings, it was usually safe, but less so on late weekday afternoons. During the night, on any day of the week, one proceeded slowly and noiselessly to avoid drunks and vandals.

Another house lay even closer to the Chapel Hill Trail than that of my grandparents. The old trail passed within ten feet of a small blue house. This was where the wide foot path—wide enough to fit a car—narrowed to fit only people walking single file. I know the width of this part of the trail because I drove my Volkswagen Beetle on it.

That little blue house on Chapel Hill was the only one on that slope. A couple of blank-faced windows looked out over the trail from behind a chain-link fence. Was somebody inside watching, hidden from view? Each window had tightly closed blinds. At night, no light escaped from those windows, so they probably had thick curtains, too. It must have been possible for the occupants to see the Third Station of the Cross from their living room windows, like us. In all the years I spent at my grandparents', I never set foot inside that house or talked with those neighbors.

I was curious about these people. Their absence from the tribe's activities made them even more mysterious. The house was nice and well kept. Sometimes there would be a car sitting in the driveway, and sometimes not. I could not tell if the owners were White or Indian from the type or condition of the car. It looked like a White Man's car, but my grandparents owned a White Man's car, too, and they were full-bloods.

I cannot remember the exact date when I learned that a girl named Mary had lived there. It was well after that girl and I had already moved away. Between the two of them, Grandma and Grandpa knew everybody within a couple of counties. Over many years, I had heard them gossip about almost everybody except for these neighbors. That was odd. Their house was only fifty feet from our house. At first, I thought that my grandparents did not think them important enough to mention.

Eventually, curiosity got the better of me. At one evening meal, I asked them point-blank about these neighbors. "The man died," Grandpa vaguely answered. "He worked for Menominee Enterprises." That was the business arm of the tribe. Few Menominees worked there. "I never knew much about him," he said. This was not Grandpa's usual long-winded answer.

But it was not until one morning forty-nine years later that I learned, via the moccasin telegraph, that when the man died, he left an attractive widow. She was not elderly. She was a youthful, middle-aged Menominee. She took in a White woman who had separated from her husband and her two children. They became a family.

Back then, in the 1950s, people who were overtly different were treated badly. Mary may have been desperate to get out of the house and be more social, but her unusual family situation would have made her a target. People left them alone.

Mary was a tall, pretty blonde. She always dressed well, and she seemed friendly enough toward me. Not gushing by any means, but when she did talk to me, she seemed genuinely happy to do so. We did not have any classes together as she was older, but we bumped into each other. I sneaked into her gym class one time and saw she was the only person who could do the balance beam. She was as graceful as a ballerina.

Mary was a study in contradictions. She was pretty, popular, and had a cute smile. Yet, she always seemed sad because, as my grandma used to say about some people, her smile never reached her eyes. In school, she seemed lonely among crowds. Although lots of people talked with her and she never sat alone, she always seemed separate from the crowd, like she was already a ghost, not quite interacting with the living.

She must have known that I lived next door to her. Perhaps she wondered why I never came to call. When I learned that she lived there all those years later, I could hardly believe that I regularly walked less than ten feet from her as she sat inside her house alone. I had always assumed that she lived in the border town of Shawano, but in reality, she was sleeping just fifty feet away from me.

Years later, I was a truck driver delivering heating and cooling equipment to Wisconsin-area construction sites. This was not a career choice. It was the inevitable track taken by an aging slacker who always chose the path of least resistance. I did this job for thirteen years. It was not hard, it did not require any deep thought, and I managed my way through it. Over time, I became well acquainted with Wisconsin highways and radio stations. My truck had only an AM radio. Reception in the Wisconsin River valley was limited and so were my program choices. I would not choose to listen to radio programs like Paul Harvey's religious talk show, *The Rest of the Story*, but programming options were few.

On one particular day, I longed for the sounds of human voices badly enough to tune in, this once, to Paul Harvey's show. This was how I found out that Mary, my one-time neighbor, had died horribly. I listened to the entire program, transfixed by the story of what I believed to be an anonymous woman's sad life, until Harvey's last words revealed that he was speaking about somebody I cared for. At the end of the program, he stated her name. Mary Herman had been fatally crushed by a circus elephant.

I pulled the truck over to the side of the road and smoked a cigarette. This was how Mary, an above-average student who never made trouble in school, had died. Unlike me, who was a below-average student and always in trouble.

Here are the facts that I later gathered from local newspaper clippings: Mary, age thirty, was seen in Baraboo, Wisconsin, on September 1, 1982, with a man named Ben Williams, a twenty-nine-year-old animal trainer from Florida. Baraboo is known as Circus City, as it was the original home of the Ringling Brothers Circus. On the evening of Friday, September 10, Mary died at a motel restaurant parking lot in Wisconsin Rapids, but her body was not found until three days later. She was reported missing after she failed to pick up her six-year-old daughter from the babysitter. Her body was found near the parking lot, fully clothed but without her shoes. Williams and his friend, a twenty-seven-year-old animal trainer named Ted Haffner, were arrested in Little Rock, Arkansas, on September 16 for her murder. On September 28, both men were released from jail when it was determined that Mary was not murdered but accidentally killed by an elephant.

According to Paul Harvey, Mary had aspirations to enter show business, and meeting a seasoned trainer like Williams had piqued her interest in becoming the star of an elephant act. As the star, she would perform dangerous tricks—just her and two thousand pounds of unpredictable animal. Harvey explained how most trainers work with elephants on their stunts before any humans are involved or at risk. For example, an elephant is taught to lift its leg on cue. After lifting its leg, the elephant will learn to lower its foot to eighteen inches above the ground, without stepping down with all its weight—that is the hard part. After the elephant can do the trick reliably, the trainers will introduce the performer—often a pretty girl in a revealing costume. She will lie down in front of the animal, the animal will lift its leg, and the lady—in this story, Mary—will put her head down beneath the elephant's foot. It is a simple trick, one of the first tricks done to whet an audience's appetite for more. It is simply one part of an entertainment routine that almost always goes according to plan—except, of course, when it does not.

When Mary's body was found, her head had been crushed. The police initially thought she had been beaten to death with a bat, and Paul Harvey speculated that she had been killed while performing a leg-lifting stunt. But there was more to this story.

Mary had moved to Wisconsin Rapids from Racine just three months before her death. At first, she worked as an interior designer and lived at a place on Witter Street. But soon she became restless and wanted brighter lights than those typically found in north-central Wisconsin. The only place to offer excitement in that region was the circus.

When Mary met Williams, the traveling animal trainer, a couple weeks before her death, she gave him her address. He said he and Haffner would be transporting an elephant and a leopard to Minnesota a couple weeks later. After they left Minnesota, they planned to go on the road with a circus. Apparently, the two men stopped in Wisconsin Rapids on their trip in the hopes of recruiting Mary to join them. On the evening of September 10, an encounter between Mary and the elephant took place in an animal trailer filled with elephant smells and surrounded by highway noise. An autopsy showed that Mary died of massive head injuries after being hit by the elephant's trunk in the narrow trailer. She had no training for working with elephants, and this was a tragic accident. She is buried among family in Clintonville.

I liked Mary and think about her a lot. We grew up across the street from each other, in the shadow of the Third Station of the Cross by Chapel Hill, but due to our respective circumstances, neither of us could ever really cross that street. I only found out her fate from Paul Harvey, who always signed off ". . . and that's the rest of the story." When I heard the sign-off that day, I pulled over to the side of the road and stayed there for a good long while, alone with my memories and regrets.

Wild Asparagus

Wild asparagus was abundant around my grandparents' house in Keshena. My pal Bud used to pick large bags of it on the highway near Banana Island. I have seen it grow in cedar swamps, in gravel pits, and along the roads in the lake country. It grows especially well on Chapel Hill, on the slope's sunny flanks. Wild asparagus looks similar to domesticated varieties except the edible stalk is much thinner and the rest of the plant is bushier. Don't worry, though; wild asparagus has a robust, buttery taste. After eating it, you will find domesticated varieties to be bland and tasteless.

Serves 4 people

1 quart asparagus, cleaned and cut into 6-inch lengths
3 quarts water
Salt, pepper, and butter, to taste

Locate, pick, and gather asparagus—it is usually locally abundant. Rinse and cut. Fill a pot with water, add a generous pinch of salt, and bring to a boil. Add asparagus and cook a few minutes until tender. Grab a stalk with a fork and check for tenderness—if the fork slides in easily, remove from heat. Do not overcook. Salt, pepper, and butter to taste. Asparagus can also be steamed or grilled, if desired.

Bowling Alley Fare in the Wisconsin Woods

Since there's no good reason to go there, driving from the Menominee Reservation to the town of Antigo is always a special occasion. This small Wisconsin town is no destination. While it is close to the reservation as the crow flies, driving fifteen miles of square corners around potato fields takes a long time. Antigo seems especially far away. My reason to be there recently? A cheap hotel deal and the need to visit the reservation.

In 2017, several months after open-heart surgery, I was able to travel again. Traveling is important for our family business of writing and selling books. You cannot write about life effectively without having any life experience, and travel is a quick way to gain life experience. Neither can you sell books without soliciting bookstores for sales. It all fits together. After a few months, I had grown bored with being close to death. I was looking forward to getting back on the road. I wanted one more adventure. I probably should have stayed in recovery for a few more months, but I wanted to stand upon the granite outcrops on the Menominee Reservation, to smell decaying pine needles, and to feel clean mist from a waterfall on my face at least one more time before I died.

Finding a place to spend a couple of days was difficult—me being the difficult part. There are no stand-alone hotels on the reservation. Although local tribal casinos all have hotels, they are distant from where I wanted to visit. Also, blissful crowds would have bothered me. I did not want to impose upon my family, either. Enough years have passed since I lived there that it would be awkward for me to drop in unannounced. As it was a cold and wet spring in early April, camping out was not an option, especially in my condition. However, for this upcoming visit I had another wild-card option. From the moccasin telegraph, I had learned that a guy I knew from the old Banana Island neighborhood managed a hotel in Antigo, just a few miles off the reservation. His mom used to live right around the corner from me, in a modest home on the river that predated the Banana Island housing development. I called him for a hotel reservation, and after a few pleasantries, he said that he would take care of me.

Thirteen hours after leaving my home in Lawrence, Kansas—including gas stops, pee breaks, and fast-food coffee—I arrived at a large poured-cement hotel in Antigo, Wisconsin. Altogether, it takes nine hours of windshield time to go through Kansas, Misery (Missouri), Iowa, and Minnesota at a steady eighty miles per hour. Then it's four more hours to get through Wisconsin at a strictly enforced sixty-five miles per hour, especially if you are a minority male with out-of-state plates driving a Korean SUV. Even more of a red flag for bored local Wisconsin police is that Kansas issues only one license plate, unlike most of the other forty-nine states. Hell, even I would pull me over.

Driving to Wisconsin requires focus and effort. There are natural insurmountable barriers on two sides of Wisconsin: Lake Michigan and Lake Superior. Man-made barriers—only slightly more permeable—are found on the other two sides of the state: Chicago and Minneapolis. Since there are no straight roads in Wisconsin, no two places are closer than a half hour by car. It takes a long time to get there, and upon arrival, there is no easy way back out. What happens in Wisconsin stays in Wisconsin.

The city of Antigo takes its name from a nearby stream, Spring Brook, or *Nequi-Antigo-sebi* in Ojibwa, meaning "water running underneath evergreens." Although I do not speak Ojibwa, I think that *Antigo* means "Evergreens." In my Menominee language, the state's name, *Wes-Koh-Sek*, means "A Good Place to Live." While there is not a sizable population of any tribe currently living in this northern community, a few scattered Menominees do call it home. My uncle and maternal aunt, Jim and Lorraine (Weso) Smith, lived their entire married life in Antigo. Uncle Jim Smith was not an Indian, but he was the best fly fisherman around and knew every secret, out-of-the-way spot to catch some trout.

The White population of Antigo is less German and more Nordic compared to the White population of Shawano. The name Shawano, or *Sha-wa-Nah-Pay-Sa* in Menominee, means "Lake to the South." It reflects the former Menominee land holdings before immigrants arrived. Germans came to Wisconsin in the early 1800s, some settling in Shawano, while Nordic peoples arrived in the late 1800s with Antigo as a destination. Antigo and Shawano are both off-rez communities, but Antigo is not a border town where mixed White and Indigenous populations live. It is just a town. In contrast, Shawano has a large Indian population made up from several tribes. It is the main border town for the Menominee Rez. Uncle Buddy used to say, "It takes a couple hours to walk from Shawano to Keshena," which is seven miles away. "But walking from Antigo to Keshena takes considerably longer." It is thirty-five miles away. In his day, walking long distances was common.

Antigo has several large Ojibwa reservations, and thus casinos, on its distant west, north, and northeast sides, in addition to the much closer Menominee Reservation to its southeast, so it is strange that it did not become a bedroom community for the casinos.

While both Shawano and Antigo are relatively close to the Menominee Reservation, these two communities are very different geologically. Downhill from Antigo, the watershed flows south. Spring Brook drains southwest into the Eau Claire River

("Clean Water" in French). It then empties into the Wisconsin River ("River That Flows Through a Red Place" in the Miami language) and then into the Mississippi River ("Big River" in Ojibwa) before ultimately draining into the Gulf of Mexico on the Atlantic Ocean.

But on the nearby Menominee Reservation, only a few miles away from the center of Antigo, water flows downhill in the opposite direction. It goes southeast into the Wolf River (*Muk-wan-wish-ta-guon,* or "Bear's Head" in Menominee) and then into Lake Winnebago ("Bad-Smelling Water" in Menominee). This lake was where most of the timber barons' sawmills were located in the nineteenth century. The Wolf River then changes direction and heads north, down the Lower Fox River (*Rivière aux Renards,* or "River of Foxes," so named because the French called members of the Meskwaki or the Sauk Tribe "foxes") and into Green Bay on Lake Michigan. The Great Lakes waters reach the St. Lawrence Seaway and finally the North Atlantic Ocean.

Antigo sits on an old Indian trail network that runs east from Chicago to Quebec, circling the shores of the Great Lakes. European trappers and traders of the seventeenth century took advantage of this ancient transportation route, which linked to trading routes that covered the continent. Indeed, precontact trade between the Southwest of the United States and the Great Lakes region is well documented.

Today, Antigo is one of the gateways to the resort areas of northern Wisconsin. A Wisconsin resort establishment is immediately recognizable. Taverns and supper clubs are filled with furred, feathered, or finned artifacts created by mad taxidermists. North Country mammals, birds, and fish are stuffed and mounted in awkward poses, sometimes with humorous titles attached. It is a type of outdoors pornography for tourists. Long, dark winter evenings provide leisure for such whimsy. And only in Wisconsin can you gamble for your next drink with the bartender by playing dice. Advanced North Country denizens can roll dice, backchat with the bartender, and maintain boozy conversation with a comely patron on the next stool—all at the same time.

These memories returned to me as I arrived at my Antigo friend's hotel. At first blush, the lobby looked nicer, cleaner, and more spacious than any of the other hotel lobbies in town, at least according to their online ads. The freshly installed carpet and lobby furniture smelled and looked clean. There was a decent-sized indoor swimming pool surrounded by plants in a glassed-in area. There were comfortable chairs arranged thoughtfully throughout the indoor arboretum. Those were the most obvious plusses. On the other hand, even without seeing any of it, I could tell the hotel's free breakfast buffet was the worst meal in town.

My buddy spotted me and beamed. He was a general manager. When I asked about coffee, he responded with silence. He just took me around the corner and pointed at a huge cardboard box in his office. Inside was a smaller box filled with coffee in opaque brown packets, ready for drip coffeemakers. All the breakfast items came straight out of the big box with shipping labels still hanging from the sides. More than anything, the makeshift pantry resembled the spoils of a hijacked vending machine. It was filled with food packages of indeterminate age, each labeled and wrapped in clear cellophane. This is how the breakfast buffet arrived from the corporate headquarters.

But still, this did not seem like a bad hotel. After all, hotel coffee is horrible everywhere, and only tourists ever eat the breakfast buffet. I asked why the hotel was empty and braced myself.

For some North Woods establishments seeking to attract hunters from the cities of Milwaukee and Chicago, a sleazy reputation is the only viable marketing plan. These hotels feature high-priced drinks made from cheap booze and served by young women recruited from Chicago. Sometimes a lucrative "bad" reputation results from a cleverly orchestrated publicity campaign created by a hotel in conjunction with the local sheriff's office, newspaper, and chamber of commerce. That notoriety can bring more deer hunters, and therefore more profits, from the annual orange army invasion—the brigades of camo-clad outdoorsmen with orange vests. One to two weeks before the start of deer season, a couple of prostitution and/or gambling arrests will occur. Prominent local citizens will then declare the area to be in the midst of an immorality epidemic with gambling, women, and booze freely available at area taverns. This story appears in the local papers, is picked up by the news wire service, and then, by golly, it appears in the Chicago newspapers. Some deer hunters are attracted more to the promise of drunken debauchery than to the actual hunting of deer. Coincidentally, many wives left at home by deer-hunting husbands across the Midwest are just as interested in their own weekend of debauchery.

When I arrived, my friend had a story to tell about the reputation of his hotel, but it was not the narrative of these resort hotels with falsified bad reputations. A few months earlier, he told me, the owner of the hotel had allegedly wired a few rooms for video recordings. This rumor circulated around town. According to the local gossips, the owner had obtained local commercial help to install the equipment. Maybe he had innocent intentions. Or maybe not. The allegations chased most local customers away, even those who had checked in just to use the pool, but that did not stop unknowing tourists like me.

Two days before I arrived, according to my friend, an incident had occurred. A tourist family with three children had checked into the hotel for the night. The couple started to drink heavily while their children ran unsupervised throughout the hotel, annoying some guests enough that they complained to the front desk. After the owner spoke to the eldest daughter, who was maybe eight years old, the girl ran away screaming to her parents. The next day, the mother called the hotel's corporate office complaining about the franchise owner and accusing him of having inappropriate contact with a minor. So far, there had been no police involvement. My buddy mused that all of this would have blown over—an intoxicated mother, an unsupervised child—had it not been for the video equipment and the fact that the owner was a person of color and, therefore, likely to experience prejudice. The North Woods are full of stories, and this one was still unfolding.

That late winter night, my friend did not give me a special discount. He told me that he could not do anything about the room rate, but he could add a few perks, like giving me a whole wing of the hotel. I was the only guest in a very large suite. All other guests had been placed in rooms around the pool. I had a third of the hotel to myself and could party like a rock star if I wanted.

This was a great perk. I enjoy—genuinely enjoy—loud music. The golden oldies of acid rock have gotten me into trouble on several occasions at home in Kansas. I had the hotel's Wi-Fi, my laptop, and powered speakers. I was grateful for this boon.

After a shower, a short nap, and a small handful of beta blockers, I was feeling ready for dinner. First, I searched the room, and especially the bathroom area, for recording devices and checked the mirrors to verify that they were not one-way mirrors. I looked at the ends of all sash cords for hidden mini-microphones. I unplugged all the clock radios and carefully inspected the lamps, light sockets, and all little boxes stuck on the ceiling. Government contract work and old spy movies have made me paranoid about such things. Besides that, I've read all kinds of stories on Facebook about people finding miniature cameras hidden or disguised as something else in bathrooms.

Once I had completed my search, I was hungry. In order to stick to my heart-friendly, restricted diet, I wanted to avoid deep-fried food restaurants. So, in the ten-degree Wisconsin night, I winced every step of the way to a local bowling alley as directed by my friend. He assured me, "They serve good comfort food."

My path took me through an empty parking lot and over eroded snowbanks, past a drive-through ATM, and around the back of a farm implement store where machinery stood like frozen dinosaurs, until finally, I emerged into a bright, full parking lot. Getting closer, I could hear loud strikes as bowling balls met ten wooden pins and an occasional high-pitched female laugh.

I was no stranger to bowling alleys. In my early youth, my grandparents had sold maple wood blanks to a firm in Chicago that made bowling pins. Grandpa and Uncle Buddy would obtain a cut of wood about eighteen inches high from a maple log. Then they would split the round maple chunk into ten pieces, each about six by six inches wide. The people buying the bowling pin blanks wanted all ten pins to come from the same maple slab. The pins had to harmonize. These blanks were then shipped to a factory in Chicago via the railroad, where they would be processed and made uniform.

While a junior in a Shawano high school, I used to bowl on Saturday afternoons. I was not that interested in the game, but the owner, an old German guy, sold beer to anyone who bowled. I had discovered the place on a gym class field trip when we were learning how to bowl, and then I stopped by the next Saturday afternoon. Some guys I knew were having beer and bowling a game. I joined them, and soon it became part of my weekend routine. I got fairly good with all the practice and under the influence of the 3.2 percent near beer.

I now found myself at the Antigo bowling alley at 8:30 on a Friday night, a night reserved for the women's bowling league. The lanes were jamming with free-styling ladies having fun. The jukebox was blasting rock and roll, and the bowling pins were flying. The bartenders were busy conducting that familiar Wisconsin symphony of drink serving and conversation. The atmosphere was thick with the delicious smells of grilled onions and hamburgers, spilled draft beer, dozens of perfumes, and perspiration.

Strangely enough, although there must have been fifty women in the place—bowling, drinking at the bar, and eating at tables—there could not have been more than six men, including me. The five other guys were scattered throughout the lounge and sitting with women. Date night, for them. I was the only single guy in the place.

Before I could order my dinner, the bartender placed a mixed drink in front of me and pointed to two women at the other end of the bar, who both waved. Directly across the bar sat three woman in team shirts, one of whom blew me a kiss. I tried to explain that I was just out of the hospital and still in pain. They laughed, and the one that had blown the kiss said, "You look all right to me." I considered lifting my shirt to expose my Frankenstein-like chest to prove her wrong, but I decided against it.

The bartender placed a drink menu in front of me. She had to look for a food menu when I asked for one. The regulars already knew what they wanted to eat, and I guessed burgers and fries were the usual. After she found a menu and gave me a few minutes, I prefaced my order by explaining my recent heart surgery and how I simply could not eat certain things. With many sets of mascaraed eyes staring at me, I ordered three tacos without any sour cream or taco sauce—just taco meat, onions, lettuce, tomatoes, and cheese. They had no soft shells, according to the bartender, only preformed hard shells. Hard-shell tortillas were—and are still—house favorites in some cold, northern outposts in the twenty-first century.

I gave the bartender a thumbs-up. My free cocktail was a Jack and Coke—Jack Daniels whiskey and Coca-Cola—and it was a generous pour. It was my first cocktail in six months. I savored it. When I came back from the bathroom a little while later, already half buzzed, I found another mixed drink next to my first, half-finished one still melting at the bar. The three women across from me smiled and waved. The one that blew me the kiss walked over. "This distance," she said, waving her arms, "isn't so good for conversation."

I did not take the bait. I lamely thanked her for the drink and told her that I was married.

She moved a little closer and looked me in the eye. She smelled good—closing-time good. "I can tell," she snorted. "Good night." I watched her walk away, then I gulped that second drink.

My dinner arrived on a thick white paper plate accompanied by black plastic silverware in a cellophane packet and two napkins. The three hard-shell tacos were lying flat with diced bits of tomato falling out of the tops. The construction of these bowling alley tacos was familiar to me. In the out-of-the-box tortilla shell was a lumpy, brownish swath of seasoned taco meat covered with thinly sliced white onions. On top of this was shredded iceberg lettuce—*lettuce* and *iceberg* are synonymous in this region—and long threads of cheddar cheese. Topping it all were diced tomatoes out of a can. All of the ingredients had come off of a shelf, out of a freezer, or down from the top of some kitchen cabinet. Cooking this meal had meant assembling and heating it.

Safe from the cold wind, I dug into my taco meal. From a vegan's perspective—or, really, from any health-conscious person's perspective—these tacos would be a no-no, as they were full of meat, salt, and preservatives. Yet, despite the grease and sodium, they were quite comforting to me. The snap of the shell resonated with the crunch of the crispy shredded lettuce. Processed cheddar cheese was the perfect counterpoint. If I could have substituted in a few fresh ingredients, like real corn tortillas or shredded beef, these tacos would have been a healthy food. Nonetheless, they were filling, as tacos are no matter their ingredients.

The two women that bought me my first drink were still sitting at the end of the bar, engrossed in deep conversation. I motioned the bartender over and asked her to give each of the ladies a drink on me. After paying the bill and waving at my two new best friends, I walked back to the hotel with a jaunty step and called my wife when I reached the lobby.

At the front desk, I saw my Banana Island buddy, ready for adventure like a kid. We were alone, so I asked, "Does the owner really have the place wired for peeping-tom videos? And did he really have inappropriate contact with a minor?"

He looked around to be sure no one was listening to—or taping—us.

"The owner has an apartment in the hotel," he said, "and it is filled with video equipment. What else would he be doing with it?" We chewed over the situation for a few more minutes, but even in the heated hotel, the winter chill crept in. My days of adventure are behind me, and I never met the hotel owner. No trophies of the hunting season remained, not even a moose head over a fireplace.

A friend of a friend had called me and left a message earlier in the evening. After returning the call, I waited in the lobby for him to swing by. He arrived, and I purchased ten pre-rolled marijuana cigarettes from him. This was medical marijuana, purchased at my doctor's suggestion. He'd said marijuana would be as beneficial to me as the blood pressure pills and beta blockers that he'd already prescribed. I went back to my room to get the keys to my truck and my winter coat. The plan was to sit in my warm running car while I smoked one of these cigarettes. At twenty below zero, it was much too cold to try to stand outside the front door and smoke.

Just as I was about to leave, my hotel manager friend knocked on my door. He stood in the hotel hallway smoking a cigarette and drinking a can of PBR. No sooner had I opened the door than he entered the room with a suitcase full of beer. "It's cold, so I keep it outside," he said. "Want a beer?"

The suitcase I could understand, and since there were Indian casinos surrounding us in all four directions—and because

Indian casinos are notorious for selling untaxed, inexpensive cigarettes—I was not surprised to see him smoking. Still, my room was a nonsmoking hotel room. "Don't worry about smoking," he told me, stepping inside. "Feel free to smoke anything you wish." I had not smoked a cigarette since my undergrad years at the University of Wisconsin–Madison, and I was too old, cold, and road-weary to drink a beer, no matter how much I wanted to Badger bond.

If this had happened to me at twenty years of age, I would have genuinely enjoyed it. I used to enjoy partying like a rock star, but at this stage in my life, I noticed only the fact that it was way past my bedtime. I longed for my flannel pajamas and slippers.

Still, his companionship was welcome. At first, our talk was jittery and halting. We had not seen each other in years, and that had been in an entirely different world. But then, we began to remember people and places. We spent the next several hours reminiscing about our Banana Island neighborhood days, just a couple of old friends telling each other stories from a shared moment in time and space. The Wolf River of our memories flowed past Banana Island and east to the Great Lakes in a continuous, unstoppable current. It felt good to return to Banana Island in conversation. It felt good to be alive.

Winter Quesadillas

Fresh ingredients for tacos, burritos, quesadillas, and enchiladas are not easy to come by during the frozen winter months in Wisconsin and other northern states. This recipe calls for grilling the tortillas directly on the burner for a smoky flavor and some flair on a cold night.

Serves 3 to 4 people

6 large tortillas, wrap size, of white flour, whole wheat flour, or corn (wheat has a higher protein content than corn)
6 ounces cheddar cheese, grated
1 (6-ounce) can white chicken meat
1 (4-ounce) can mild, diced green chilis, drained well
Black olives, sliced (optional)
Grilled onions (optional)

Spread out 3 of the 6 tortillas. Sprinkle 2 ounces cheese, 2 ounces chicken meat, and ⅓ of the chilis onto each tortilla. Add canned black olives, sliced, or grilled onions, if desired. Cover each tortilla with 1 of the remaining tortillas, sandwich-style. Heat the largest burner on the range to low. Place the quesadilla on it for 1 minute, turn over, and cook another 30 seconds, or until cheese is melted. Alternately, put all three quesadillas on a baking sheet in a 300-degree oven for 15 minutes or until cheese melts.

My Menominee Mom's Death

The sixty-five-year relationship between my mother and me came to an abrupt end in 2018, upon her death. Our times together could be characterized as problematic at best. Yet, here I am in the future, sitting on a futon in my comfortable home, and without even trying, I know more about her now that she is gone. The evidence of her life, of her existence, was all around me. It was within me. She gave me life, fed me, and kept me alive through many desperate times.

For the last thirty-five years of her life, my mother lived in a small house between Crow's Nest and Camp Four Hill on the Menominee Reservation. Her modest home stood across the highway from the Neopit Cemetery and overlooked the Little West Branch of the Wolf River. It was easy to find.

At the end of one of my infrequent visits, I perfunctorily verbalized my love to her as I walked to my waiting motorcycle, ready for the ride back to my life in Madison. A motorcycle is a solitary vehicle, demanding focus to navigate and with no room for any extra thoughts. By the time I reached Madison, I had forgotten about the rez and my mother. Once, and I am not sure why it worked out this way, I did not see my mother for a thirteen-year stretch. I was not angry with her. But any time the idea of a meeting was raised, something else always came up instead. Neither did she play much part in my daughter's life. That one was on me, though. I did not want her to influence my daughter. I guess I was angry.

My mom died in a nursing home in Shawano. She did not have a terminal illness. What killed her at the age of eighty-seven was a combination of old age and a hard reservation life, a relatively common cause of death for American Indians. About eight months earlier, my siblings and I had put her in the nursing home. It was not an easy thing. Those of us still speaking to each other mutually agreed that we could not provide the level of care that Mom needed. Her declining health exceeded our ability to provide for her. Three years before this, we had recognized that she could no longer stay in her own home. A retirement home or nursing home with a full-time staff was the logical decision then. Instead, we decided to move Mom into my sister's home. A nursing home was too big of a leap. After some time, our mother required a level of care that was simply beyond what my sister could provide. None of us wanted to face the simple realization that she needed professional assisted living care.

We all knew—as my mom knew, too—that this building was the last place she would ever wake and dream. All of us shared unspoken guilt. Once upon a time, at least in our stories from the olden days, the elderly were honored leaders. They were the last word in all discussions. Perhaps we once put our old ones upon the ice floes and sent them off into the uncharted Hudson Bay waters to die quickly rather than incrementally, but there were no stories left about that. Today, we put our old ones into nursing homes, emotional ice floes.

Once my siblings and I realized that we needed to institutionalize my mother, the actual decision of where to move her was easy. There simply are not that many places in north-central Wisconsin. Indeed, there was only one facility serving several counties.

This home's resident population, as well as the staff, are diverse and completely integrated—much more so than in the surrounding local towns and villages. I saw just a couple of Black people there, but few Black people live in this part of the state. I saw lots of Whites and Latinos/Latinas, and all of the local tribes were well represented—Ho-Chunk, Menominee, Ojibwa, Oneida, and Potawatomi, as well as a couple of Pine Ridge Sioux. Because of too-frequent deaths on the rez, I knew that upon death, most corpses tend to resemble each other. Their skin turns from a normal, living color into the same shade of pale bluish gray. They all acquire the same thousand-yard stare, and they all wear the same slack-jawed expression. Death does not discriminate.

The facility was home to a hundred people at any given moment. Since both staff and residents were locals, it was natural that there were many relatives among them. Visits became quick reunions with friends and family members.

I would guess that fewer than half of these residents had any chance of becoming healthy enough to walk away. For the semi-healthy, this facility was like a jail—three hots and a cot, with medical. The length of stay was determined by the body's ability to heal. For the terminal residents, the majority of the facility's population, this place was a fluorescent-lit waiting room, a windowless train station located halfway between boredom and death.

Supervised activities were offered throughout the day, and each one usually had several participants. Sometimes the room would be filled with patients in wheelchairs unable to escape on their own. They even had satellite television in the lounge areas, and the remote controls for the big-screen televisions were kept within easy reach. Still, it would be hard to make this place attractive to residents and visitors with interior decorating touches.

The plated meals, however, passed the smell test when I walked by, and they certainly looked better than the food at the local Golden Corral where we were finding sustenance. One night, Mom's dinner platter had a scoop of mashed potatoes, a slice of animal protein covered in brown gravy, and a ladle of colored vegetable bits. To the left of the dinner setting, in the ten o'clock position, a small plate held a dinner roll and a butter pat. A small lettuce salad sat expiring in a bowl on the right side in the two o'clock position. In the middle, at high noon, was dessert, white cake with brown frosting. The nutrition expert at the facility made sure to check all the boxes, and the result was a reliable, balanced meal, and not unappetizing.

Meals were most often joyless occasions for patient, staff, and visitor alike, though. Nutritious meals went uneaten. Ambulatory residents sat alone by choice. People were not unfriendly; they just did not form friendships. Very few people other than the staff watched the big televisions located in the group living areas. It seemed like most everyone, even those who would eventually heal and leave, were just marking time. The place reminded me of the human autopsy labs I attended while an anthropology student at the University of Kansas. There was an actual odor of death permeating the hallways.

Some of the residents looked like they were already dead. They lay on their beds listening to subdued sounds emanating from the bedside speakers wired to their small wall-mounted televisions while staring at the doors to their rooms. The only sign of life from many of them, the only flicker coming into their eyes, was when a living person walked past the door. The lucky ones were still able to sit on their own or plant themselves in the doorways. It was hard to think of my mother in this place.

Two weeks before my mom died, I got a late-night phone call telling me that I needed to come, as her time was near. My wife and I threw a couple of overnight bags into our car and drove north for thirteen hours. For the next two weeks, until the moment that my mother died, we lived in a series of budget hotel rooms located around the Shawano area—each one cheaper than the last. We learned to navigate the local WalMarts and hotel bar budget happy hours.

Mom was a tough old lady, and she got tougher even as she became more frail. At the end of her life, her strength of spirit filled the entire room. She died slowly, and I think she died hard. It sure did not look easy. She was not in physical pain. She just did not want to go.

I made sure Mom received morphine well before she actually needed it. The attending nurse did not put her on a morphine drip, the usual step in cases like this, since Mom was not already on a saline drip. Instead, she got a dose of morphine smeared on a popsicle stick, which was then placed under her tongue. Her suffering was kept to a minimum. I could have used that morphine myself. I was pretty old (in my midsixties), I had various ailments and pains, and I had seen death walk into the room far too many times, including during my recent open-heart surgery. But at least I was still able to live on my own.

There is a big difference between a quick death and a slow, years-long, waning death. Mom's death was especially hard because she clung to those whisper-thin threads of life so tenaciously. Like a falling, desperate climber, she managed to find another grip just as the previous ones failed. In this manner, she lived longer than seemed possible.

I was not there at the exact moment of her death. I was maybe ten minutes late, coming back from a much-needed break at the hotel. Upon entering the room, ten minutes after she passed away, I saw her form in the corner, suspended a few feet off the floor, not bound by earthly laws. Her lifeless eyes followed me, accusing me of not being a good son.

About two hours earlier, a nurse had come into the room and, after a quick examination, told my brother and me that her time was coming soon. My brother, bless him, looked at me and asked if we should try to get her home, up to Crow's Nest, to die. I looked at Mom lying there. Her eyes fluttered behind her closed lids. She was listening.

I looked back at my brother thinking, *Yes, we should do this.* But I heard myself say, "No, Brother, we can't do this. There is a good chance that you and I would kill her trying to get her from here to there, and even if we did get her home alive, it would be putting her death on our sister to handle. You and I can't make that decision without Sister being here." For the length of a thought, my mom opened both her almost lifeless eyes and looked directly into mine. I had failed her for the final time.

My brother missed that moment between my mother and me. It was eight in the morning, and suddenly I needed a drink—really bad. I drove the five minutes across town through the industrial district, across the railroad tracks, to our hotel just off the old military road, and back to my fifth of Johnnie Walker Red. When I held it to the lamp light, I could see just a few amber ounces of scotch left. I gulped them down, straight out of the bottle. Then my wife, Denise, drove us back to the nursing home.

When we arrived, my mother was dead. But she had not actually left—not her spirit, anyway. Maybe she really did not want to go, or maybe she could not. I could feel her presence there, with her disappointment in me quite palpable. So I left the room. There were phone calls to make and members of the living to care for, and I had stories to remember.

My mom, Frances "Babe" Weso, was born just after the end of the War to End All Wars. Her dad, born Kesōq Wesho (or Sun, also known as Grandpa Moon) had recently returned from his post with the United States Army Indian Cavalry stationed at Haskell Institute in Lawrence, Kansas. Grandpa had narrowly missed active service in both world wars. He was too young for the first war and too old for the second, he told me. Grandpa, Grandma, and my mother were living in Neopit right after her birth, at the old hotel next to the railroad tracks near the sawmill. This same hotel was my first home, too. My mom brought me there a couple of days after I was born.

The truth about Grandpa's military service was complicated. Grandpa served his stint in the US Army while he attended high school at Haskell Institute in Kansas, just before the war. Many young Indian men from distant reservations joined this same cavalry unit stationed at Haskell. It was not parade-ground duty. This was a federal intertribal cavalry unit. The Kansas State National Guard units spent months training with them on Daisy Hill, where the University of Kansas dormitories are currently located. Over and over again, the mounted Indian Cavalry would have mock battles, advances on machine-gun positions manned by members of the Kansas National Guard. One of the US Army's original war strategies was to send Indians to the European front lines in an attempt to break the trench warfare stalemate. These Indians, mounted on horses, were being trained to attack enemy machine guns. At some point, the military decided to send regular troops to Europe instead of the Indian Cavalry. As a result, Grandpa Moon survived World War I and graduated from high school in Kansas before returning home to Wisconsin. My mom, the oldest of six children, was his and my Grandma Jennie's first child.

Grandpa Moon, my mother, and all of her siblings attended high school at Haskell. I earned an associate of arts degree in business there, and years later, my daughter attended and earned an associate's degree in science. Perhaps my grandchildren will attend Haskell in their turn.

By coincidence, one of the other residents in the nursing home where my mother died was a cousin that I had not seen in over fifty years. Back in the day, though, we had been close. He was one of my mom's first cousins, younger than her and several years older than me. He was one of the lucky ones in the home, as he was just there to recover from an ailment. The day Mom died, this cousin named Shebokly (his Menominee name) sat on one side of my mom while I sat on the other—just the three of us.

He talked to me for an hour or so about those olden, happy days when we were all living in Zoar, when it was fair time in Keshena in the late summer, when the family gathered at the stockade. He was one of the best traditional dancers in his day. Eventually, he stood, bent over, and kissed my mom's cheek. Suddenly, I realized with more than a twinge of guilt that he knew my mother better than I. He was familiar enough to kiss her. After following him to the door, I shook his hand and thanked him for sharing my grief. Now, one year later and a thousand miles away, I realize that I will never see him alive again.

I do not know very many personal things about my mother. That sounds horrible, but my grandparents mostly raised me. They never spoke of my mother. Sure, I could have asked one of her sisters, but I did not. Once, Mom did tell me a story that stuck with me about when she was young and attending the old St. Joe's school in Keshena. This was not at the nearby Indian Agency Catholic boarding school, which was destined to become a tavern where my friend lived. That school was also called St. Joe's. Instead, Mom attended the Gothic-looking school on the hill overlooking our small town. It was a castle, complete with turrets and guarded by a moat. Inside the walls of this massive brick building, all of the romance, mysticism, and horror of eighteenth-century Catholicism took place. The Catholics had built this school on top of the graves of the original inhabitants, my Menominee ancestors.

Keshena Creek flows below the highest side of this multifloor castle, the side with the best view. Despite the magnificent vista, the building presents a massive blank face on this side. No doors or windows break up the bricks. It is as though the Catholics chose to ignore the natural world.

Three sandy hills force Keshena Creek into sweeping curves. The first is the one with St. Joe's, the second is Bean Hill, and the last, the original site of Chief Keshena's band, is the hill on the southeast. A spring that we called Keshena's Spring once lay between Bean Hill and Keshena's Hill, before farmers dammed the spring. The water from this spring once flowed to Keshena Creek. At that time, the half mile from the spring to the creek's confluence with the Wolf River was the site of prime wild rice beds. It was the main reason that the Keshena band of Menominee settled here in the first place. The Catholics turned these waterlogged rice beds into grassy meadows for cattle by building a dam below the blind brick building. This caused the spring's outflow to change direction and run into Keshena Lake, which dried out the rice beds. Without their mainstay food, that band of Menominee were trapped by this Catholic dam, and they became dependent on the Catholic officials.

The front entrance of my mom's old school, long since closed down, faced the state highway three hundred yards away. That side of the building sat upon a low-rising hill. The effect, then, was a level front side of the school. Another side, the southeast side, opened to a small gymnasium and sat on a gentle, paved hill. Once, a road had run through the schoolyard along this hill.

There was no egress at the rear of the building, which abutted Keshena Creek. A narrow pathway ran around the back of the school. On one side of the path was a boulder-strewn, flowing creek where our family once caught brook trout. On the other side of the trail was a four-story, sheer brick wall.

The last side of the school, the north side, was on a very steep hill. It would make a good horror movie setting. A steep sidewalk and stairs led from the school down the hill. Suddenly, at the very bottom, just yards from the creek, the sidewalk made an abrupt right turn and led down another steep flight of stairs enclosed by narrow cement walls. There were no handrails on the stairs, and the sidewalk was decorated with concrete Gothic religious statuettes set beside the sidewalk. At the very bottom of the walled staircase, leading outside to the creek, a thick wooden door was located. It was as though that door was the absolute last chance to stay inside the Catholic sanctuary before tumbling all the way down into hell.

Where the sidewalk turned right, there was a cement ledge across the pathway to alert you that you had reached the bottom. This ledge was like one of those concrete barriers that keep you from pulling too far ahead in a city parking lot. If you allowed inertia to take over your movements as you went down those stairs, you would trip over that cement ledge and fly headlong another ten craggy feet into the creek. If you were careful, however, you turned right and negotiated another steep stairway to the door.

When I was a small child, this campus had been part of my playground. The dangerous path was an especially wonderful destination, even though the nuns prohibited anybody from even standing on that side of the building. Reminiscing about St. Joe's once, Mom told me why.

When my mom was a young girl, the school was still relatively new and in all its glory. It promised sanctuary—in this world and the next—to anybody who would accept the White God. This new God explained everything in a book. It was the written word versus the unknown Great Mystery. Anyway, the Menominee people had little choice but to comply with all these new commandments. They learned all the mortal and venal sins. All Indian children on this northern Indian reservation had to attend the Catholic school and, therefore, the Catholic church. All three Catholic schools on the reservation enjoyed record attendance in this age when residents had no other choice. The United States government authorized the three Catholic churches on the reservation to carry out assimilation policies, and required Catholic schooling was an essential step. The Native American Religious Freedom Act was not passed until 1978.

When my mother attended the school in the 1930s, the nuns did not allow girls and boys to play together. Some of the younger girls played hopscotch in the front of the building near the main entrance. But most of the girls, especially the older ones, played on the side of the school with the sheer stairs. The hillside is dotted with boulders that provide numerous nooks and crannies in which children can play. The nuns left the girls to play by themselves, preferring to spend time breaking up fights on the boys' side of the school. While steep, the hill where the girls played was not dangerous—but the concrete steps were.

Inevitably, there were accidents. For the most part, these were skinned knees, torn dresses, scraped elbows, and some bloody noses. These minor injuries took place on the dirt hillside. But accidents closer to the building on the steep concrete stairs were more serious. These included things like broken teeth and broken bones. In retrospect, two things should have been obvious. First, the steep concrete stairway represented a very real physical danger, and second, there was a lack of adult supervision.

One characteristic of the Menominees is that they are an egalitarian people. Gender roles tend to be fluid. Women can be warriors, and men can be great homemakers. About the only thing that divides male culture from female is that women are not allowed to handle drums. This belief in human equality was not adopted by incoming Catholics. They expected Indian girls to behave like White girls—to be demure and require only a minimum amount of supervision. But Menominee girls did not fit this stereotype. Like Menominee boys, the girls needed to decide among themselves who was king of the hill. Indian girls did not do this by comparing whose boyfriend had the nicest car. They did it like Indian boys, using physical ability as a measure. Sometimes they used fists.

Queen of the hill could be decided by racing to the bottom of the dangerous concrete stairs. The young girls raced down the steps to be first in line at the door, and the nuns did nothing to stop this. After all, the nuns probably thought, these Indian children should be encouraged to rush back into the school building. They should have expected that this race would become a shoving contest as much as a contest of speed and balance. It was inevitable that something horrible would happen.

One day, before the start of school, the bigger girls decided among themselves who would be first. As the pack raced downward, one girl started to tumble down the concrete steps. This started an avalanche of bodies. I do not know the unfortunate girl's name who must have died, and my mother did not either. Neither could I find her name, or even the incident, in the available archives, but it must have been a fatal accident. There was never any mention of this accident in public. The girl disappeared. The only evidence that something major happened is the fact that the nuns stopped allowing children to use that side of the building. Girls and boys began to use the same playground. This integration of the sexes, something no good Catholic would ever approve of, proves how bad the accident must have been. Anyway, this explains why the concrete stairways on the north side of the building and the small doorway down at the bottom were no longer used.

Years later, when I was a child attending St. Joe's in the early 1960s, the playground was on the paved side of the school. In the winter, the nuns broke out the big sleds, which had been fashioned out of old school benches that had been replaced by desks. The benches must have been built with eight-foot-long boards, as long as a freshly hewn log. The thrifty church brothers attached long wooden runners to their bottoms, making eight-foot-long toboggans. Ten to twenty kids would pile on and ride these sleds downhill in the winter snow. Since there was no way to steer the sleds, there were severe crashes and injuries. At some point, the nuns stopped bringing out those sleds in the winters. I assume a major accident made them change their policy.

One of the weirder things I remember about my mom was

that she had a plug-in aluminum water heater for many years. It was a heating element attached to an electric cord. I remember that particular water heater because she carried it with us on our numerous moves from the big city to the rez, back to the city, to a village, and back to the rez. She used it to heat water in a big metal washtub. Many of our homes did not have hot water. Sometimes, the hot water she made in the washtub was for dishwashing. At other times, it was for clothes washing. We also used that same metal tub when we cleaned fish and when we bathed.

That water heater was dangerous. I learned this at a young age after reaching into the tub of water as it was heating. The electric shock was exactly the same as the one I experienced when using a butter knife to pry a stubborn piece of bread out of a plugged-in toaster. It was a learning curve.

After a divorce in my thirties, like many insecure men, I moved back into my mother's home. This was the first time that we had lived as mother and son, with the exception of a few months here and there. For the first time in my life, I felt like a son.

During this interlude, our homelife routine involved weekly trips to the laundromat in Shawano. Eventually, this chore became the exclusive responsibility of my brother and me. We did family laundry about two hundred times, once a week for five years. It took one hour of driving and twenty bucks in change to do our laundry. We got there around 7 a.m. and always used the same machines. With washing, smoking joints, drying, and folding, the whole thing usually took us more than three hours. We would return home just before noon, ready for lunch.

The day before my mom died, and before I left her spirit glaring at me, clean laundry was something my wife and I needed. It was early morning and Denise was still asleep, so I grabbed the pile of dirty laundry off the floor, added it to the pile in the back seat, and drove to town. I knew exactly what to do. I went back to that same laundromat from my distant past. I walked in around 7 a.m. and used the very same machines that I did thirty years earlier. Yes, the coin slots were different—they took several more quarters—but as far as I could tell, these were the very same machines. Even the signs warning people not to use the machines to dye clothing were the same signs from thirty years earlier.

On the day my mother died, I was wearing a clean shirt. The next hours were a blur, and it was 11:30 a.m. before I could leave the nursing home. The coroner examined her, the funeral home people arrived, and Mom was washed and placed in a coffin. With great solemnity, the entire nursing staff escorted my mother's body down the long hallways in a procession. The staff take the deaths of their patients very seriously and were part of this death parade, except for the upper management types, the suits, who remained at their desks behind open doors. We proceeded out the front door to a waiting hearse. The funeral director and assistants loaded the coffin, and the hearse drove off.

I needed to be alone. There was nothing left to say to the small group of relatives standing where the hearse had just been. We had already said everything that needed to be said during the two-week death watch, and I was tired.

The family decided to hold a ceremony for my mom at a later date. There was no other reason, then, to stick around. Denise and I began our long drive back home to Kansas. We drove the rest of the day, and all night long, too. We spelled each other, let each other sleep, stopping only for gas and to grab a cup of coffee and a sandwich. I drove the final three hours from Des Moines to Kansas City at ninety miles an hour. In Missouri, you can drive fast.

On the trip home, my wife and I did not speak much beyond a few required grunts and facial gestures. In fact, for the next few days after getting home, we hardly spoke. During those two weeks that we had waited for my mother to die, we had clung to each other and told each other every secret that we ever had. But now I had more memories to digest.

The Shawano nursing home is a one-story, meandering, nondescript building that needs painting. I always thought it resembled a 1960s ranch house, just bigger and with parking lots. It is near the edge of town, close to the former location of Pops Reilly's outdoor theater, an entertainment mecca in its day like other outdoor theaters in many small Midwestern towns. When my brother, his wife, my friend Bud, and I saw *Vanishing Point* at that theater back in 1971, we drove past the nursing home. We even pulled into the parking lot to put our beer into the trunk for the movie. None of us except my brother was old enough to have beer. None of us looked at the nursing home as anything but a place for a quick turnaround. Now it is a landmark in my emotional life that will never be forgotten. It is another place, like Banana Island, St. Joe's school, and my grandparents' house, that has significance beyond its geographic location. This is a geography of the emotions, which runs deeper than the Wolf River.

Wild Rice Soup

The St. Joe's rice beds are long gone, but wild rice continues to be the signature dish of the Menominees. My mother and grandmother both cooked wild rice soup. This recipe calls for one whole chicken, or one whole partridge, or a couple pounds of venison. My mom used pork hocks, my favorite, to make this dish. She told how dried wild rice was a survival food—nutritious, easy to keep, and easy to transport. This is the quintessential tribal meal.

Makes 5 quarts, or 10 2-cup servings

1 whole chicken, 1 whole partridge, 2 pounds of venison stew meat, or 1 pork hock (the pork hock will add another 15 minutes of cooking time)
1 gallon water, plus more if needed to thin soup
1 medium onion, roughly chopped

2 teaspoons salt
½ pound wild rice
2 cups carrots, diced medium
2 cups celery, diced medium
Salt and pepper, to taste

Put the chicken, partridge, venison, or pork hock into a stockpot and fill two-thirds full of water. Add onion and salt. Bring to a boil, then simmer until cooked—about half an hour for poultry, a bit longer for venison or pork. Remove chicken, debone, and return meat to the pot. Add wild rice, carrots, and celery. Simmer on low heat until vegetables are tender, about 20 minutes. Add more water, if necessary. If using poultry, do not overcook or the meat will get tough. Serve with salt and pepper to taste.

Acknowledgments

I am grateful to my wife, Denise Low, for thirty years of companionship. She was an attentive first reader with invaluable suggestions. My appreciation to the staff of the Wisconsin Historical Society Press, especially my editor, Elizabeth Wyckoff, and to my copyeditor, Katherine Pickett. I am grateful to Kate Thompson, who encouraged me to continue work on the manuscript after a presentation at the Green Bay book event Untitled Town. I am grateful to the family and friends who had parts in these stories—too many to name.

Index

About the Author

MARCIA EPSTEIN

Thomas Pecore Weso (1953–2023) was an author, educator, artist, and enrolled member of the Menominee Indian Nation of Wisconsin. His book *Good Seeds: A Menominee Indian Food Memoir,* published by the Wisconsin Historical Society Press in 2016, was reviewed widely and won a national Gourmand Award. He also wrote many articles and personal essays, a biography of Langston Hughes with coauthor Denise Low, and the children's book *Native American Stories for Kids* (Rockridge Press, 2022), which was named a 2023 Kansas Notable Book. Weso was an alumnus of Haskell Indian Nations University and the University of Kansas, where he earned a master's degree in Indigenous studies. He died in Sonoma County, California, on July 14, 2023.